Little Theatre *of* Gestures

Introduction
Nikola Dietrich and Jacob Fabricius

> *"The man, who holds his head with his hands and touches his hair, is apparently listening to a lecture. He is stained and tired and wants to make sure by this gesture that his brain still works all right."*[1]

The text of chirological researcher Charlotte Wolff (1897–1986), *A Psychology of Gesture*, systematically examines our gestures of early childhood, especially hand gestures, from where preverbal movements start at birth, and remain the most important means of expression until the age of five or six, to adult gestures of power and powerlessness. There are many types of gestures, they may be different dependent on our background and origin, but as Wolff states, "gesture-language is practically the same in all human beings, and it follows that it must correspond to the primary level of existence, comprising instincts and emotions, on the one hand, and an elementary knowledge of objects on the other. It is only abstract thought which cannot be expressed in the language of gesture."[2] Undoubtedly, what can be said is that our gestures change many times daily; we pose continuously, and our gestures and poses change according to our situation. We also rehearse these actions when alone.[3] Before walking out the door, we practice a look in the mirror, a gesture that might be useful later in the day, our workday, and in public appearances. Like a baby looking and being unsure of what to do with her or his hands, with those disconnected elements of the "foreign body," we also practice small scenarios—movements and gestures of power and powerlessness—even though we may not know how these movements and gestures can be used, and in which situations they might be appropriate. At times, "we turn up the volume" of our gestures and poses, or our surroundings become the stage for part of our daily theater.

Much has been written about gestures, and comprehensive research clarifying the subject was undertaken. In a broader sense, everyone would agree with regarding gestures as movements of the body. It becomes more complex where we to try to understand what physical, physiological, psychological, social, economic, cultural, or other implications stand behind a specific, stereotypical, conventionalized gesture. We might argue that it is our free will which makes us pose in this or that way. The theatricality of dramatic gestures was applied to art of previous epochs, and placed on the same level as the sensual painted drama of the Baroque. The modern age, by necessity, had to overcome the powerful, sensual theatricality. As a consequence, these gestures were increasingly replaced by mechanical and reflexive movements, and reduced to small, shortened, stiff, and less significant motions. These small actions, some of the more involuntary body movements that remained in our daily life, is but one aspect on which the artists in the exhibition reflect.

When we first began talking about a possible exhibition between Museum für Gegenwartskunst Basel and Malmö Konsthall, we considered a number of artists and approaches. We talked about how some artists record, transform, and alter everyday gestures into small, new ones. We talked about "abstract thought," which according to Wolff, "cannot be expressed in the language of gesture," and we wondered if it could. Through these early talks, we encircled three words: *theater, representation,* and *gestures,* namely, the importance of certain everyday gestures. We also discussed how the latter's small actions can be extremely revealing, and how, from early childhood, we rely on skills of gestural interpretation. Small gestures.

The Jewish Jamaican painter Isaac Mendes Belisario (born 1795, Kingston, Jamaica – died 1849, London, England) was among the first artists of which we thought, due to his interest in recording and describing the social realities of slavery at a pivotal moment in Jamaican history. Working in times of change and rebellion, his images record the cultural responses of the enslaved and emancipated, the economic, materialistic, and cultural interests of the land- and slave-owning elite, and the beauty of a land shaped by the sugar economy. In his most well-known *Sketches of Character, In Illustration of the Habits, Occupation, and Costume of the Negro Population in the Island of Jamaica,* published in collaboration with the lithographer Adolphe Duperly in 1837–1838, Belisario depicts the mixed, urban population of Jamaica and its folklore traditions and celebrations through twelve hand-colored lithographs.

Belisario's *Sketches of Character* provides the first detailed visual representation of the celebrated Afro-Jamaican masquerade, or *Jonkonnu* (or John Canoe), of enslaved performers dancing, performing drama, and creating music during the Christmas and New Year holidays. Isaac Mendes Belisario soon became a turning point in our discussions. Our interest could well have been socio-political and post-colonial, or we could have looked at the practice of slavery and the legacy of its economy, still being felt today. As relevant and obvious as this latter subject is, we decided to abandon this track. Instead, we discussed the importance of how Belisario portrayed, documented, and staged the Creolization and theatrical gestures of Jamaican folklore during the mid-eighteen-thirties.[4]

Inspired by Belisario, we turned toward modern gestures. The twenty-first century has seen the introduction of many new tools for self-representation and gestures. Media and access to information have clearly escalated in the last ten to twenty years, and have increasingly become personalized. On diverse social www-platforms such as Facebook, MySpace, etc., we exchange opinions and images of our self, stage ourselves, and present our own private theater of images from our daily life. We show how we would like to be viewed, with whom we would like to be associated, or befriended. These new tools would have been Andy Warhol's wet dream due to their immediate and constantly changing or changeable window to the outside world. Faster than ever, we can be anyone we want, and can create different personas in different media. The created stage, platform, or theater can be seen, more or less, anywhere on the planet. The ways of understanding distance have become distorted and abstract, but on an individual level, our *Little Theatre of Gestures* seems somewhat closer.

We have invited eight artists who deal with theatricality and gestures: within art, daily surroundings, or with gestures of "abstract thought." *Little Theatre of Gestures* is not aiming to give an overview of the formal and informal codes that constitute our communication in daily life, but instead to gather artistic positions for a mutual play on smaller or larger deeds. The traditional focus and issue of gestures in theater and performance is too vast a field to enter within this exhibition. Our focus is concentrated on a few artists who deal with gestures on a rather conceptual level. A broad category of visual expression is based on the attempt to present and represent reality. In *Little Theatre of Gestures*, the eight artists' expressions are just as broad. Yet, they often present and mirror each other's interests and approaches: from documentary-like staging to self-staged personas, from staged objects to daily abstractions. One focus point winks at the use of found material, plays with reworked and "second-hand" theatricality, while another examines the play of staged gestures.

1   Charlotte Wolff, *A Psychology of Gesture* (London, 1945), p. 205.
2   Ibid., p. 1.
3   Recently, in February 2009, when Kate Winslet received the Academy Award for Best Actress as the character Hanna Schmitz in *The Reader*, she gave her thanks and told the story of how she had practiced this speech with a shampoo bottle when she was eight years old. "Well, it ain't a shampoo bottle anymore," she ended.
4   The African ancestral spirit changes, becomes different in essence and loses part of its original nature, absorbing a new, Eurocolonial identity. "The figures whom Belisario sketched were suspended in a historical and legal limbo—a moment between slavery and freedom, when they were still bound to labor for their former masters." See Tim Barringer, Gillian Forrester, and Barbaro Martinez Ruiz, *Art and Emancipation in Jamaica. Isaac Mendes Belisario and His Worlds* (New Haven, Conn., 2007), p. 2.

A Glossary for *Little Theatre of Gestures*

Dominic Eichler

The production, dissemination, and reception of contemporary art is a form of modern drama involving a cast of thousands, lavish sets and costumes, complex scene changes, and plots ranging from the comic to the tragic. With its incessant comings and goings, doors and discoveries, the farce is particularly prevalent. The production of this drama now has a long history, and its forms and codes are steeped in tradition. Art is, and seems likely to remain, despite fluctuations in economic conditions, bigger than *Ben Hur.* As shown in the generally unsatisfactory depictions, in television, film, and other media, the sophistication of the.art drama is notoriously difficult to reproduce convincingly. Entering the art world of your own choice or design, involves an initiation and an understanding of not only the gestures and manners, but also the plot. A certain amount of stage fright and performance anxiety is inevitable. (I am reminded of a friend whose first theatrical role was a nonspeaking part in a play in which the shy fellow was cast to stand around nude holding a heavy stone for the entirety of the piece.) It matters not if one is destined to remain backstage, wait in the wings, or bathe in the footlights. The actors on the other side of the proscenium —the viewing audience—are equally as important, and also playing a role, whether in the front row or with a limited view in the cheap seats up the back. Everybody needs to know his or her lines in the little theater of art. Of course, as contemporary art is a modern drama, some improvisation and adlibbing is permitted if one can carry it off. Some knowledge or familiarity with key terms can help—hence this glossary, which regrettably is by no (Pilates-)stretch of the imagination complete. It has also been drafted specifically with the group exhibition *Little Theatre of Gestures* in mind. In frankly diverse and contrary ways, the works in the exhibition revel in different kinds of performance. This glossary could also be considered as a kind of performance—or, at least, as a little gesture in its own right.

-A-

Akimbo—typically one hand on a hip, the other indicating, holding something, or, otherwise, engaged. In the bygone centuries, this posture was visually promulgated by artists as a manly, Western European aristocratic pose. In the twentieth century, it was increasingly a high fashion and/or campy pose (Bette Davis to Yves Saint Laurent). For the relation between these vainglorious pasts and contemporary thinking, see Henrik Olesen's book *Some Faggy Gestures* (Zurich, 2008). The bent elbow is the key, suggesting a modicum of defiance, and an entitlement to a certain amount of contested space. The artist Hilary Lloyd's slide installation *Untitled (Cut-Outs)* (2006) has an akimbo attitude about looking at male crotches. When your hands are on your hips, your fingers are still pointing.

Assistants—perform roles and are often candidates for Best Supporting Actors. They are sometimes helpful, but who pays them what? Be aware that they are here to judge and eventually replace you. Thus, the more assistants at work in any given art setting—the studio, the gallery, the museum, the editorial office—the more danger is actually lurking. It's not their fault. Russian stacking dolls—nearly everyone is or has been an assistant. Always side with the assistants!

-B-
Being Looked at While Looking at Exhibitions—self-centered creatures that we are, most people imagine going to look at exhibitions to look at art *and* to look at other people looking at art (important conceptual and pictorial subject matter for the artist Peter Tyndall). Since the nineteen-nineties, this scene has extended into museum cafés and shops. In the wider world, our delicate subjectivity is usually outnumbered in purely democratic terms by those who make us objects amongst other objects. Thus, the viewer of an exhibition (except blockbusters), often enjoys a solacing rectification of subject and object relations. Sometimes, this can be erotic. See, for example, Brian De Palma's film *Dressed to Kill* (1980). At least, intuitively, we know this and our poses and gestures may reflect a different sense of belonging and purpose at an exhibition. For instance, the drinking of a glass of white wine in the morning is quite different to a wine of inferior quality from a plastic cup in a white cube.

-C-
Catalogue—the remains of an exhibition. Sometimes an *exquisite corpse*. Thus, a keepsake resembling a theater program, but not necessarily a script. Common wisdom has it that a catalogue essay, like the pitch of a theatrical agent, always praises—or does it?

Curatorial Posse—a group of curators and their assistants who commonly make studio visits with artists prior to large-scale art events, such as Biennales. Allhough their hierarchy is strict and often inscrutable, the curatorial posse moves as one organism. Divining the meaning of their actions and utterances—in curatorial code—may reveal a "curatorial stance." Typically signaling "freethinking" and "reserved creativity," curatorial sartorial is a key feature of their visual manifestation.

Cornerists—a corner in an art space is the equivalent of the kitchen at a house party. It is a place to be a part of things and, at the same time, set yourself apart. Cornerists are those who always do this, spatially or otherwise. Architect Mies van der Rohe and others imagined the art stage as a corner-less, level playing-field or piazza. That was idealistic. When forced in or onto one such field, art protagonists clump, but it is the space between people and groups of people that is the most telling. People mingle to ease the tension of social geometry. Abstractly, corners are virtually everywhere, and so too are cornerists. Some work hangs out in corners. For example, strange vitrines standing like sentinels around the edge of the amphitheater. See also *Jay*.

-D-
Discomfort—unlike the rest of the world, a certain amount of non-life threatening, physical discomfort is a positive attribute of much art.

Dandy—defies definitions, perhaps needs a break from art glossaries.

Exasperation—often felt, but hard to express in and around art. Arms seldom rise above the head. Related to its opposite *elation;* also rare.

-F-

Family—in the same way that art is sometimes referred to as a secular religion, social groupings in the art world are comparable to families and the soap operas that their inner workings engender.

Fashion—i.e. costumes: Art and fashion have been known to cannibalize each other. Art worlds have strict fashion codes. Artists have a certain amount of leeway, but less than they used to. Following the logic of a chessboard, white walls seem to demand black dress. Different roles in the art world entail specific costumes. For inspiration and inspiring demonstrations about how to command attention and construct "realness," see the documentary film *Paris is Burning* (1990)—a celebration of "vogueing," walking the walk and talking the talk.

Fetish—a term art borrows too much from psychoanalysis, used casually to add sexiness while, in fact, paying lip service to the idea that one should not love art objects unnaturally.

-G-

Gallery Gallop—a gait for the terminally busy, applied while swinging by and through a number of art galleries, one after another.

Gender—despite the fact that art often professes to deal with gender in a progressive manner, it is actually performed by most art practitioners in a rather orthodox and unquestioning way.

-H-

Hanging—an activity, which manifests underlying power relationships between those who bring what is to be hung and those who organize what is to be hung. See also *Hardware.*

Hardware—the tools and technology that enable the transcendence of the work. If you are an artist and one day take a work to a future Venice Biennale, you would be well advised to bring your own hammer.

Hygiene and Hair—also make-up. The approach to these personal attributes are both good indications of the age of an artwork, or of any given, particular actor in a particular art world.

-I-

Introspective—a feeling artists have at other artists' retrospectives. The feeling curators have when the show is up and the opening has passed.

Identity—an itemized list of achievements, belongings, talents, and contacts, which together describe who we are. A role given to everyone, however unclear the director may be about our character. In Iñaki Bonillas's installation *A sombra e o brilho* (2007), the result is of a fantasy construction as demonstrated by the story of his Portuguese grandfather's Wild West dreams.

-J-

Juggling—done mentally when faced with a clash of interests. An unpopular pastime in the art world.

Jay—one part of the collaborative duo Jay Chung & Q Takeki Maeda, often referred to affectionately as "J & Q." In the exhibition, they can be seen awkwardly pretending to be Daryl Hall and John Oates in their work *She's Gone* (2009). See also *Reenactment.*

-K-

Koo-Koo or Actor-Boy—a lithograph with watercolor by Isaac Mendes Belisario (Kingston, 1795 – London, 1849), from his series *Sketches of Character, In Illustration of the Habits, Occupation, and Costume of the Negro Population, in the Island of Jamaica* (1837–1838). A rare and joyous document of a dress-up parade.

-L-

Laptop Lethargy—a condition increasingly prevalent in the last decade amongst art professionals.

Late Career Comeback—a way for artists to have another chance at getting what they might have deserved earlier.

-M-

Mobile Communications—the great irony of mobile communications is that they attach and tie you down more firmly. The devices are social shields and swords. See also *Fashion* and *Identity.*

Movement—a clumping together or grouping to increase the historical importance of two or more artists. Any action, however small, of a living body.

-N-

NOT Available—a description applied to both people and things. A verbal wall. Not always the truth, but, usually, rather happily conveyed. Embodies a kind of desire that was or should be.

-O-

Opening—doors, windows, or escape hatches. See also John Cassavetes's film *Opening Night* (1977), and consider whether there could be a remake set in an art context.

One Last Drink—euphemism for continuing until morning. The lubricant for late night bacchanals when art method actors reveal their true motivations to each other in an informal but public setting. Such gatherings often feature free atonal interpretations of operatic arias such as the Queen of the Night's, *Der Hölle Rache kocht in meinem Herzen (The Vengeance of Hell Boils in My Heart)*. Beware of the difference between being *a part of* a scene and *making* one.

-P-

Podium and Panel—and also *Press Conference*, a place where the distance between those who attend and those who are present is measured using a secret equation with variables, including: the faraway look, a sense of necessity, and conceptual palpability. If art speak is the world of the shadow's shadow, what does that make its agents?

Pursed Lips—is commonly observed when someone disagrees with something around them, for example, while looking at a work of art or being asked an opinion about something that they disagree with. The pursing of lips indicates the person is reflecting how to couch their response. Perhaps no response will ensue. It is harder to get words out of a tight opening, which is sometimes a good thing.

-Q-

Q—see *Jay*.

Queues—for example, at the food stalls at Art Basel, which are inexplicably dysfunctional. A favorite anecdote from high times in 2008: A woman screams to the congested bunch of well-heeled people waiting for their unmanageable coffees and cakes, "Let me through, I'm a collector." One of the people near the front turns and pronounces: "But darling, we are all collectors."

-R-

Reenactment—art mirroring and recycling other art or culture in order to critique or pay uneasy homage or something in between. Gerard Byrne's three-monitor video installation *New Sexual Lifestyles* (2003), for example, consists of an animated transcription of a symposium printed in the September 1973 issue of *Playboy*, restaged in a late-modernist setting. Rodney Graham's series of paintings *Picasso, My Master* (2005), is a spoof of painterly ambition discovered late in life by "a gifted amateur." According to the artist, his alter ego is "an upper-middle-class guy from West Vancouver in his first or second mid-life crisis, who sees a show of paintings by Morris Louis and decides this looks fun, and easy. He doesn't have a profound sense of culture, so educates himself by buying art books and becomes this Hugh Heffner dandy, making paintings in his pyjamas."

Residency—a place to go to be an artist and nothing else. Conditions vary wildly. Typically engenders a sense of displacement which is a key method in contemporary art, but which can be personally taxing.

Rubber Dinghy—part of a performance and installation by Kirsten Pieroth's *Untitled* (2008). The rubber dinghy is inflated via a hose connected to a piano accordion on which a musician plays Eastern European folk tunes. More than hot air, the work might be read as a metaphor between concept and the physical manifestation of art. An idea inflates things.

-S-

Stage—"All the world's a stage, And all the men and women merely players: They have their exits and their entrances; And one man in his time plays many parts … " (taken from William Shakespeare's *As You Like It* (1623)), but also Judith Butler's *Gender Trouble* (1990).

Steady Stare—a way of looking when listening in order to convey genuine involvement and interest.

Sale—never used. Art is often "sold" but is never on sale. It may be still available.

-T-

Touching—not usually encouraged, but various techniques for touching art include pulling the bubble wrap off like it's a pair of underpants. See also *White Gloves.*

Titles—The following sentence is exasperating (see *Exasperation* above): I don't like to title my works because it overdetermines their reading. Everything overdetermines everything and working in that daunting framework is one of the things art does best.

Tattoo—a permanent costume worn on the arm of one of the arm wrestling women in Susanne M. Winterling's new 16mm film *Untitled (the pressure behind your nail colour my dear)* (2009). These two opposites are arranged in a constellation making use of theatrical lighting.

-U-

Undergraduate Artist Groups—share many attributes of *Assistants* (see above), except their group manifestation and point of entry is different. Tend to see art as a theatrical production in which the drama surrounds their fledging identity, both personal and artistic. Buds on their professor's tree or future acid rain?

Up, Up, and Away, Low-Cost Airlines—unofficial sponsors of many international exhibitions.

-V-

Very Interesting—two useful non-words when others fail. In American English: "*great*" or "*amazing.*"

-W-

White Gloves—important prop and costume, not only in the film *Dressed to Kill,* but also the daily operations of galleries, auction houses, et. al. Used to signify a value that the work itself may or may not have.

Wig—a versatile head covering with profound socio-cultural implications, as demonstrated in the multiple screen video installation work of artist Kutluğ Ataman *Women Who Wear Wigs* (1999).

-X-

Exoskeleton—a hard crust. Develops naturally over time. For a nightmarish satirical vision of one, read artist Alasdair Gray's novel *Lanark* (1981).

-Y-

WhY?—a short question, short form of "Why bother?" or "I don't understand why this work was made." Alternatively, the beginning of everything, and the prodigal return.

Yesterday—i.e. Last Night, a preface for excuses, myths, and embarrassing tales.

-Z-

ZZz: Sleepwalking & Insomniacs—as filmmaker and artist Jack Smith once suggested, museums should open at midnight.

Fragment, Mediality, Gag

Sarah Pierce

> *"Alas," said the mouse, "the whole world is growing smaller every day. At the beginning it was so big that I was afraid, I kept running and running, and I was glad when I at last saw walls far away to the right and left, but these long walls have narrowed so quickly that I am in the last chamber already, and there in the corner stands the trap that I must run into."*
> *"You only need to change your direction," said the cat, and ate it up.*
> —Franz Kafka, "A Little Fable"

After first reading the short tale above, "A Little Fable" as Franz Kafka named it, it may be that you will automatically read it again. It is because the last line is so stupefying. As with our friend the mouse, the end traps us and swallows us up. *Gulp!* So we return to the beginning to escape an inescapable ending that will only repeat, inevitably with each return, again rereading and returning, arriving each time at the ending, and its inevitable *swallowing up!* It is said that when reading his stories aloud to his friends, Kafka used to laugh so hard that he would have to stop reading to catch his breath. Gasping for air, what kind of release might such a tale bring? Indeed, when the convulsions are involuntary, perhaps it is more akin to being violently tickled. Anyone who was teased this way as a child remembers that as the attack subsided, we would catch our breath, and it would begin again.

With repetition in mind, I would like to present some thoughts about "gesture"—a term that has received much attention of late in contemporary art. With each return, there is a reappearance, something made visible by or through gesture. Yet, in considering gesture, it is also important to address what is lost, and how loss, in particular, continues through the staged impulses that cause us to rethink, retrace, and repeat.

With reference to painting, and at least in art historical terms, gesture or the gestural has traditionally referred to individualized marks on a canvas. With a particular category of Abstract Expressionism developed after World War II, gesture is the visual traces of an artist's movements thought to be unique and fundamentally non-repeatable, although sometimes occurring in sequence or as a series. I would like to set aside this view of gesture, which not only describes the artist as the individual with a distinct relationship to a work of art, but also describes gesture as indicative of an artist's presence in a work. We can also forego the usage of terms such as "curatorial gesture" to describe the recognizable "mark" of a particular curator on a particular exhibition. Instead, I would like to consider gesture via the writings of Italian philosopher Giorgio Agamben. I am thinking of a collection of essays entitled *Means without Ends*, which introduces a number of political paradigms, some clearly understood as belonging to politics and others just marginally so, including a sphere of gestures. Agamben suggests there exists a politics of gesture—where means, freed from any relation to an end, yet still remaining means (and not purely aesthetics), posits a proper sphere of politics. In a short and dense essay called "Notes on Gesture," Agamben opens up this much needed discussion to art, dance, theater, and cinema, a discussion that moves us into a complex zone of collectively account-able relationships.

Illusion to Fragment

In these circles where trifles are of such importance, a gesture or a word at the outset is enough to ruin a newcomer. It is the principal merit of fine manners and the highest breeding that they produce the effect of a harmonious whole, in which every element is so blended that nothing is startling or obtrusive. Even those who break the laws of this science, either through ignorance or carried away by some impulse, must comprehend that it is with social intercourse as with music, a single discordant note is a complete negation of the art itself, for the harmony exists only when all its conditions are observed down to the least particular.
—Honoré de Balzac, *Lost Illusions* (1837)

Agamben begins "Notes on Gesture" by citing a remarkable disappearance: "By the end of the nineteenth century, the Western bourgeoisie had definitely lost its gestures."[1] Gesture has ties to class, in particular, to a class preoccupied with rules of etiquette and style as the outward expressions of inner worlds. Gesture, as a mannered, ritualized manifestation of shared attitudes, gives public way to one's private self. In the English translation to Honoré de Balzac's *Lost Illusions*, references to gesture are numerous if not utterly vague. Characters mingle amidst a world of gestures, gestures the author never seems compelled to describe physically, as though any reader would know or should know what he means by phrases like: "She comforted him with an adorable gesture," and "He expressed his thanks by one of those gestures that speak more eloquently than words."[2] People ponder other people's gestures with affection, but never confusion, never questioning their meaning, through an exhaustive inventory of scornful gestures "that seemed charming to the provincial," a gesture "worthy of Talma," regal gestures, queenly gestures, comical gestures, gestures of denial, gestures of the beloved, gestures of protest. Today's reader can only imagine what bodily movements might accompany each subsequent representation.

Half a century after Balzac wrote *Lost Illusions*, Gilles de la Tourette famously observed nine patients that displayed the symptoms of a strange neuropsychiatric disorder, which would come to bear his name. With thousands of cases to follow, Tourette's syndrome described a spectrum of sudden, repetitive, non-rhythmic motor and vocal "tics." Yet, by the beginning of the twentieth century, recorded cases of Tourette's practically ceased to exist. Agamben presents this phenomenon as a postulation, not as the *disappearance* of a syndrome, but as its extreme proliferation. "At some point, everybody had lost control of their gestures and was walking and gesticulating frantically."[3] An impression was re-affirmed for Agamben when viewing the early cinema of Étienne-Jules Marey and the Lumière brothers, which began during these same years. With no one ever completely starting or finishing any gesture, the illusion of a "harmonious whole," espoused by Balzac, yields to fragments. Gesture breaks down and we arrive, not coincidentally, at the creation of early cinema: "In the cinema, the society that has lost its gestures tries, at once, to reclaim what it has lost and to record its loss."[4]

I cannot help being reminded of the Russian filmmaker Sergei Eisenstein, who wrote an essay in 1929, "The Unexpected," which enthusiastically describes a visit to Moscow by a Japanese kabuki theater troupe. Kabuki, of course, is a theater of gestures. Each movement made on stage is stylized and "readable" to an audience schooled in its meaning. A character's exaggerated wiping of a sword after committing murder, functions in a larger system of codes and sounds, costumes and sets. No one gesture stands out alone, nor can gesture be read in isolation, but rather, meaning in a kabuki play is produced by the sheer physical form of the ensemble. Plot cannot be construed by following gesture alone. Gesture does not narrate, as in language. What excited Eisenstein were the "mechanical" cuts *between* gestures, when an actor would change character without leaving stage. These cuts produced something unexpected, an effect that Eisenstein likened to his theory of dialectic montage. Two conflicting shots, when placed together will create unexpected meaning. Like Agamben's example, which cites Walter Benjamin, the single image of the flipbook, delivered frozen and in isolation, is meaningless. Meaning requires the flicking of pages, and it is through a shortening of the gaps in-between turning that the flipbook's pages perform collectively, and always collectively through motion. Agamben concludes that the element of cinema is gesture and not the image; image is but a fragment of gesture.

The Exhibition of a Mediality

Agamben's sense of the fragment is an extension of Gilles Deleuze's description in *Cinema 1* of the "movement-image," which develops a form of spatialized cinema, of time determined and measured by movement. Movement in early cinema does not render holistic time, but a "mobile section of duration." Although modernity has given a certain status to the image, every image is part of a larger whole, a fragment that never exists in isolation. The rigidity of the image as singular and discrete, gives way to the collectivity of gesture. And it is here that Agamben shifts his discussion from aesthetics to ethics. "The gesture is the exhibition of a mediality: It is the process of making a means visible as such. It allows the emergence of a being-in-a-medium of human beings, and thus, it opens the ethical dimension for them."[5] Like image is to gesture, we already and always exist in relation with one another, never in isolation. For what is a being-in-a-medium of human beings, if not a reminder that no singular self pre-exists our relations with others? To exist is to coexist.

If gesture is the exhibition of a mediality, then through gesture, something is expressed. This is very different to a notion of gesture as expression. Gesture does not communicate, it does not express something *in* language. It is the "communication of a communicability."[6] In gesture, there is the potential for something to be communicated, but only potentially, and always something that language cannot express. Literally, lacking words, gesture compensates for this loss.

If we think about how curious it seems that Balzac's readers would have had a handle on so many gestures that he leaves undescribed, we need to remember that at the end of *Lost Illusions*, our hero Lucien, whose life in Paris relies on his ability to read the gestures of those in his close company, is left utterly duped and alone. Visibility is not the same as legibility. Misrecognition leads to lost illusions, or, disillusionment.

So then, how might we consider gesture as the exhibition of loss, or lost meaning? In a most extraordinary passage from Atom Egoyan's 1994 film *Exotica*, Christina, an erotic dancer, enters the stage of an upscale nightclub. Against a soundtrack of Leonard Cohen's "Everybody Knows", wearing a schoolgirl's uniform, white blouse, kilt, and knee socks, she performs a slow, ritualized routine, made all the more striking due to interstices of odd sequences of hand movements repeated throughout the course of the dance. These occur "out of sync" with the music, and as such, they not only interrupt the typically seamless flow of erotic dance, they reveal something *beyond* the erotic. Each movement exceeds visual codes of pleasure and titillation. On the one hand, Christina's hand gestures may be read as pure affect, a kind of representation of a representation that mimics sign language without actually saying anything. Yet, Christina's performance, more than being a medium for the pleasure of others, is the exhibition of mediality. What she makes visible through her dance is the depth of an *incommunicability* (to play with Agamben's description)—Francis's suspension in grief over the murders of his wife and daughter. We come to understand that his obsession with watching Christina perform her schoolgirl act is bound to the intimacy of this loss.

Gesture in *Exotica* moves us beyond morality and into a sphere of human relations: the "ethical dimension." For Emmanuel Levinas, ethics is our obligation to the other *in the absence* of any regulating, reducible, totalizing, or anterior imperative. For Agamben, "What characterizes gesture is that, in it, nothing is being produced or acted, but rather, something is being endured and supported. The gesture, in other words, opens the sphere of *ethos* as the more proper sphere of that which is human."[7] Without mistaking Christina's dance as an aesthetic "act," we can understand it as an unspoken intimacy, shared, endured, supported between her and Francis. It is her attention to another's grief, despite the distance between them. Importantly, it is not intimacy with an "end." It does not claim, recuperate, or redeem. Agamben's consideration of ethics in *The Coming Community* also emphasizes this way of being together in the absence of any direct imperative, which, for him, evolves as the simple fact of existence, "as possibility," in the absence of destiny: "The fact that must constitute the point of departure for any discourse on ethics is that there is no essence, no historical or spiritual vocation, no biological destiny that humans must enact or realize."[8] *Possibility* is what complicates the sphere of human relations, and this complication makes ethics possible. For Agamben, ethics exists as potentiality—it is the possibility of acting without prescription in the absence of a language of good and evil.

With What Words

At the very moment that we arrive at "the communication of a communicability," Agamben introduces a caveat: the "gag." "The gesture is essentially always a gesture of not being able to figure something out in language; it is always a gag in the proper meaning of the term."[9] For Agamben, gag has a double meaning. It is that which literally hinders speech by being placed in the mouth, and it is a type of improvisation, as in the actor's gag, which compensates for a loss of memory on stage, when one cannot remember the words. But, there is a third meaning of gag, the "gag order," which legally restricts a person from speaking publicly. It is a tool to prevent speech, to suppress it. The gag is the limit.

The films of Robert Bresson convey worlds of wordless gestures, but perhaps none more so than *Pickpocket* (1959). We follow Michel, the lead, through a series of encounters, many of which take place with little or no dialogue. Those that are invariably "silent" involve a ballet of intricate hand gestures, which disclose Michel's crimes, both as they take place, and as he practices his craft alone in his apartment. As the template for the infamous scene in Paul Schrader's *Taxi Driver* (1976), where Robert de Niro as Travis Bickle postures in front of a mirror while repeating the words, "Are you talking to me?," Michel calculates his crimes wordlessly, yet with equally merciless repetition. In austere, unadorned silence, he works over the suited hanger that represents his victim, mounting his attack from behind and to the side, where Bickle addresses his imaginary adversary frontally, and with pungent violence.

The scene that introduces Michel begins with a voiceover, "Men who do these things keep silent. Those who talk haven't done them. Yet, I have done them." Ludwig Wittgenstein once wrote that confession has to be a part of one's new life. He also wrote, "Whereof one cannot speak, thereof one must be silent." An accomplished logician, Wittgenstein sought to find the logic behind misunderstood language. Yet, to say that something cannot be spoken of, is already to speak of it. Likewise, gesture is a condition that both silences and allows us to speak. The artist Terre Thaemlitz introduces his compendium of writings, entitled *Nuisance*, by cataloguing the condition in which he writes and is writing against—incessant optimism. He describes this optimism within critical fields (commercial, academic, artistic, or otherwise) as a continual desire "to make things better."[10] We fixate our discussions in culture on hypothetical notions of what could be or what should be, while remaining silent about an immediate material need to simply end what exists but is unacceptable. Here, Thaemlitz enters a lengthy discussion of pessimism and nuisance, as ways to contest optimism's critical claims on the future, by seeding one's critique in an immediate present. In characterizing the conditions that we operate within, that we, in turn, reproduce, we need to consider what the compulsion to produce, indeed, to *over produce*, says about the extent of communicability. What do all these publications, and exhibitions, and discussions tell us about the limits of language? What kind of discourse can be produced and acted when discourse is neither endured nor supported? Within a sphere of gesture, a sphere of pure means leads down a corridor whose long walls have narrowed. There, in the corner, stands the trap. We only need to change our direction, and then, to change it again.

1   Giorgio Agamben, "Notes on Gesture," in *Means without Ends* (Minneapolis, 2000), p. 49.
2   Honoré de Balzac, *Lost Illusions* (1837). Project Gutenberg ebook: 2004 #13159.
3   Agamben (see note 1), p. 50.
4   Ibid., p. 53.
5   Ibid., p. 58.
6   Ibid., p. 59.
7   Ibid., p. 57.
8   Giorgio Agamben, *The Coming Community*, trans. M. Hardt (Minneapolis, 1983), p. 43.
9   Agamben (see note 1), p. 59.
10   Terre Thaemlitz, "Introduction to Nuisance," in *Nuisance: Writings on Identity Jamming and Digital Audio Production* (upcoming). www.comatonse.com/writings/nuisance.html

Isaac Mendes **Belisario**

Isaac Mendes **Belisario**

SKETCHES OF CHARACTER,

In Illustration of the Habits, Occupation, and Costume

OF THE

NEGRO POPULATION,

IN THE

ISLAND OF JAMAICA,

Drawn from Nature, and in Lithography,

BY

I. M. BELISARIO.

" Nothing extenuate, nor set down aught in malice."

Price { To Subscribers . . . . £1 6 8 } Per Number, Colored.
{ To Non-Subscribers . . . . 1 13 4 }

PUBLISHED BY THE ARTIST, AT HIS RESIDENCE, NO. 21, KING-STREET.

KINGSTON, JAMAICA:

SOLD ALSO BY MESSRS. JAMES WALLACE & CO.
MESSRS. SMITH & CLARK ; MESSRS. JORDON & OSBORN ; L. TREADWAY ;
F. EGAN ; AND MATTHEW HYMAN, PORT-MARIA.

Printed by J. R. De Cordova, at the Gleaner's Office, No. 36, Harbour-Street.

1838.

PREFACE.

Various have been the reasons, or rather apologies, frequently advanced by writers, for presenting their works to the public : conveying thereby for the most part, evident distrust of their legitimate pretension to favor.

Such precaution, may in some few instances, have a tendency to disarm criticism, or at least, to cause its lash to fall more lightly ; but surely claimants for indulgence, would be spared the humiliation of either craving mercy, or having recourse to subterfuge, were they openly to avow their motives for having embarked on the perilous voyage of public approval, and at the same time stipulate for the privilege due to authors, "viz," that of not seeking more in their works, than they themselves intend.

Shielded as this production it is hoped will be, from the severity of criticism with which a literary work might probably have been visited, still the Artist is not altogether free from apprehension, for the safety of his Bark, launched as it is on the like troubled Sea.

His motives for having intruded on public attention, he unreservedly states to be, firstly, the ambition to acquire repute in his favorite occupation—the Arts; secondly, a desire to hand down faithful delineations of a people, whose habits, manners, and costume, bear the stamp of originality, and in which changes are being daily effected by the rapid strides of civilization ; and lastly, the hope of reaping an abundant harvest from the undertaking, to compensate for the toil, anxiety, and time bestowed on its completion, in a clime so inimical to the furtherance of such an object.

It will be borne in mind, as set forth in the Prospectus, that, he purposes to furnish but " *Sketches of Character*," steering clear of *Caricature* : nature in her ordinary form alone, having been the source from whence all the original drawings were derived, and however amusing her accidental deviations from that course of moulding the human shape, may prove to the admirers of the ludicrous, it behoves not an Artist in this instance, to lend himself to the portraying of deformity !

Whilst your Purveyor, Gentle Reader, disclaims all intention of becoming a Satirist with his pencil, he confidently indulges the hope of being enabled, nevertheless, to provide a series of mirthful, and otherwise interesting designs, combined with strict attention to costume, so varied and picturesque in the Negro Population.

To those friends who have aided him either by useful hints, or the loan of Works, conveying valuable information on the various subjects, on which he will have occasion to touch in the progress of the publication, the Artist thus publicly begs to tender his acknowledgments, such timely assistance having afforded him considerable facilities.

In conclusion, he has also to express his sense of the obligation conferred by the Subscribers, in the liberal support extended to the Work; this he trusts may augur favorably of their future encouragement, by kindly naming it in their several circles—to merit which, his best energies, and close study, shall be unceasingly employed.

KINGSTON, JAMAICA, JUNE 1837.

RED SET-GIRLS, AND JACK-IN-THE-GREEN.

Having paid all due respect to the Queen, these Damsels, and their embowered companion, next claim attention ; but previously to entering into detailed particulars regarding them, it may not prove altogether uninteresting to the reader to be informed, whence the origin of term " Set-girls."

It is thus given in a popular work* :—

" Many years ago, an Admiral of the " Red," was superseded on the Jamaica station, by an Ad-" miral of the " Blue," and both of them gave balls at Kingston to the *Brown Girls :* for the *fair-sex* " elsewhere, are called *Brown Girls* in Jamaica.   " In consequence of these balls, all Kingston was di-" vided into parties : from thence, the division spread into other districts, and ever since, the whole is-" land, at Christmas, is separated into the rival factions of the " Blues" and the " Reds," (the " Reds" re-" presenting the English, the " Blues" " the Scotch,) who contend for setting forth their processions with " the greatest taste and magnificence."

On the correctness of this traditionary account, it is presumed, reliance may be placed, considering the authority quoted : we shall therefore at once proceed with our notice of these capering, whirling and light-hearted creatures.

All their dresses, it may be observed, correspond in color, &c. agreeably to established rule, those of their Queen, and other Leaders, differing only in the *superior texture* of the materials.   These latter also display a greater profusion of Jewellery than their young followers can boast ; yet, however homely may be the earrings and bracelets, they are never dispensed with by the Set-girls—such lovers are they of ornaments.   Thus gaily attired then, they sally forth in the morning at ten or eleven o'clock, properly marshalled, and attended by a Band, *(*as shewn in the " Order of Procession") and parade the town, with little intermission, till night, when they are invited to enter private houses, to dance and sing, (this is likewise their practice during their excursions by day.)   Refreshments, and a gratuity are presented them for the amusement so afforded the families, and they retire to repeat the same elsewhere, till a late hour.   There is another Set, denominated " House-Keepers," who never *dance* in their progress through the streets.

The sums thus collected, frequently amounting to eight or ten pounds per day, are either divided amongst the Set, or employed in defraying the expences of a Ball and Supper given at the termination of the Christmas Holidays, the season of these merry-doings, when they are allowed three days, and also New Years'-day, for their celebration.

The degree of jealousy heretofore existing between the rival Sets, can scarcely be conceived.   The writer has been credibly informed, their animosity some twenty years back, was of so inveterate a nature, that their meetings in public, seldom passed without violent affrays : proving fatal in most instances, to their articles of dress, if not also to their persons, in the struggle for pre-eminence.   Such *unlady-like conduct* in the present day, being regarded as highly indecorous, this description of warfare is rarely witnessed—the parties contenting themselves with the expression of epithets only, without resorting to more *striking* proofs of their hatred.   Profound secrecy is even enjoined the Dress-Maker, on the pattern of the printed cotton selected, and on pain of their displeasure, dare she divulge *that* or the *fashion* of their dress, (differing every year) to the opposite set.

Strange as it may appear, they constantly carry *opened* umbrellas in their *nocturnal*, as well as day-light rambles.   N. B. Stockings in very few instances constitute a part of their attire, with the exception of the *Leaders* of the Set, who invariably wear them.

The Jack-in-the-Green of Jamaica, differs in very few points from the same description of personage, who accompanies the chimney-sweepers on the 1st May in England—they both travel *in cog.*   The covering of the former, is composed of portions of the leaves of the cocoa-nut tree, attached to hoops, diminishing in circumference to the top, which is crowned by a large bow, with the addition of a couple of flags.

ORDER OF PROCESSION OF THE SET-GIRLS.
Four Grand Masters, to protect the Set.

Adjutant bearing Flag. } Hand-drum. Singer.† Tambourine. Violin. Queen. Triangle. Tambourine. Maam. Hand-drum. { Adjutant bearing Flag.

Commodore.‡

Set-Girls in equal numbers.   Set-Girls in equal numbers.

Jack-in-the-Green.

---

* " Journal of a West-India Proprietor," by the late Matthew Gregory Lewis, Esq. M. P.

† Or leader of the chorus, the Set-girls always singing some unconnected ditty—the specimen given will convey a just idea of these compositions.

‡ A very stout woman is usually chosen to fill this post of honor, but no satisfactory reason has ever been assigned, for the jumble of naval, military, and other distinctions, bestowed on these Commanders.

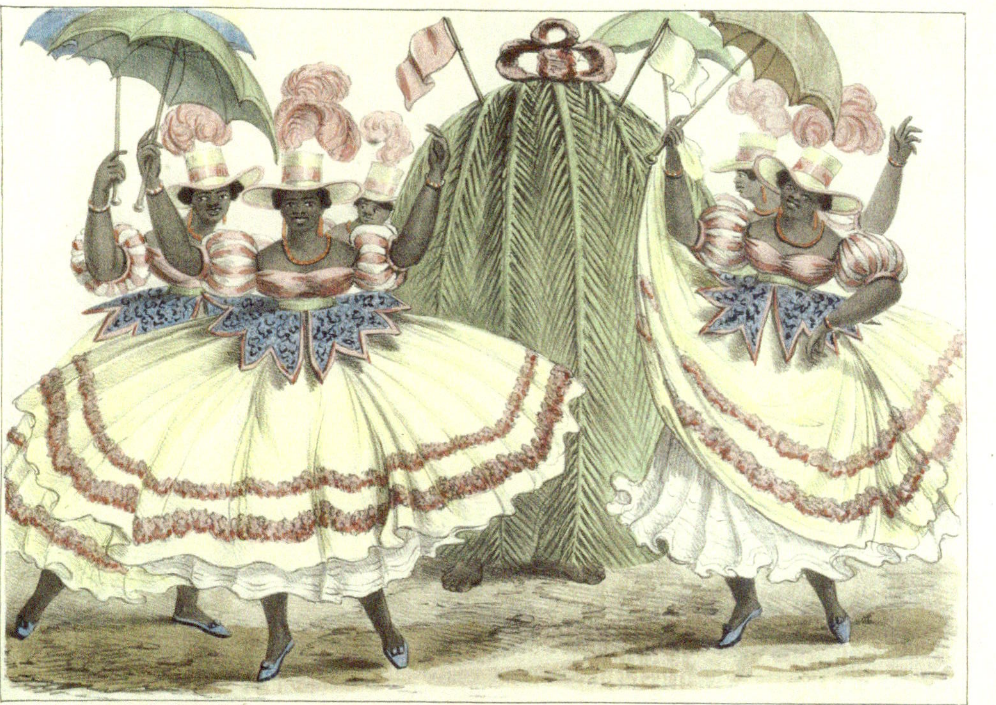

Drawn after Nature & on Stone by J. M. Belisario.

Print'd by A. Duperly.

RED SET-GIRLS, and JACK-in-the-GREEN.

Kingston Jamaica   June 1837

SONG.

> " There is a Regiment of the 64th, we expect from home,
> From London to Scotland away they must go,
> There was one among them, that I really love well,
> With his bonny Scotch plaid, and his bayonet so shining,
> Now pray my noble King, if you really love me well,
> Disband us from slavery, and set us at large."
> Chorus.—La la la, la la la.

Perhaps the reader's quickness of perception, may enable him to discover the meaning in this choice scrap, the writer pleads inability, and therefore retires from the attempt. The incongruities to be found almost in every line, never strike these folks, on the contrary, they are perfectly satisfied with this style of arranging their ideas, without for a moment stopping to consider, if it be prose, or poetry.—Here we have a love-sick *fair-one*, absolutely enamoured of a soldier she has *never seen*, and in conclusion, presuming the King is in love with her.

These Songs are chanted at the top of their voice, with an accompaniment of instruments, for the most part out of tune, and played by musicians, *rather* carelessly dressed.

JAW-BONE, OR HOUSE JOHN-CANOE.

It might perhaps prove almost as fruitless, as it would be a difficult task, to trace the origin of the "John-Canoe." In the absence then of more positive information on the subject, it is presumed, we may be allowed to hazard the opinion that, this description of *Merry-Andrew*, was introduced into the Island with the Slave-Trade, having since undergone certain changes in costume, &c. produced, no doubt, by the nearer approach this people had made towards civilization. Yet, with all such attempts at improvement on their own rude mode of habiting these grotesque figures, sufficient still remained for a long series of years, so monstrous and uncouth in their general character, as to induce the belief, they were derived from an untutored, and savage nation.

By the powerful influence of the *March of Intellect*, this Christmas amusement, with many others, has been nearly abandoned, leaving but a catalogue of names, to remind one of the by-gone days of merriment in Jamaica, when the streets were thronged with forms as varied, and hideous, as a mind disturbed by " Blue Devils," could well have conjured up, and the scene might not inaptly have been styled a *Tropical Carnival*. Some few tribes of Africans, may still be found enjoying their song and dance to the *Gumbay*, after the manner of their native country, but such instances are rare.

The most conspicuous of those who *annually* attract public notice, are the " Koo-Koo," or " Actor-Boy," and the " Jaw-Bone John-Canoe." Of the former *Buskined Hero*, more in the second number of the Work. The latter, non-descript compound, in half-military, half-mountebank attire, comes under present consideration. His regimental coat and sash, are invariably retained, whatever changes may take place in the other parts of his costume—and as a rule without exception, he (in common with the whole of the John-Canoe fraternity) always wears a mask, with a profusion of dark hair, which is suffered to fall in large wild ringlets over his face and shoulders, giving to his appearance an extraordinary and savage air—scaring, and creating wonderment in the gaping crowd around him.

The* house is usually constructed of pasteboard and colored papers—it is also frequently highly ornamented with beads, tinsel, spangles, pieces of looking-glass, &c. &c. and being firmly fixed on a board, the bearer is enabled to balance it, whilst going through many strange contortions of body and limbs, *miscalled*, dancing : the position in which he is drawn, will convey a tolerably accurate idea of one of his favorite steps, consisting of rapid crossings of his legs, several times repeated, and terminating in a sudden stoppage, at which point, it requires all the ability of this *Posture-Master*, to poise his body at one and the same moment, with his paper castle borne aloft, and indeed, it is truly astonishing to witness the celerity, and precision with which this feat of agility is performed : not *altogether* unlike the movement so *rapturously applauded* in the Foreign Dancers at the the Opera-House, who, after having executed an extraordinary *pirouette*, remain, as it were, transfixed to the stage.—Pardon the comparison ye *Artistes ! ! !*

---

* The specimen as given in the print, although *a plain one*, has been selected, to shew an evident attempt (however humble) at West Indian architecture—the scallopped pillars, being intended as imitations of the same kinds of supporters in wood, to the balconies so universally attached to dwellings in warm climates,

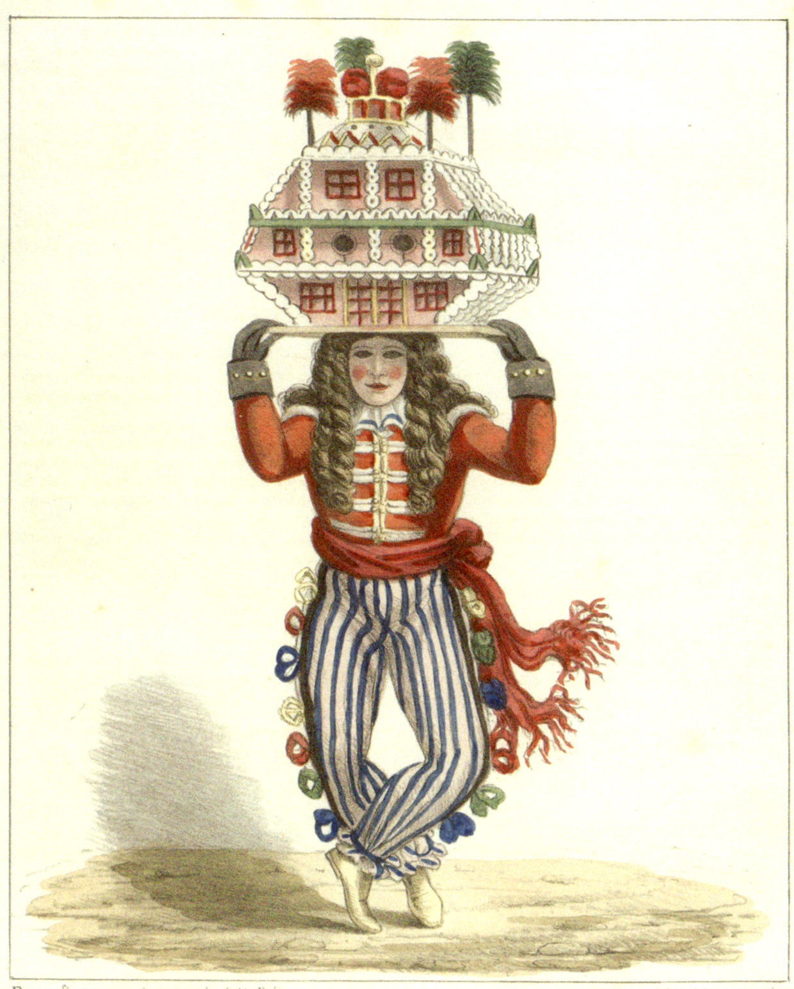

JAW-BONE, or HOUSE JOHN-CANOE.

Kingston, Jamaica, July 1837.

A *rather* discordant chorus of female voices, added to the stunning and harsh grating sounds produced by the instruments in the band, constitute the only *music*.

" And when with none of these they meet,
They dance to the echo of their feet."

It would appear, that *sound*, without the slightest attention to *harmony*, delights these personages, for they are in no way annoyed, should the vibration of a drum even be destroyed by a fracture in the parchment. Their perambulations through the streets, are rendered profitable, by the generosity of the house-keepers and passengers, and the funds thus raised, are, as usual, expended in feasting and carousing. To relieve the chief actor in the scene, one of his attendants carries the house occasionally, and when it is considered that, his head is covered with false hair, weighing four or five pounds, and his face concealed by a mask, it will be readily admitted, said relief must prove both requisite, and acceptable in a *meridian* temperature, ranging between *eighty and ninety degrees*, not to mention, the constant and violent action, into which his whole frame is thrown.

BAND OF THE " JAW-BONE JOHN-CANOE."

More primitive instruments in form, (to be styled *musical*) than those before us, could not well be conceived, and it must be admitted, they are in *most excellent keeping* with the musicians, whose appearance, clearly proves them, non-observers of the requisites to the outer-man.

The small square wooden frame, over which a goat's skin is tightly strained, is termed a " Gumbay,"* " Box," or " Bench-drum," and by being briskly struck several times in quick succession with one hand, and once only with the other, produces a monotonous sound with but little vibration :—it is supported by a Bass-Drum : *very unlike* that in the band at the " Horse-Guards" in London, certainly, either in its tone, fashion, or the style in which it is played upon by the stately, and noble-looking Black, attached to the regiment. The tattered urchin who upholds the "Gumbay" in front, is by no means an *exaggerated* sketch, many such half-attired ramblers being daily seen in the streets of Kingston—indeed, female, as well as male negro children, and youths, who are not constantly about the persons of respectable house-keepers, seldom, or never wear but one article of dress.

The instrument from which the " John-Canoe" in the foregoing print derives his title (a *novel* mode of conferring distinction) is simply the lower jaw of a horse, on the teeth of which, a piece of wood is passed quickly up and down, occassioning a rattling noise†—this would not prove an inappropriate prelude, to the entrance of a gibbering spectre in some theatrical representation. It may be observed of these *peripatetic orchestras* that, they in general *follow*, instead of *preceding*, in the procession.

* Under the same denomination, the African Tribes have an instrument, *barrelled-shaped*, and of great length, used also as a drum,
† To loosen the teeth, the Jaw is hung in the smoke for several days.

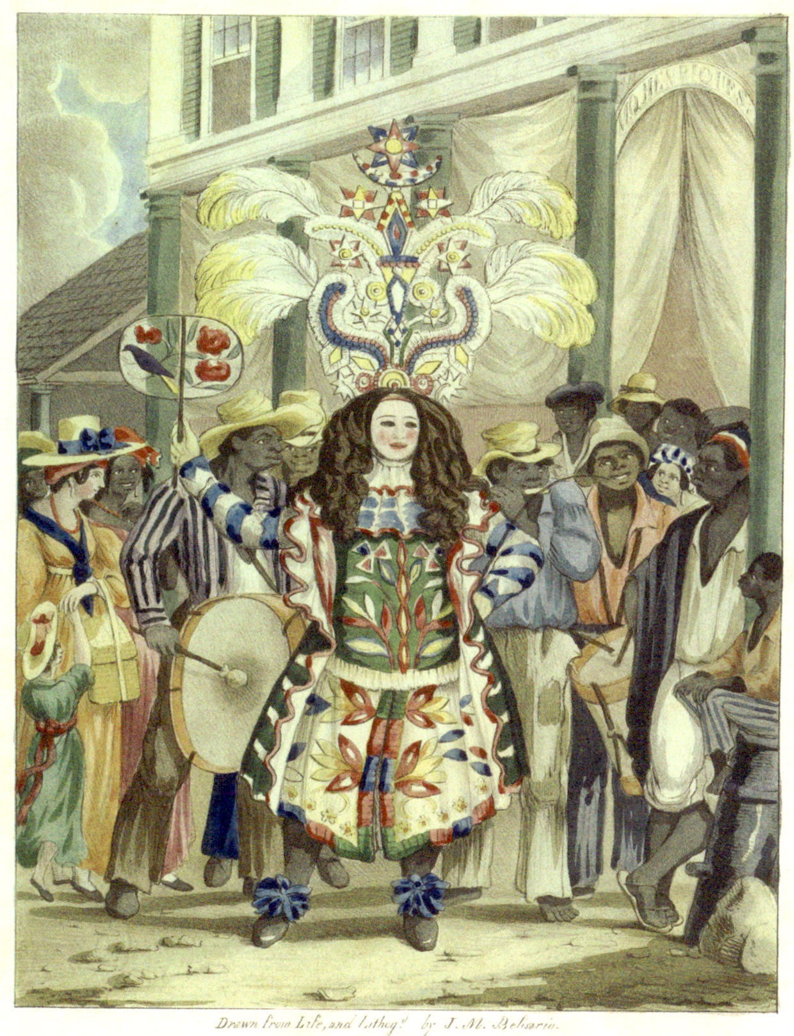

Drawn from Life, and Lithog.ᵈ by J. M. Belisario.

"KOO, KOO, OR ACTOR-BOY."

Kingston . Jamaica , Oct.ʳ 1837.

Printed by A. Duperly.

" KOO, KOO,* OR ACTOR-BOY."

Such is the strange title, by which this Aspirant to Histrionic honors is designated. Ten or twelve years back, several companies of these self-styled Performers, envious of each other's abilities, strolled through the streets, habited in varied costumes, considered by them however, as having been in strict accordance with the *characters* they were called upon to sustain—for be it known, they dared to perpetrate " murder most foul," even on the plays of Shakspeare.

Of late years, this class of *John-Canoe*† has found but little inducement for the exercise of his talent, wanting that grand stimulant to energy—Competition—candidates for *Dramatic* fame among his brethren, having gradually decreased in numbers, leaving the field open to a few only of these heroes of the *Sock and Buskin* who, from having once figured prominently in the *higher walks of their art*, now descend from their pedestals, and content themselves annually with the public exhibition of their finery, and the performance of certain unmeaning pantomimic actions, which are also repeated at private dwellings,—whereby they contrive to draw largely on the bounty of the parties inviting them.

In order to qualify themselves for the representations above alluded to, a negro who could *read*, and instruct them in committing their parts to memory, was pressed into the service for the purpose— *that portion* of his Pupils' education, having been *unfortunately omitted*—a remunerating sum was paid him for the four or five weeks so occupied, previous to the Christmas Holidays, at which period, the effect of his labours was manifested to a wondering and admiring audience. " Richard the Third" was a favorite Tragedy with them ; but *selections* only were made from it, without paying the slightest regard to the *order* in which the " Bard of Avon" had deemed it proper to arrange his subject: Pizarro was also one of their Stock pieces ; but whatever might have been the performance, a Combat and Death invariably ensued, when a ludicrous contrast was produced between the smiling mask, and the actions of the dying man. At this Tragical point, there was always a general call for music—and dancing immediately commenced—this proved too great a provocative usually to be resisted even by the slain, and he accordingly became resuscitated, and joined the merry throng. Scenery was of necessity dispensed with, from the removal of such appendage, proving extremely inconvenient to a Company strolling only from street to street.

If competitors for *Dramatic excellence* be wanting in the present day, the *vanity of excelling* in costliness of attire at least, has not expired, as may be annually seen, when a struggle for superiority in that respect amongst these " Actor Boys," takes place on the Parade, a large and much frequented thoroughfare in Kingston, near the immediate scene of business, or in front of one of the principal Taverns. Gentlemen who may be passing, are requested to decide which is the smartest dressed.

The majority of voices is considered definitive as by previous arrangement, and the individual thus distinguished, then retires " with all his blushing honors thick upon him :" *gratification of feeling alone* forming the prize gained on the occasion, and we may here enquire, what greater reward frequently awaits the achievement of exalted actions in higher life ?

* Through the kindness of a friend, we are enabled to furnish the following derivation of the term *Koo-Koo*. It appears that many years back, this *John-Canoe* performed in pantomimic actions *only*, consisting of supplications for food—as being demanded by his empty stomach. At each request, an attendant chorus repeated " Koo-Koo ;" this was intended in imitation of the rumbling sound of the bowels, when in a hungry state.

† The term *John-Canoe* has had many derivations applied to it, amongst others, that it has arisen from the circumstance of negroes having formerly carried a house in a boat, or canoe ; but it is perhaps more consistent to regard it, as a corruption of *Gens inconnus*, signifying, " unknown folks," from their always wearing masks. We are strengthened in this opinion, by the frequent occurrence of foreign appellations, being attached to the various grades of people of colour, fruits, &c. in this Island.

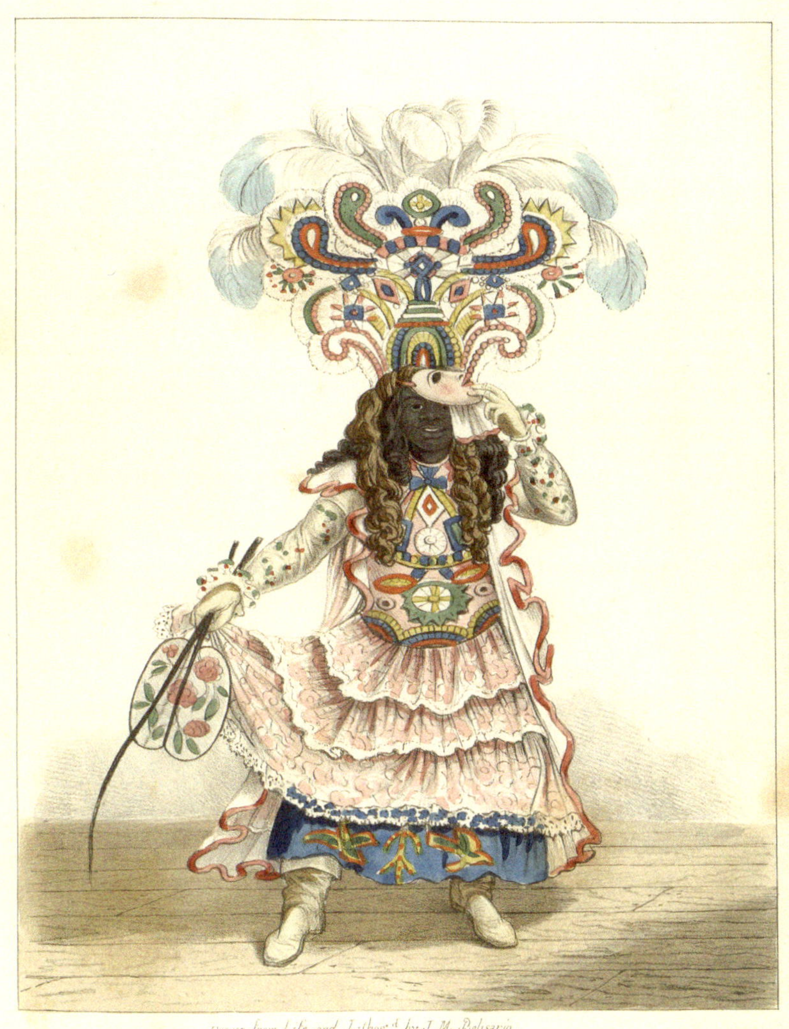

"KOO, KOO, OR ACTOR-BOY."

Kingston Jamaica.

On being asked if he were a * married man, he replied " *yes Massa ; but me wife no tay wid me again—†him gone, so lef me.*"   Did he cry on losing her ?   " *What for cry,—him no bin go from me ? me no send him away.*   But were she to die, would he then cry ?   " *Oh yes Massa fe true, 'cause all done ! ! !*"

This was uttered in a tone so expressive of forgiveness for injury sustained, as to leave no doubt on our minds of his sincerity—and afforded as excellent a moral lesson as could have been inculcated—that with death, all animosity of feeling should cease !

‡ SUNG BY LOVEY WHILST DANCING HIS PUPPETS.

" Tang ding, ding dang, tiggi dang, ding dang,"
" John-crow pick me dandy eye out,"
" When me come to you, you come to me,"
" Me love you, you love me"
" John-crown pick me dandy eye out,"
            " Tiggi ding, &c. &c. &c.

" Man-a-war Buckra, man-a-war Buckra, never, never do for me"
" When me go to man-a-war ship, me get a doubloon,"
" When me go to Soldier Barrack, me get a piece of pork,"
" Man-a-war Buckra, good for the ladies"
            " Ting a rang dang, tiggi dang, &c. &c.

" Please me Massa, tanky me Missis."
" Love and fancy good for the ladies,"

NAMES GIVEN TO HIS BOUQUETS.

" Kiss your love, and please your heart"
    " Touch your heart"
    " It smell so sweet"

" Miss Nancy in the room,"
" Mr. Brazen in the hall"
" Captain Buckra"
" Young Miss, (applied to the *buds* of flowers)"
" Old Missis, (ditto,   *full blown*   ditto.)"

* We have been given to understand, Lovey is *not* married ; but *considers* himself united in wedlock, on the principle we suppose, of
            " If you loves I, as I loves you,"
            " No knife can cut our love in two."

† The Masculine pronoun, is frequently substituted for the Feminine, by Negroes.

‡ These choice scraps, absolutely forming part, and parcel of Lovey, must be our apology for their insertion. In vocal powers, *he fancies himself second to none in Jamaica*—and is also an excellent mimic—imitating the cough of the aged, equally well with the voice of youth.

Kutluğ Ataman

*Nikola **Dietrich**: With reference to your words "identity is not something that you possess, but something that people make you wear," the four women in your early work* Women Who Wear Wigs *(1999) literally shows this. The irony seems to be that it is the concealment (here the wigs) that allows for a revelation—under the wigs, a sort of freedom is possible. On the other hand, there is, of course, also the aspect of hiding. How do you see this? What were your initial thoughts before producing this work? How did you meet, or rather approach the women?*

*Kutluğ **Ataman**:* Wigs, in this specific work, are shown as one way of manipulating one's identity and this is, in no way, the only means for these women. I do not think so much of concealment, exclusively, but also of manipulation, in the sense of constructing. Identity is a construction. It is a role that is played by actors, actors being everyday people. All of us. *Women Who Wear Wigs* is, to me at least, not about wigs at all. Wigs are only an excuse here to point to or attempt to reveal how identity is something that is constructed, like a dress that is tailored, and worn.

When I first started thinking about it, I did not start with a set of ideas. I came across one of the women and started to think about other possibilities and, suddenly, the puzzle revealed itself to me. I knew about all of these women, but had never thought of them before within the same context. And now, suddenly, they were connected with wigs.

*N**D**: The way that certain everyday gestures can create and control a situation is something that we wanted to articulate with the exhibition. Would you say that with the characters you are looking at in your work, you lay open life itself as a construction and a fiction?*

KA: Life is a construct. That is why we invented fiction. Fiction gives us a chance to reflect on our own lives. That is why we are spectators: We are curious of ourselves. Who am I? What am I doing on this stage? What is my role? Can I change it if I wanted? And so on ...

*N**D**: Yes. Everybody is playing a role whether on the front stage or, in a more subtle way, behind the curtain. Equally, everybody needs to know his or her role (through poses, mimics, gestures, lines) in the little theater of daily life.*

The 4 Seasons of Veronica Read *(2002) or* Stefan's Room *(2004) are good examples. In your film and video work, you stage ordinary people with obsessive interests. The viewer becomes an observant of the wondrous curiosities of other people's lives. One reading is that by collecting all these characters and putting them together in a whole, they constitute one possible self-portrait of you (see Emre Baykal, in* Kutluğ Ataman, you tell me about yourself anyway! *(Istanbul, 2008)). How would you see it?*

KA: The simplest explanation of it is that I am a looker. I hold the camera and the viewer accesses the subjects' story only through me. I frame the subject as I see. Therefore, any claims of objectivity become obsolete; everything is subjective. Moreover, I deal with my subjects in areas that really are my concerns. I often feel that I show them playing out concerns that are my own. My subjectivity makes them my own. In a way, I steal part of their lives by filming, and only the part that is important to me. So I am not surprised that they mirror me.

*N**D**: Does this also describe the way you find/choose your actors? The people who you feel closest to?*

KA: The subjects of my art works are real people. I have known most of them before I became an artist. If, however, you mean the actors, I mean professional actors who work on my movies, this is a completely different ball game altogether. In this case, I do proper casting that would best fit the fictive character in my mind.

ND: Could your art practice be seen as a group portrait of people with various activities and particular ways of living that, cumulatively, reflect on the diverse ways identity is constructed?

KA: I used to think of them as pieces of the puzzle which, when completed, would become a portrait of myself, a self-portrait.

ND: You have worked with films and storytelling for many years now. When was it clear to you that you wanted to work with the camera?

KA: When I was in high school, I acquired a camera. It was the best thing I ever owned. I loved it. I was completely obsessed by it. I don't think I ever thought of any other activity, in fact. And I still love it the same way as before. To this date, the capabilities of a camera are magical, like that Douglas Sirk movie, *Imitation of Life*. It is a magical tool.

ND: Metamorphosis, transformation, recreation, and reincarnation are they subjects that link your works together: as symbols of the many fluctuations we go through in our lives?

KA: All these juicy notions and concepts are one way or another of how we look at life itself, from many different angles. It is like holding an object in your hands and trying to understand it, trying to decipher it; and you need methods to penetrate into its structure and chemistry and mechanisms. Metamorphosis, transformation, recreation, and reincarnation are all aiding in offering different ways of dissecting.

ND: Right now you are working on a new feature film. I am most curious to hear what it is about. Could you tell me about the main subject and the protagonists?

KA: I am writing about a women writer who creates her own killer. One day, the doorbell rings and he appears at the door with a gun. He can't kill her and leaves. She continues to write and kills him. It is called *Yaşamak*, which, in Turkish, means "Living."

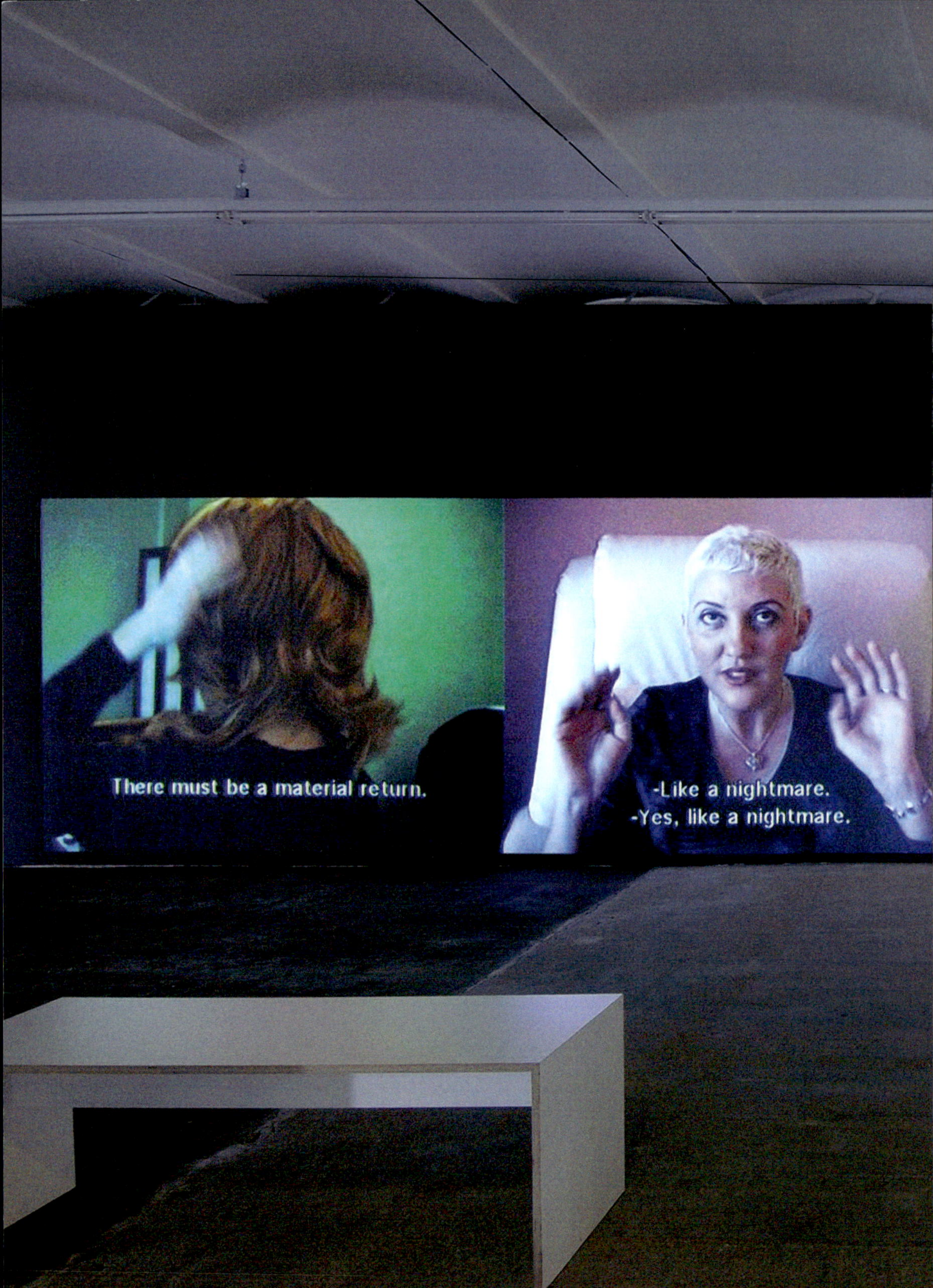
There must be a material return.
-Like a nightmare.
-Yes, like a nightmare.

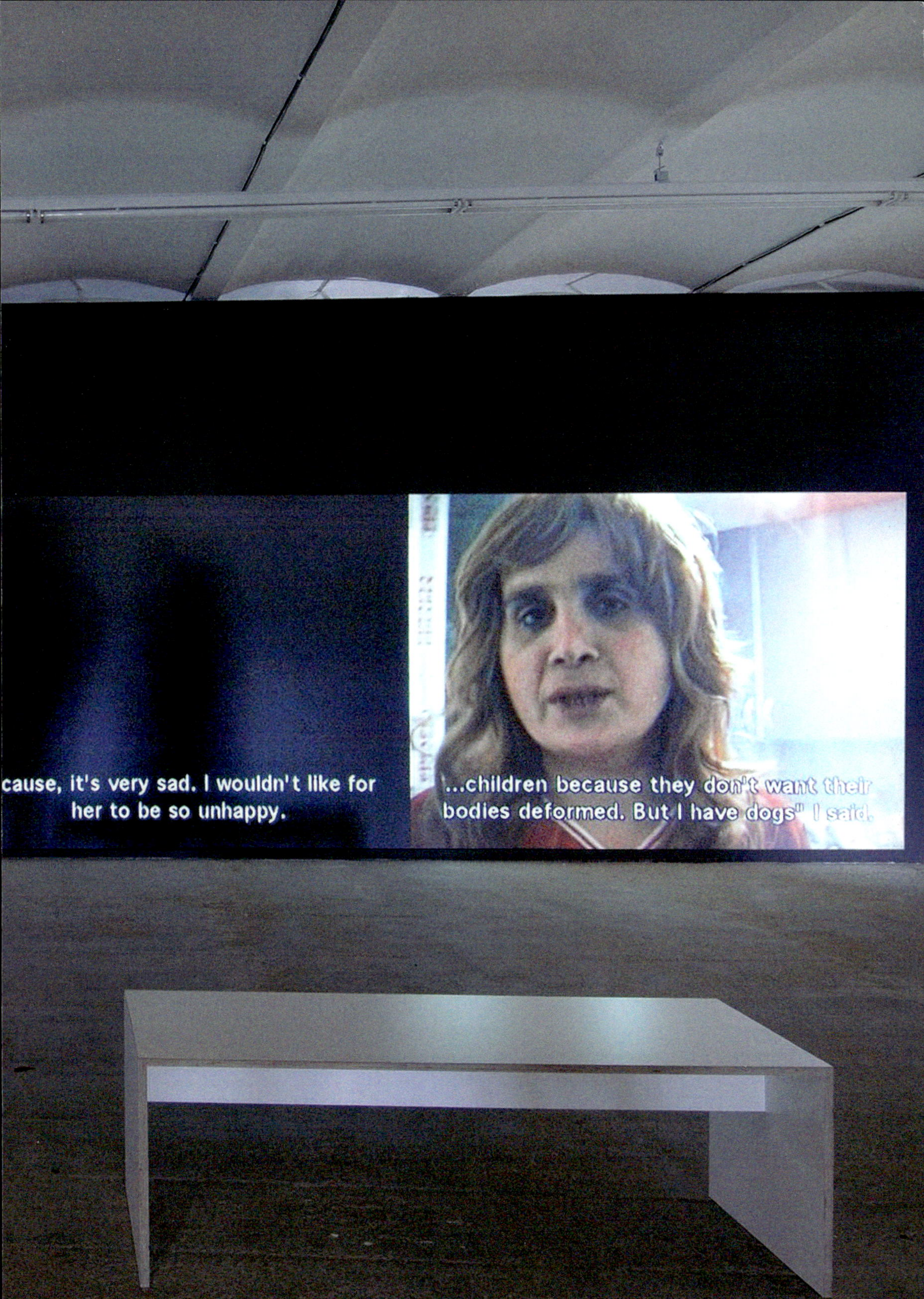
cause, it's very sad. I wouldn't like for
her to be so unhappy.
...children because they don't want their
bodies deformed. But I have dogs" I said.

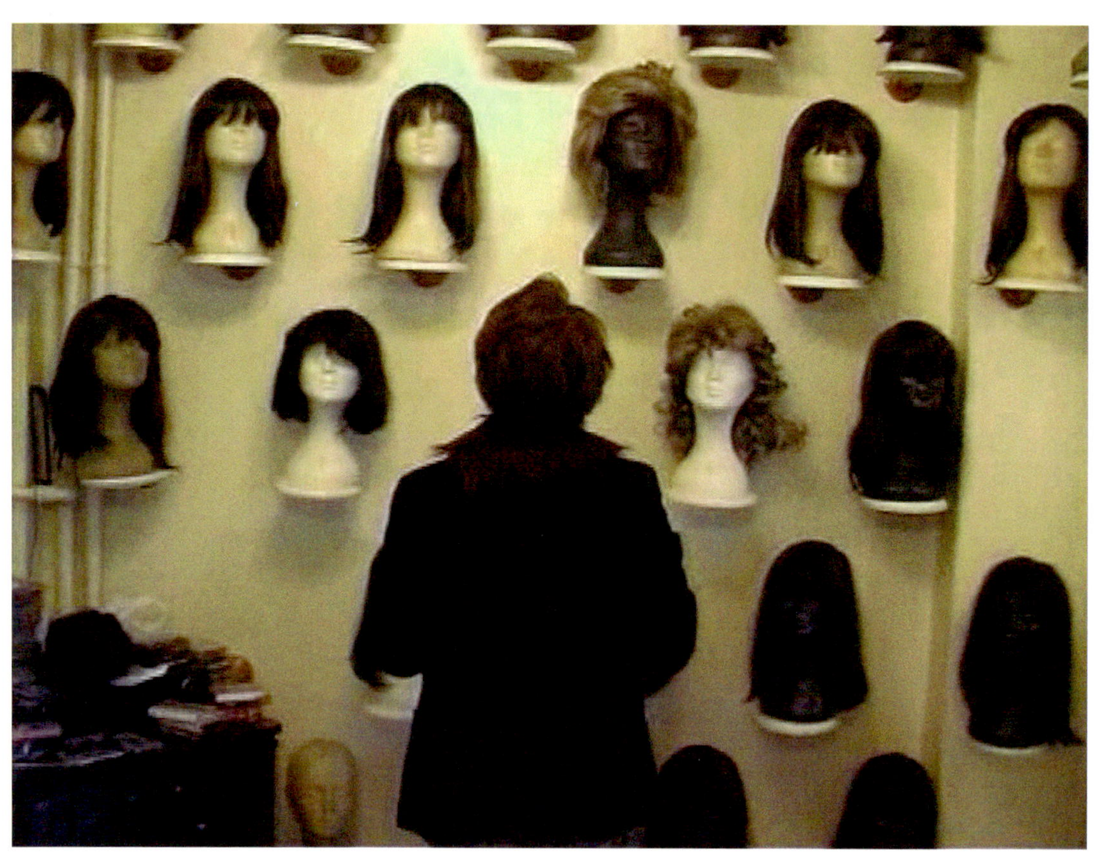

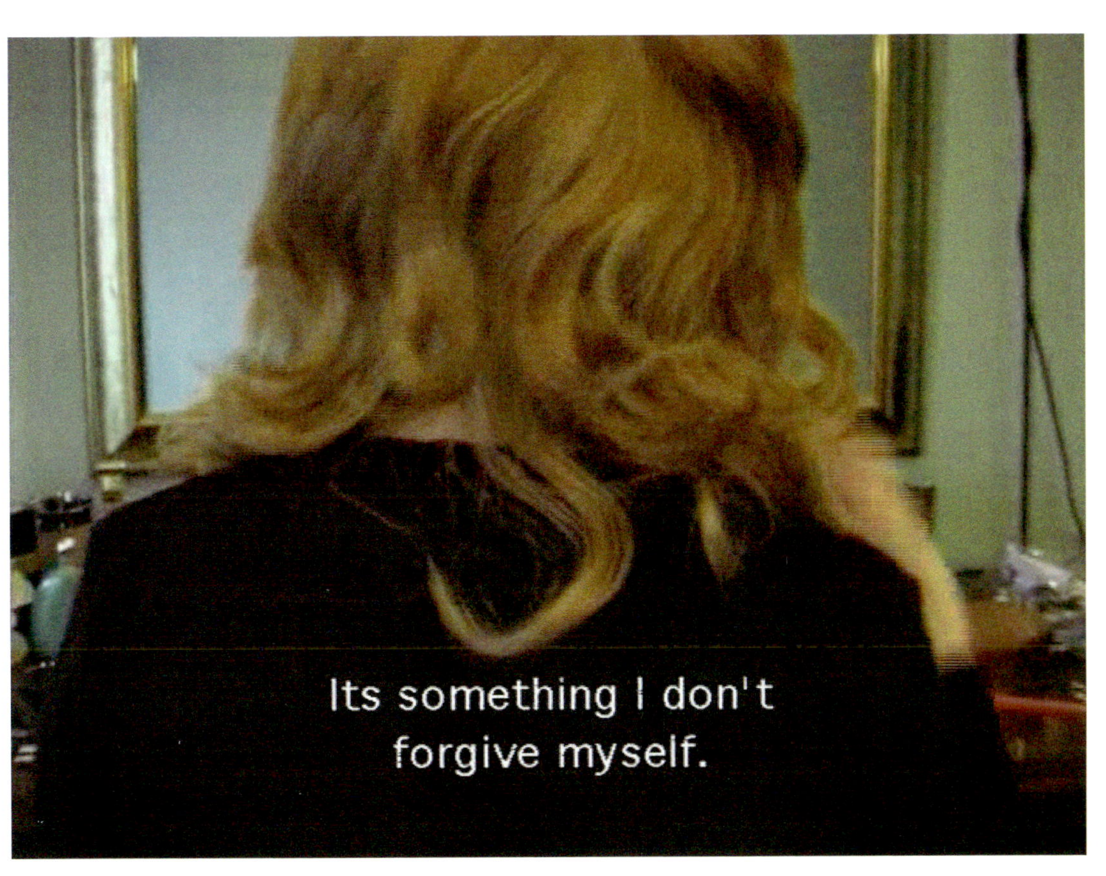
Its something I don't
forgive myself.

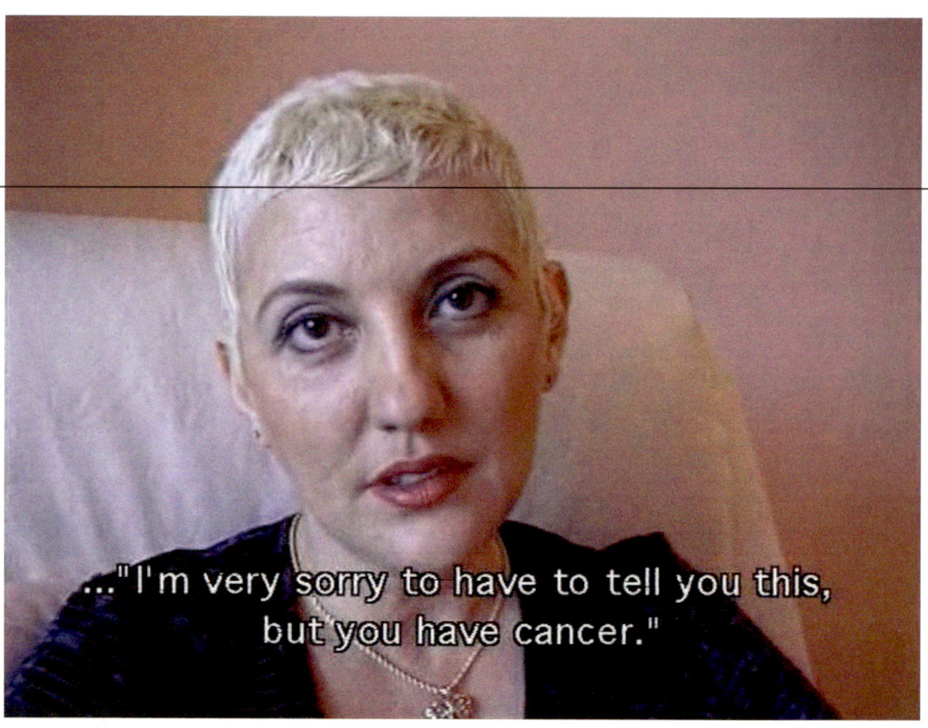
..."I'm very sorry to have to tell you this,
but you have cancer."

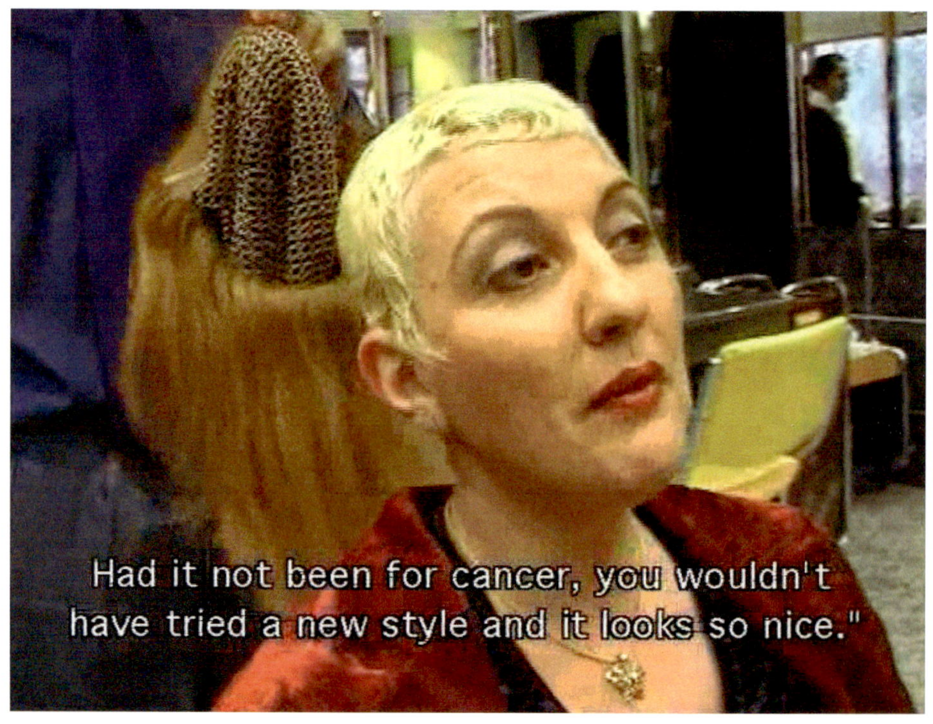
Had it not been for cancer, you wouldn't
have tried a new style and it looks so nice."

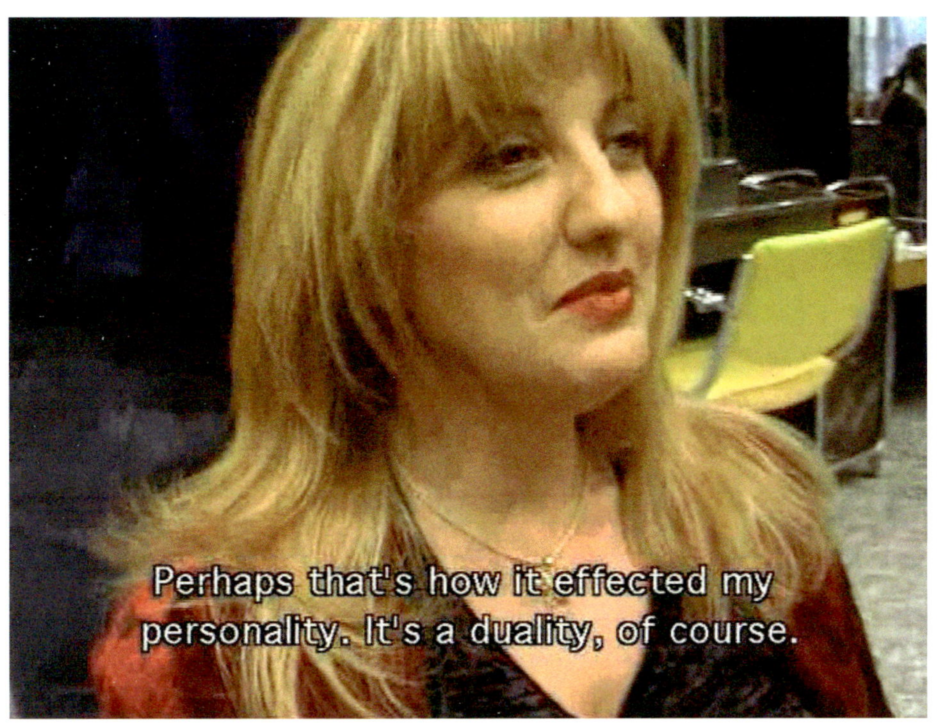
Perhaps that's how it effected my
personality. It's a duality, of course.

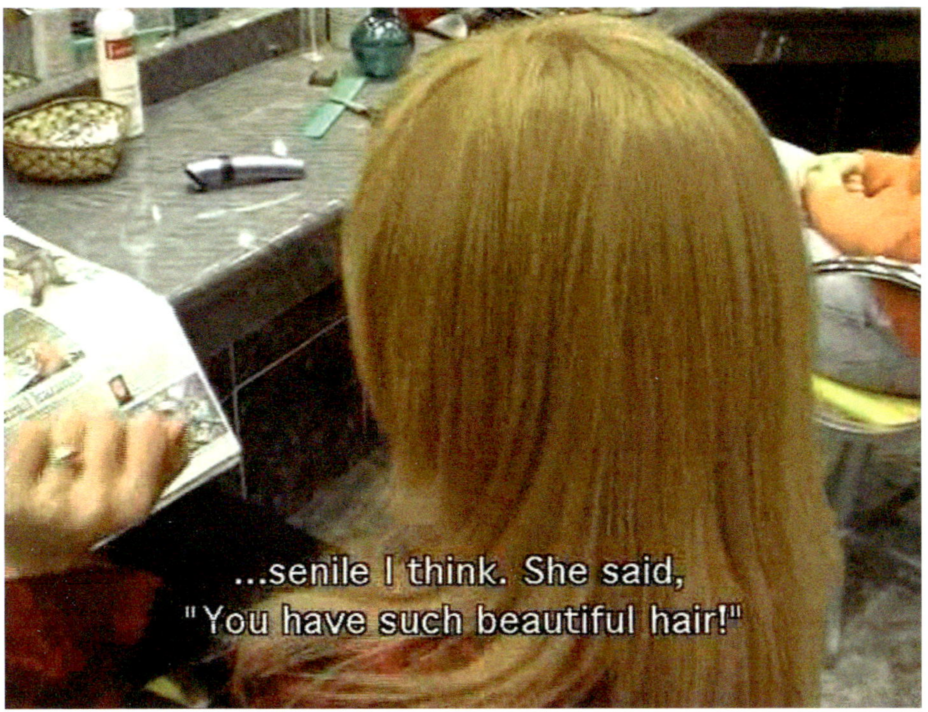
...senile I think. She said,
"You have such beautiful hair!"

At the beginning, I t

able to look an

ught I would not be
ne in the eye...

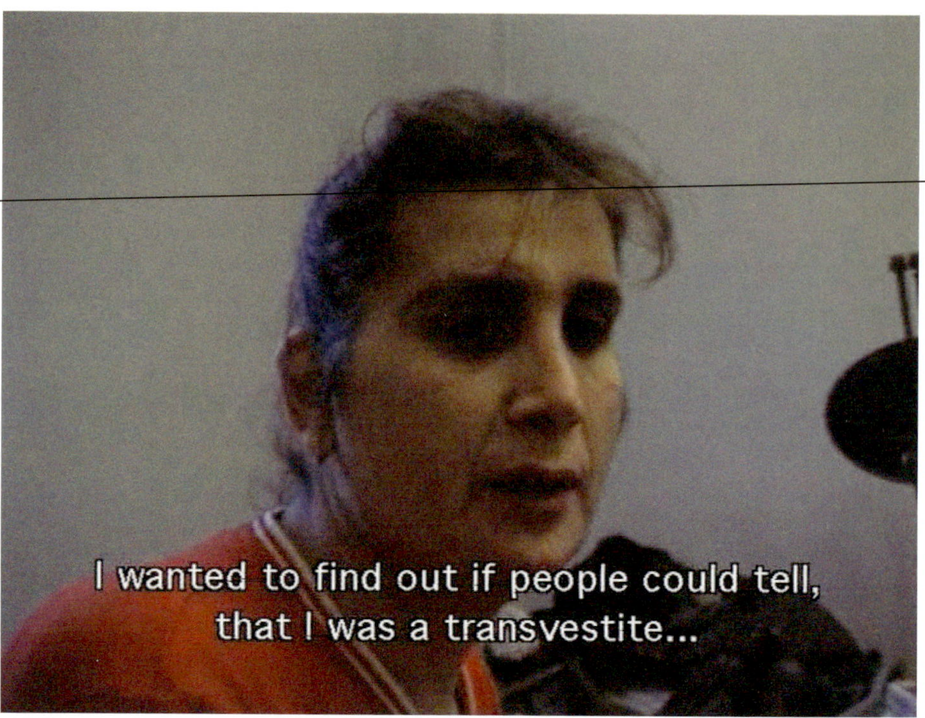
I wanted to find out if people could tell,
that I was a transvestite...

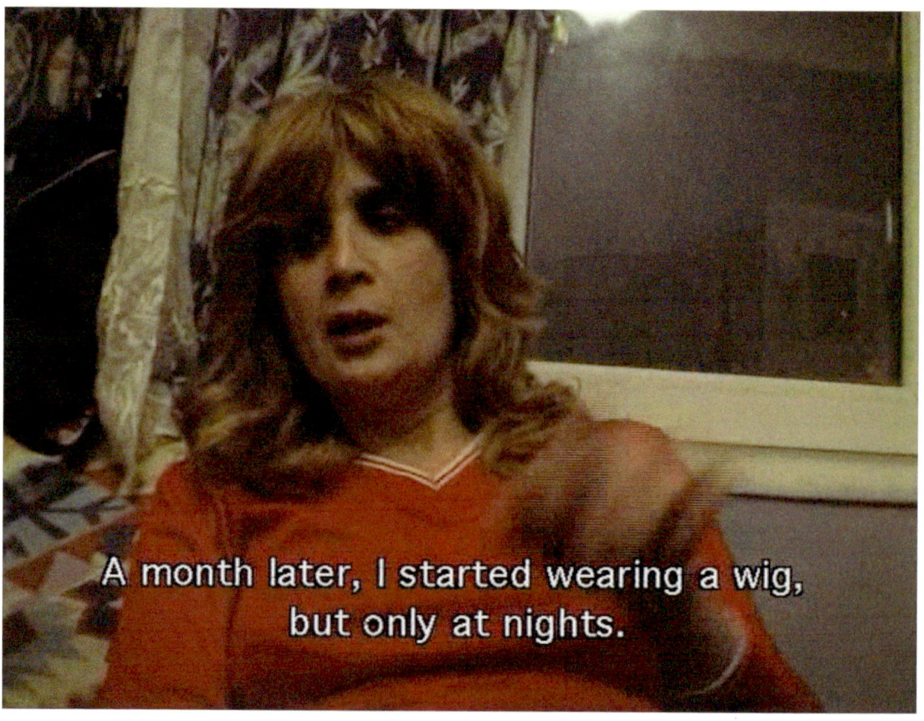
A month later, I started wearing a wig,
but only at nights.

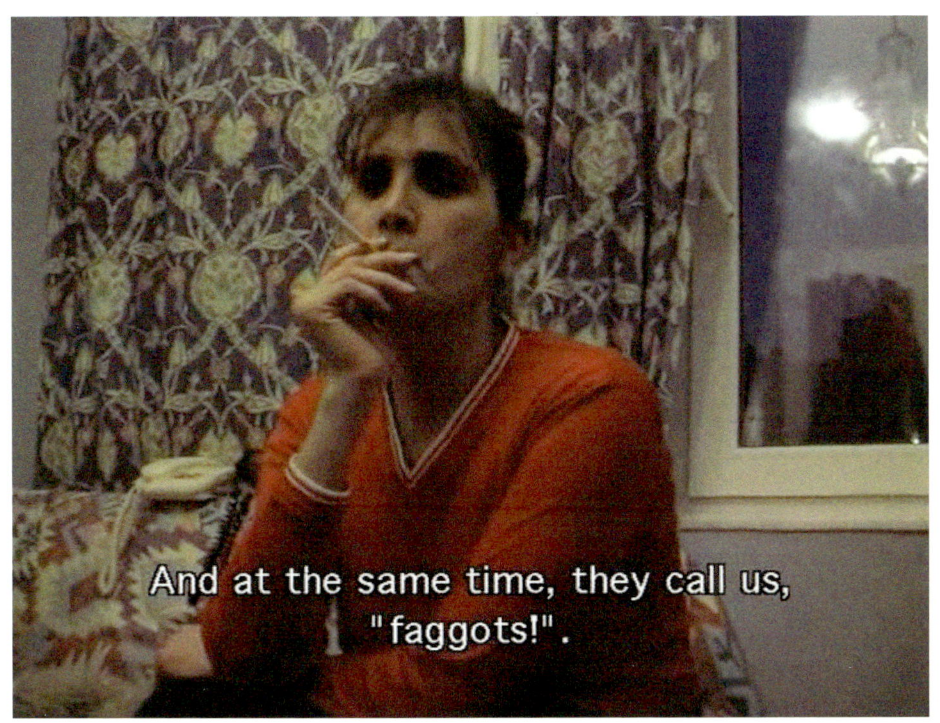
And at the same time, they call us,
"faggots!".

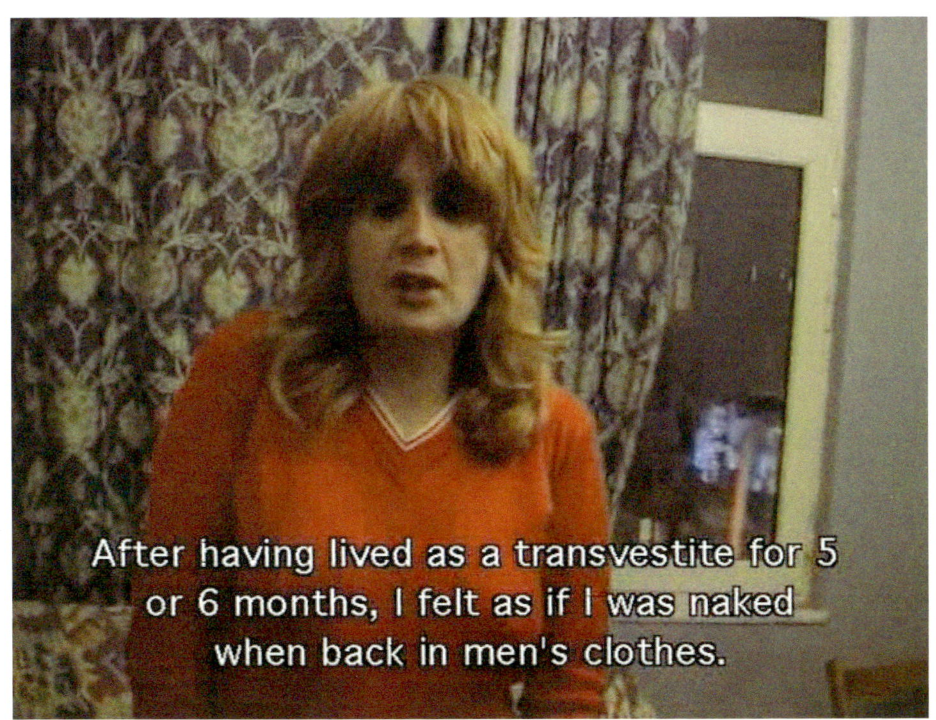
After having lived as a transvestite for 5
or 6 months, I felt as if I was naked
when back in men's clothes.

Iñaki
Bonillas

Jacob **Fabricius***: When and why did your interest in found material begin?*
Iñaki **Bonillas***:* It began in my early days working as an assistant photographer. I used to collect all the phototests that the photographer did before the photographic session. That material seemed to me much more interesting than the final result: the light and exposure variations, the different film proofs, the Polaroid, the background color examinations ...

*J***F***: What was it about your greatgrandfather's photographs you liked?*
*I***B***:* It was something intuitive. In the beginning, I didn't even like the photographs themselves. I was more attracted by his precise arrangement of the collection: thirty identical black leather files, numbered and ordered chronologically, and placed on top of a wooden shelf. It reminded me of On Kawara, whom I was already interested in.

*J***F***: Did you ever talk to your greatgrandfather about all the different male characters that he performed?*
*I***B***:* Unfortunately, I didn't. My greatgrandfather passed away in 2000 and I went on living with my grandmother for several months, and it was up to this period that I got close to the photographs, and learned a lot about him, his "incarnations," and about photography in general.

*J***F***: The works* A sombra e o brilho *(2007) and* Una tarjeta para J. R. Plaza *(2007) are both a mixture of facts and fiction. Is it possible to say that they create a dual personality represented by your great-grandfather?*
*I***B***:* Yes. In *A sombra e o brilho,* I try to confront dreams and reality, and the different ways in which we perceive them. Here, reality is represented by the diary that my great-grandfather wrote during his three months' stay in Wyoming, in which he tells us about the bitter reality of his life as a shepherd (life that my great-grandfather imagined would be like in a cowboy movie). And dreams are conveyed by the photographs he took of himself disguised as a cowboy, which shows us his desire of living a romantic and adventurous life, similar to the one John Wayne performed for the big screen.

In *Una tarjeta para J. R Plaza,* this dual personality gets even more accentuated, since in the fictive side, my great-grandfather acquired not one but many personalities. He, for instance, pictured himself, literally and in his mind, as a model, as a mechanic, and as a cane cutter, among other things. He was, in a way, all of those characters: in some cases, in his dreams and fantasies, and in some others, in daily practice or sudden moments.

*J***F***: The photographs seem like male dreams mixed with ordinary life. Could you tell the story behind your great-grandfather's poses? Why do you think your great-grandfather acts out these roles?*
*I***B***:* During his youth, he used to watch two or three films daily, and I guess he secretly fantasized with the idea of being an actor. Maybe, that's why we see so many pictures of him being conscious of the camera, although in many others he is completely unaware of it; all of this gives the impression as if he had hired one photographer to document his everyday life, and another photographer to register him posing as he wished his life should be like. In reality, though, he had an awful job, a lot less glamorous than acting: a salesman for an aluminum company. But, instead of getting depressed, he took pictures —he acted—and in that way, fulfilled his dream. At the end, perhaps, it

also has to do with some, now dated, cultural identities that my great-grandfather couldn't escape from. For him, as for many men of his time, cowboys—with their bravery and bold way—were the "real" men, not like all those silly and sad little salesmen.

JF: You mentioned that you wanted to reveal part of the process of the construction from both works in the catalogue. Maybe you could explain the process here?

IB: Searching for inscriptions on the backside of the photographs from my great-grandfather's archive, I came across a torn-off magazine page with a drawing of the exact same scene (a duel scene) portrayed in the picture right on top of it. It was then I discovered that my great-grandfather had—in his enactment of the magazine illustration—transcribed a "hand-made drawing" into a "light drawing." That observation triggered the idea of "transcribing" the positive images of him dressed as a cowboy onto negatives, and his own hand-written Wyoming diary, to a machine typed letter.

Apart from the photographic archive, I also inherited a black leather folder with some documents that were of personal importance to my great-grand-father. Among them, my attention was specially attracted by a collection of presentation cards pasted in a cardboard page. After carefully looking at them, I noticed that some were made by him and others were "professional cards." Suddenly, I understood that my great-grandfather had gathered together the jobs he actually had, with the jobs for which he had longed. It was not until some years later, while working with all the vertical photographs of the archive, that I realized there was a missing card in his collection, that one of the "Self-Portrait Photographer." So I made it, using the same technique as he used before (and with his own typewriter). In addition to that, I related each of the "fictive cards" made by him with a matching self-portrait, a picture of him enacting a given job, taken from the archive.

JF: Your approach to making your works goes through many stages—it is a process. In your new work Doble claroscuro *(2009) you rework a portrait of your great-grandfather, that your grandmother has already re-worked once. Could you tell me about this work?*

IB: I was working during a time period with underlined books. Most of them were underlined with a pencil, and I used to spend long hours scanning the pages of the books and then carefully erasing the text, leaving only visible the traces and marks left by the readers. At that time, I thought I had finished working with the archive of my great-grandfather. In fact, every time I finish a work around it, I feel it is the last one to come. Strangely, however, an image from one of the albums appeared in my mind: a portrait of my great-grandfather that had been altered with a pencil grid. After I found it, I looked at it and realized that my great-grandfather had done that intervention to the photograph so my grandmother, who is an amateur painter, could copy it as a drawing. Afterward, I realized that the portrait had been taken under a very curious lighting condition: The face presents a *chiaroscuro* that goes from lightness to darkness, and the background shows another one that goes the other way around. Those crossed light degradations, and the fact that the photograph was "divided" in various imperfect squares, gave

birth to a long term project that
consists of rearranging the squares
in different gradation principles.

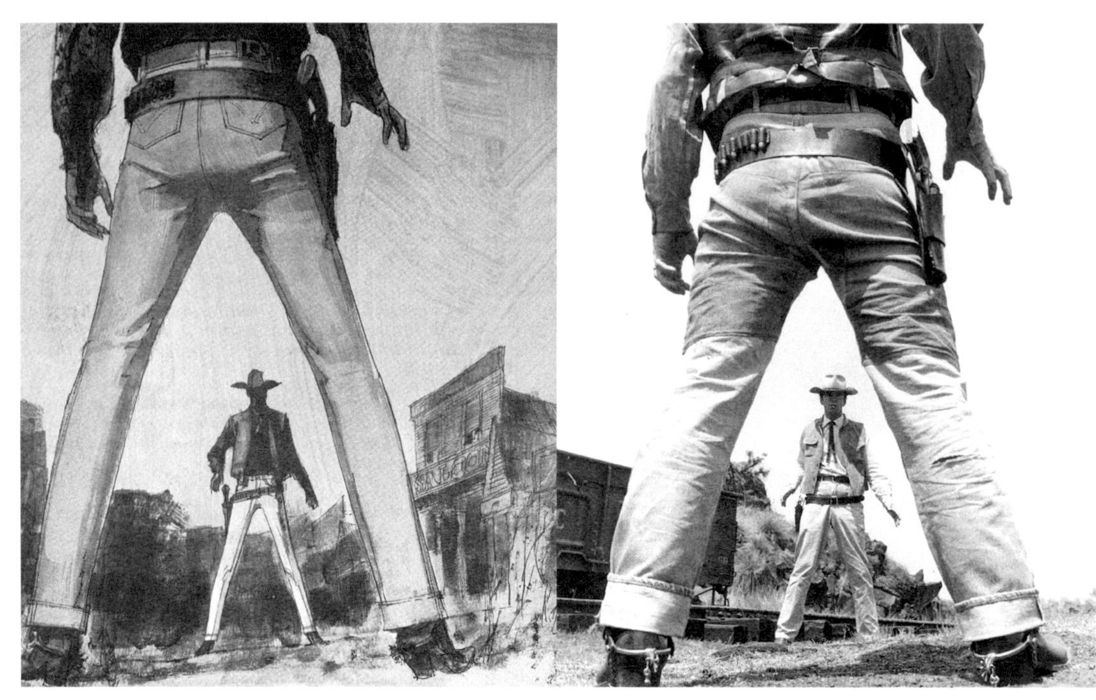

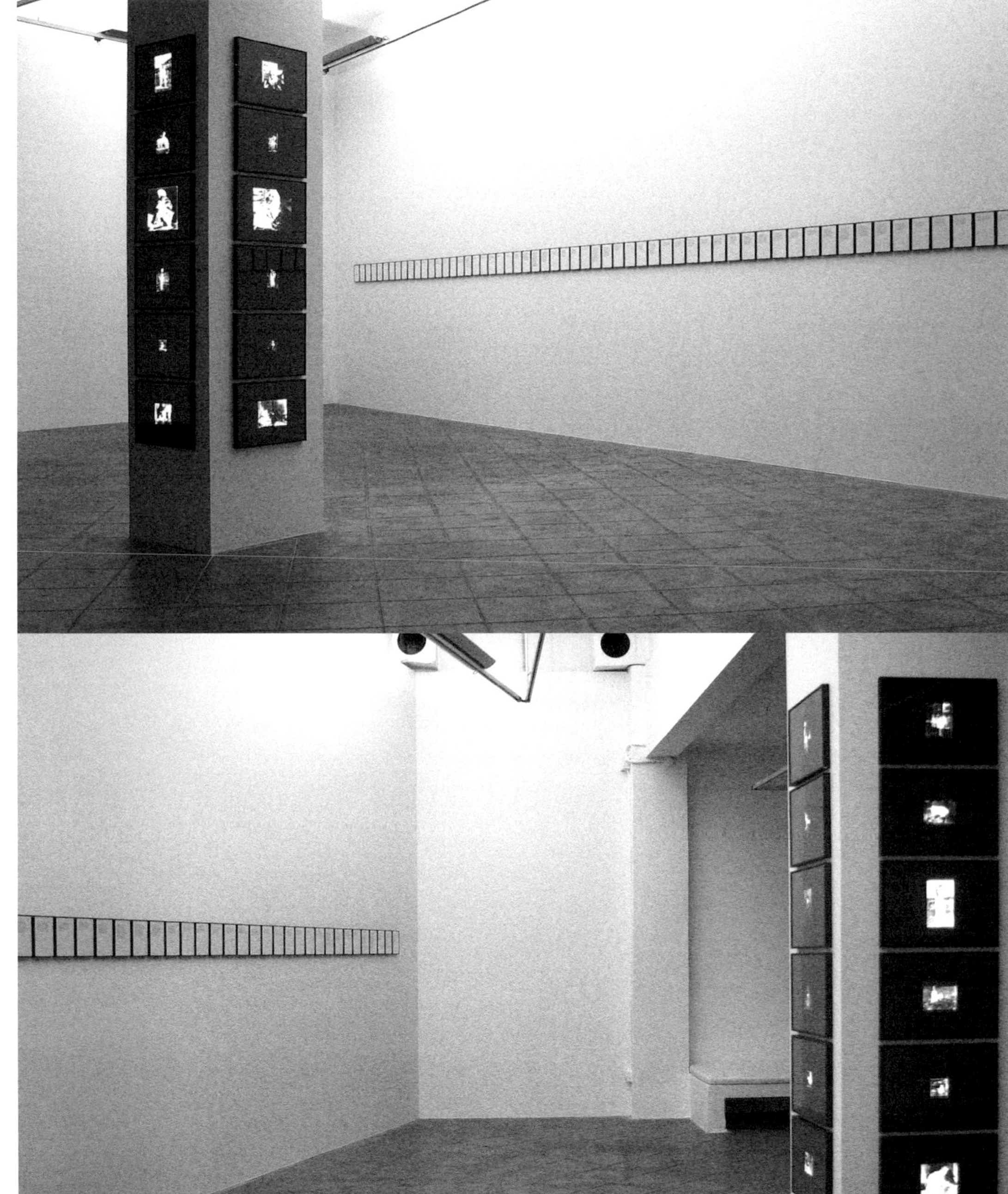

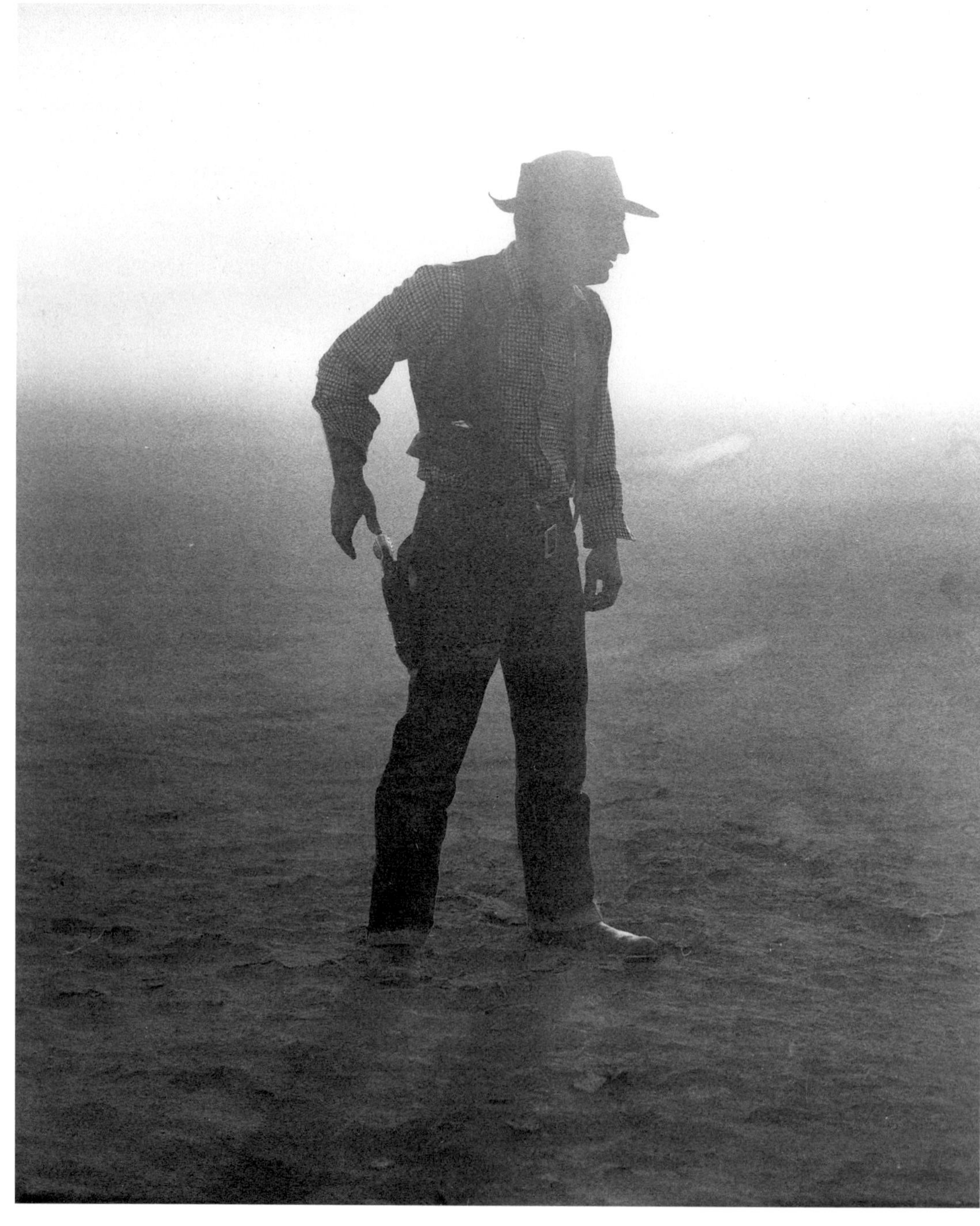

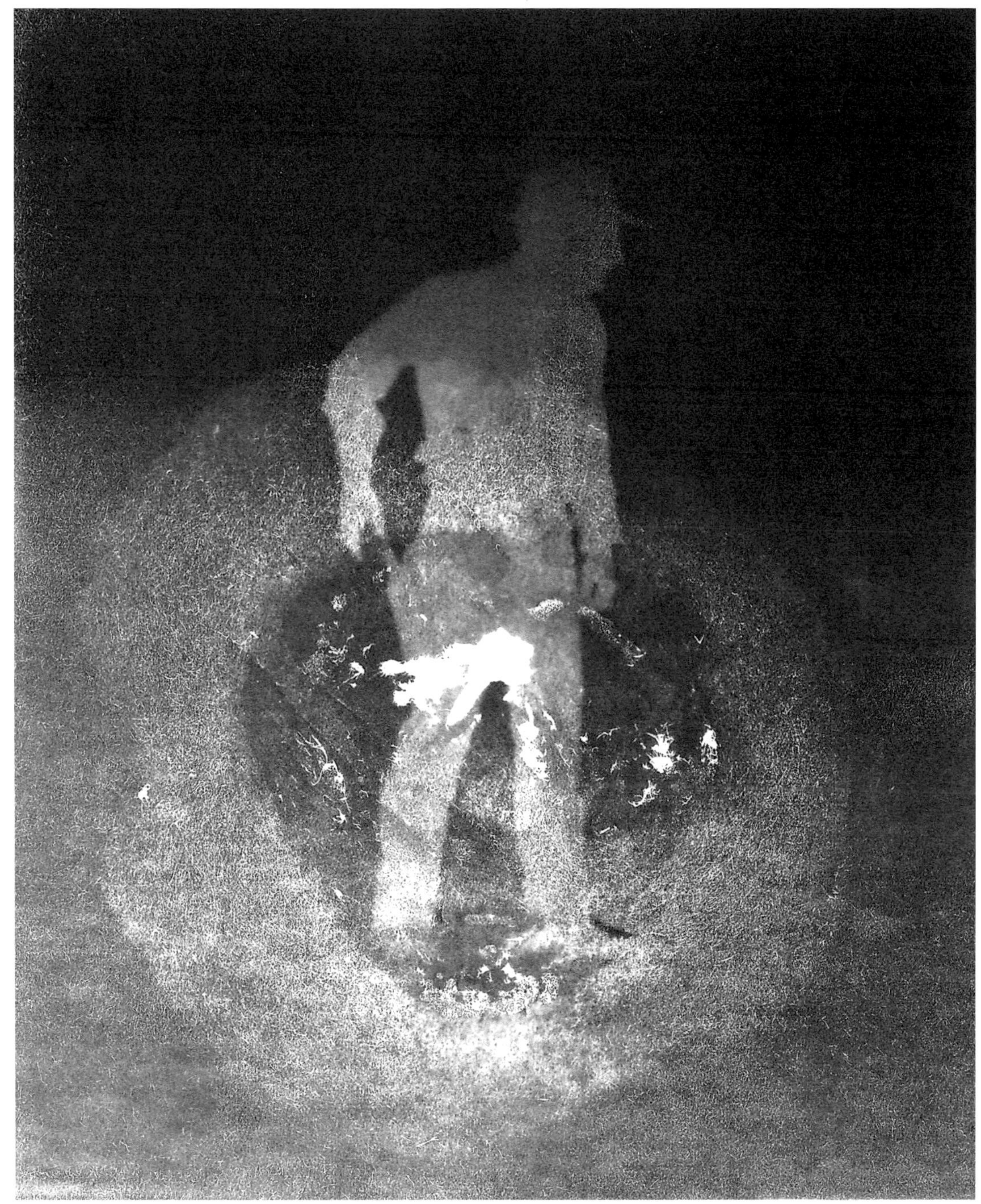

Simón, cuando los 2 "ranchés" se estaban juntando, el campe-
ro se va, no + sufrir. De nuevo
al rancho, mucho trabajo. Me
dá tabaco muy malo el patrón
Jesús Peres se "fué" a México
el 31. ¡Que suerte!
2 y 3·11·45 Ayer tuve el día
de + trabajo. Me acosté rendido
sin ganas de escribir por no
recordar lo amargo que fué.
Hoy domingo recibí carta y
foto de casa. Varela enfermo,
no le querían bajar al pueblo.
Esto parece trata de negros. Se
guram. lo mandarán a Mé-
xico. Mañana empesamos
a capar ¡aleluya! Tengo las
manos llenas de heridas con
pus. Perfectam. de salud.

4 y 5·11·45 Ayer he pasado todo
el día bajo la lluvia y sobre
un lodasal. Enlodada, ensan-
grentada, enbarrada y mo-
jada toda la ropa. Hoy estuve
a punto de romperme la cris-
ma al ir a recoger los ca-
ballos, arriba del burro con
nombre de caballo q. yo mon-
to. En la tarde chaparrón. Lo
aguanté debajo de unas tablas,
llegué calado. En las borregas
me tocó granizo. Todo el día
con fiebre, x ir con las ropas
mojadas; no tengo para cam-
biarme. Parió una vaca. Ca-
pamos y marcamos 4 bece-
rros, yo hice de cow-boy. Recibí la carta de papá, está
algo desanimado.

...bía ser a causa del es-
paradrapo q. llevaba 7
días sin quitarlo. Se aca-
ba la tinta.
6·M·45 y 7·4·45 ESCRIBO ESTO
EL 8·M·45. ESTUVE ENFERMO

11-M-45 Pasó otro día. Estoy
hecho un chulo. 18 días sin
bañarme y 15 con la mis-
ma ropa; pero debe ser
el clima frío, pues nadie
se daría cuenta, no pare-
ce q. estoy sucio. Aprendo
+ cosas.

J. R. Plaza
Autorretratos

8 de Septiembre No. 42
Tel: 5896714

ADDRESSOGRAPH · MULTIGRAPH · MULTILITH

Floyd D. Ransom e Hijos
S. A. de C. V.
DISTRIBUIDORES EXCLUSIVOS PARA LA REPUBLICA MEXICANA DE
ADDRESSOGRAPH · MULTIGRAPH · CORPORATION
ESQ. EDISON Y ROSALES
MEXICO 1, D. F.

JOSE RODRIGUEZ PLAZA

OFICINAS GENERALES:
TELEFONOS: 21-30-97 / 35-75-42 / 36-77-59

Collins
GINEBRA SECA
LONDON

London Liquors Co. de México, S. A.

José Ma. R. Plaza

TEL. 12-30-31
DR. ANDRADE 128-2º
MEXICO, D. F.

J. R. PLAZA

ABASTECEDORES ELECTRICOS, S. A.
JUAREZ Y RAMON CORONA
TELEFONO: 2-74-87   TORREON, COAH.

T. V. ALTA FIDELIDAD
TOCADISCOS · RADIOS
IEM · WESTINGHOUSE

AE
ECATEPEC

JOSE RODRIGUEZ PLAZA
DEPTO. DE VENTAS

ACEROS ECATEPEC, S. A.
REFORMA Nº 122-7º PISO
MEXICO 6, D. F.

TELEFONOS:
35-17-87
CON 4 LINEAS
DIRECTAS

J. R. Plaza
Encargado Mostrador

Ferr. Los Dos Leones
Rib. San Cosme No. 116   Tel: 3580

Almexsa

JOSE R. PLAZA

ALUMINIO INDUSTRIAL MEXICANO, S. A.
FABRICANTES NACIONALES DE ALUMINIO
LAFRAGUA NO. 4-202
MEXICO I, D. F.   TEL. 46-91-92

José Rodriguez
DEPTO. DE PLOMERIA

SEARS, ROEBUCK DE MEXICO, S. A. DE C. V.
TEL. 20-34-40 EXT. 142

AV. EJERCITO NACIONAL 980
MEXICO 5, D. F.

J. R. Plaza
Modelo

Dinamarca No. 25,16
Tel: 46-09-64

José R. Plaza
Vendedor

BENJAMIN FRANKLIN No. 9
CONJUNTO INDUSTRIAL LA JOYA
CUAUTITLAN EDO. DE MEXICO
TELS.(91) (591) 22651 / 23055 / 23144

TELS. 21-96-00 / 10-03-33
DEPTO. HERRAMIENTAS 12-51-90

LOUIS MULÁS, SUCS., S. A.
DISTRIBUIDORES EXCLUSIVOS
DE
THE GARLOCK PACKING CO.

I. LA CATOLICA 49
MEXICO, D. F.

J. R. Plaza
Armador

Dinamrca No. 25,16
Tel : 46-09-64

872-61-00

JOSE MA. RODRIGUEZ PLAZA
REPRESENTANTE DE VENTAS

BENJAMIN FRANKLIN Nº 9
CONJUNTO INDUSTRIAL LA JOYA
54730 CUAUTITLAN. EDO. DE MEXICO
TELS. 872-3144 872-3050-872-3242
TELEX: 171327 LASAME

J. R. Plaza
Modelo

Dinamarca No. 25,16
Tel: 46-09-64

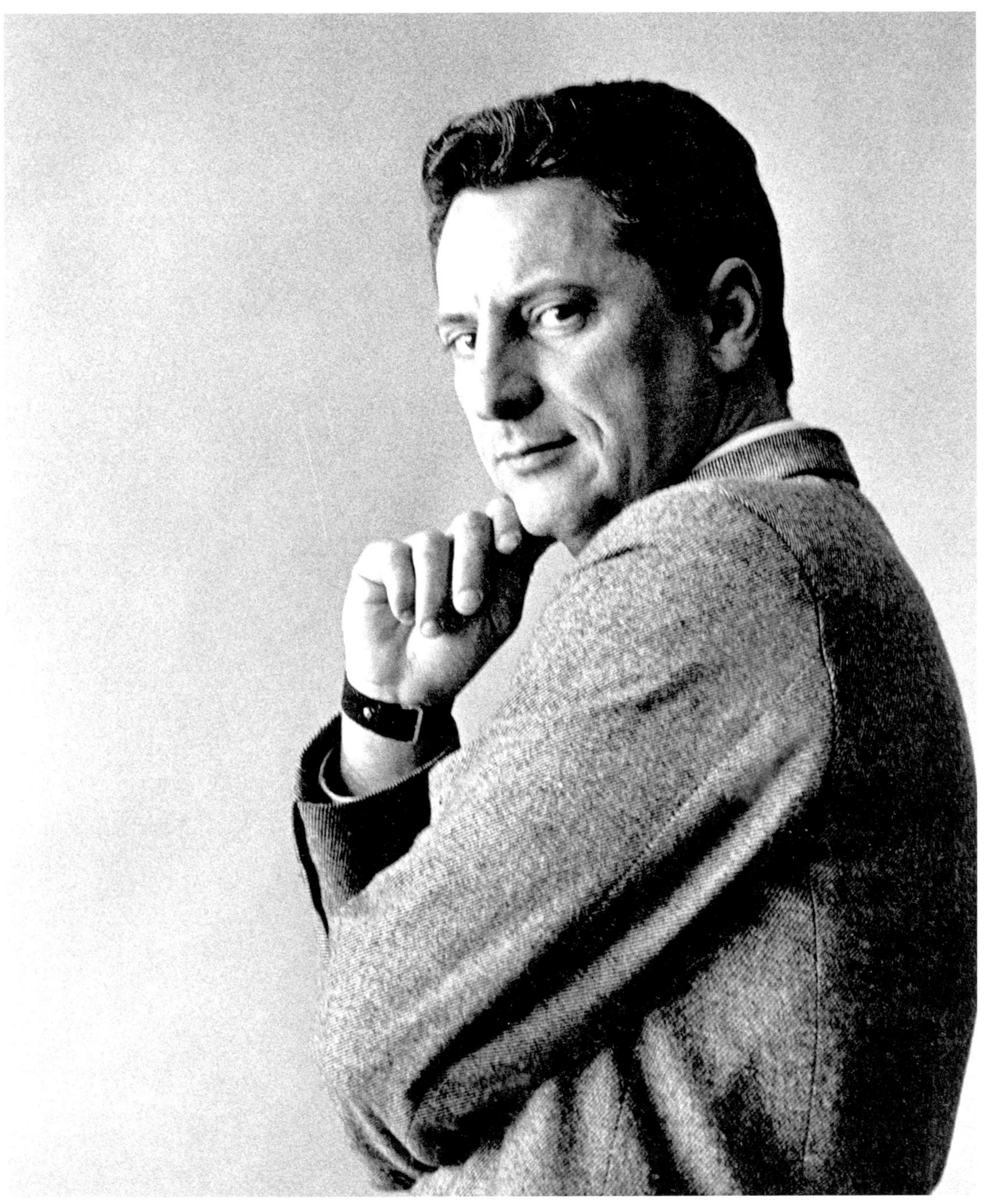

Gerard
Byrne

*Jacob **Fabricius***: *When you create fiction, you use simple tricks: Subtle replacements and reenactments of texts, films, books, advertisements, etc. Many of your film works bring past, present, and in some sense, future together. Often, your point of departure is found material that has a very specific relation to the time it was produced. Seen in the present light and time, it becomes more theatrical. Or, would you say that you make it (even more) theatrical?*

*Gerard **Byrne***: To answer the question asked, I'd say that an uncanny theatricality is unavoidable given the temporal moment in which my works are realized. Texts that represent cultural moments (the "base material" of these projects) exist "in time" and are subject to temporality—which has many consequences, amongst which is a certain uncanniness when the material is read out of its time, as in my reconstructed readings. I've been interested in theater as a model for other art forms for a while, mainly because I'm interested in theater's relationship with time. It's both archaic and always contingent, never fixed. I guess it's not a question of "making" things (even more) theatrical, but more a question of how the theatrical becomes the only means of grasping historical moments, even when they are from within living memory.

JF: You have worked with films and storytelling for many years now. The story's narrative is important, however, how it is staged seems often more important than what is staged. How have you worked with and incorporated Brecht in your work and storytelling?

GB: I'm interested in the formal means by which works are resolved, but the "story" itself is always part of what constitutes the "form" of the work. I think it's a false opposition—these facets are essentially one and the same. Forms and stories are equally idiomatic. In speaking of stories and how they are staged, I'd say that Brecht's legacy seems exemplary in terms of how it values stories whilst also being formally disruptive of conventional configurations of theatrical storytelling. Brecht saw theater as a communal art form—deeply idiomatic. Historically, he is synonymous with the idea of theater as a tool for social change. I think the potential for social change through artistic means is differently understood right now, although Brecht remains a central reference in the discussion.

JF: Could you describe your interest for the found material, the fictive magazine ads versus the staged discussion, as in Why it is Time for Imperial, Again *(1998–2002) or* New Sexual Lifestyles *(2003)?*

GB: Generally, the works you refer to are rooted in old magazines, which were all widely distributed. *National Geographic, Playboy, Interview* magazine, and *Le Nouvel Observateur* have all been sources for works. Part of my interest has always been in how mainstream magazines, whose commercial *raison d'être* has always struggled to be prescient at the moment of their publication, can produce disruptive meanings when read out of the forum of their original market. What can emerge from reading something as culturally representative as a mainstream magazine, when you are not actively identifying with the consumer or subject position the magazines' editors are speaking to?

JF: How do you choose your setting and actors for these productions?

GB: Circumstances are a big factor. I'm very precise about differing elements in different works—sometimes costumes are really important, and sometimes they are not. It depends on the project. My working model is closer to theater than to film, so jarring accents might not be an issue in the way it would be in film. I'm much more interested in contingency, provisionality. I take a sort of collage-like approach to representation—Cubism as opposed to naturalism!

JF: The title of your recent book suggests a collage-like interest in time. Is there a story behind your catalogue title The Present Tense through the Ages—On the Recent Work of Gerard Byrne *(2007)?*

GB: "The present tense through the ages" is a purposely awkward way of suggesting that the work discussed in the book addresses ideas of how coherent constructions of a present tense are regulated through media representation, and continuously revised over time. Of course, there is also a sort of literary contrivance to the whole thing. Although I don't generally write, like many artists, I quite enjoy playing around with words.

JF: Tell me about your ongoing Loch Ness interest? What tickles your fascination about this particular lake, and how did it begin? Is it its representation of the unknown?

GB: I was drawn to Loch Ness because of its exemplary history as a site of collective fantasy and as a cardinal point in the use of photography in newspapers. Secret monsters hiding in deep lakes is a standard archetypal myth that recurs around the globe. What distinguishes Loch Ness from the rest is the role the newspaper industry played. "Sightings" have been chronicled there for a millennium, but essentially, the history of Loch Ness as it is known, dates to 1933, when British and then international newspapers used it as a way of selling newspapers during the Great Depression. When I began thinking about it, I wondered how to characterize the popular desire the monster would have fulfilled at that time, which loosely coincided with the moment when theorists like Walter Benjamin and Siegfried Kracauer were responding to a perceived need to critically identify the talismanic role of the photograph in the nascent mass-media culture. I can only speculate that the popular desire for the existence of a primeval monster at that moment, was connected to a fantasy that there could still persist spaces, times, and indeed living things, which defied the increasingly claustrophobic reality of a mass media modernity with its attendant downside—the Great Depression. Hopefully, that answers at least one of your questions.

JF: Indeed it does. The photographs A Country Road. A Tree. Evening ... *(2005–ongoing) certainly also have an uncanniness to them—almost as if it is a document of Unidentified Aerial Phenomena. It appears almost as artificial as* In Repertory *(2004–2006). Though the two works are quite different—a series of photographs and objects in installation—they both use theater lights as an important element and appear almost as empty stages, where something is about to happen. Could you compare these two works or their theatricality?*

GB: They are distinct projects begun around the same time, so it's not unreasonable that they would share interests. The series of photographic works *A Country Road. A Tree. Evening ...* make use of conventions of theatrical lighting as a means of reconstructing a type of literary space, the *mise-en-scène* from *Waiting for Godot*'s, in specific locations that could conceivably have been a source reference for Samuel Beckett's scenario. Each work is a distinct hypothesis. As such, the works accumulate to form a spatial typology defined by Beckett's script. The photographs are exactingly detailed depictions of each location, and simultaneously heavily stylized theatrical constructions. In a sense, the works depict each site as imminently theatrical, whilst doggedly testing the "credibility" of the play itself as a construction.

In Repertory is, of course, related, but the terms of artistic investigation are displaced to the gallery space, which is transformed into a space of literary citation. The fact that settings from multiple plays are combined and overlapped in the installation implies that the focus is not so much on an exemplary theatrical work such as *Waiting for Godot,* but rather, on a sort of exemplary condition of the theatrical itself, exhibited conspicuously out of its original context—in an art gallery! *In Repertory* refers to the idea of the theatrical moment banished to a state of perpetual historical suspension.

*J**F**: Regarding* In Repertory, *would you say that you, by layering props from these different plays, open up the plays—how we perceive them—and the idea of theater?*

The audience, who usually sits afar and watches the props on stage, now all of a sudden is on stage (in the gallery space), walking inside the plays, has to fill out the gaps, appears as actors, right? Is that the only work where you have used the audience as actors?

*G**B**:* Much of my work involves eroding clear distinctions between "actors" and "non-actors" and between "acting" and "not acting."

Maybe the most notable gesture in *In Repertory* is an inversion whereby the "audience" enters to find itself inhabiting the space of a literary citation; but a space where the ability to "read" may not necessarily be a useful means to quantify the work. In this inversion the finite length of the play or the novel is replaced by a sort of unquantifiable temporal experience of duration not dissimilar to the experience of Minimalism Michael Fried described in his infamous essay "Art and Objecthood" (1967). When I film the audience inhabiting the literary *mise-en-scène* constructed in the gallery, I am chronicling through the time-based medium of video, something of the ambivalent experience of duration the audience is experiencing. The video also chronicles the audiences' efforts to narrate or rationalize their experience of the *mise-en-scène.* Editing the video material together is an important controlling phase in the formation of the project, because it is a process whereby I attempt to rationalize the material gathered into a sort of narrative, where each piece of footage has a causal relationship with the shot that precedes or follows it in the edit, even though the material was not at all orchestrated in that way. What emerges is a context-specific video "play" in which the audience serves as protagonists, I assume a directorial role after the fact, and the rectangle of the video screen serves as a sort of procenium arch, demarcating a fictive space. When the video edit is ultimately presented in the exhibition space, it is a sort of tangible fruition of the dramatic potential of the *mise-en-scène,* fixed in duration, and circumscribed in fictive space. Its audience looks on from a distinct and dark space—and sometimes they are watching themselves.

*J**F**: Does the devil live in the details?*

*G**B**:* I think you already know the answer to that one—I've been sparing you here.

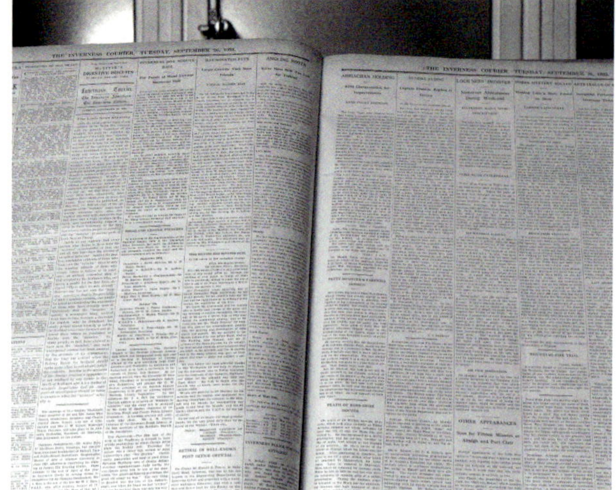

Fig. 1

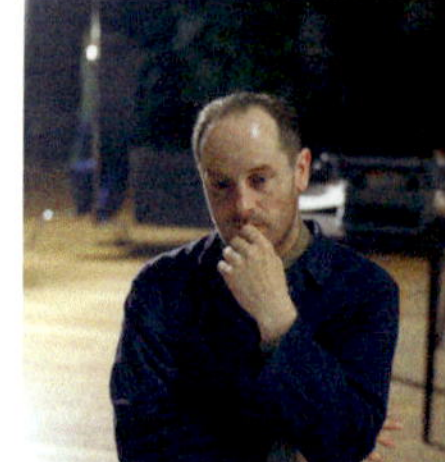

Fig. 2

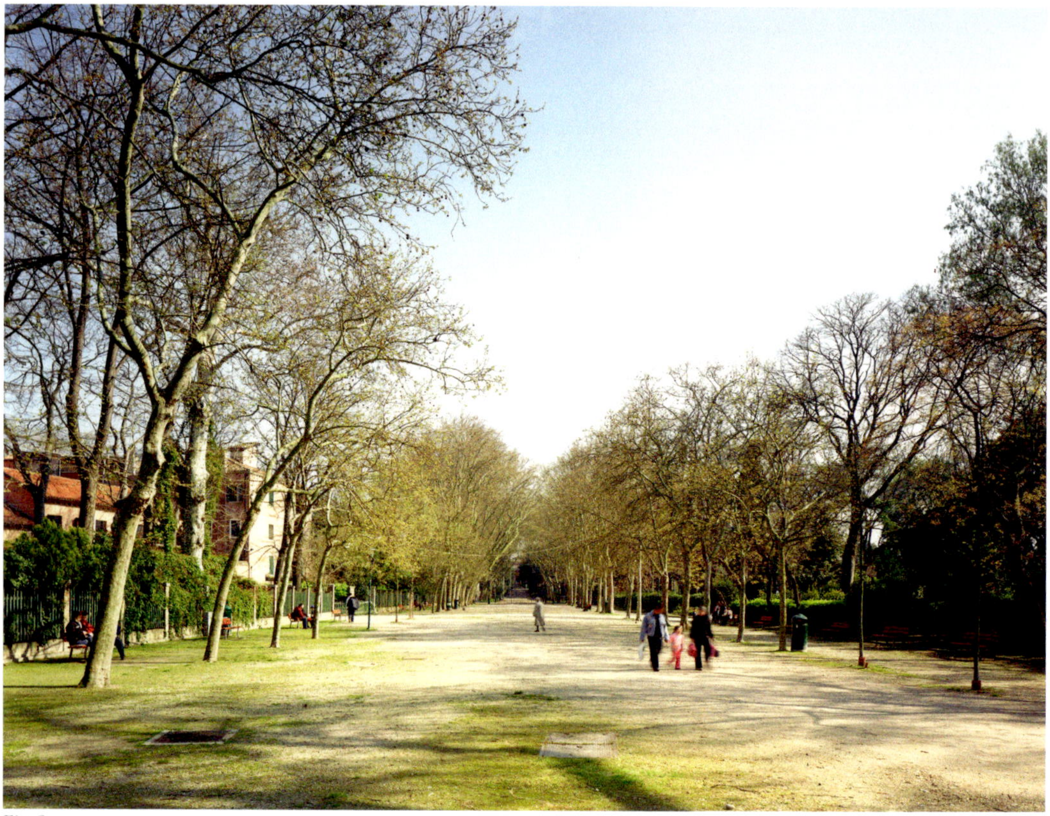

Fig. 3

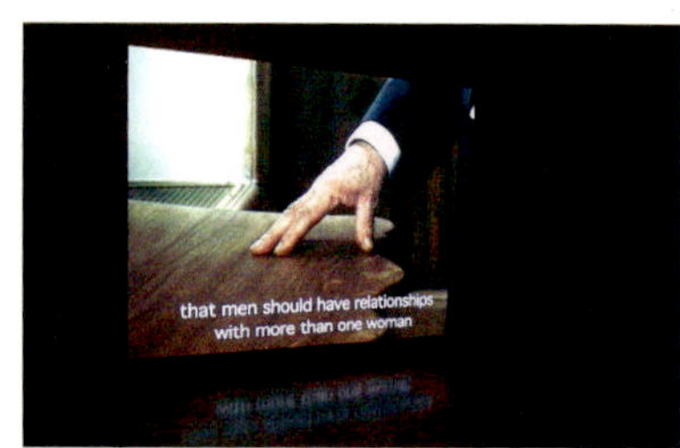

Fig. 4

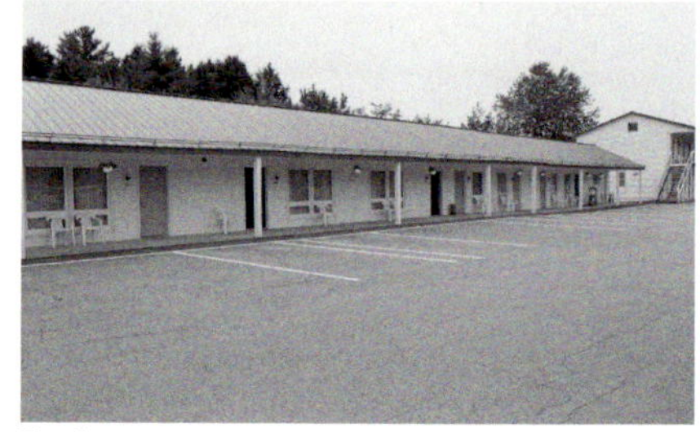

Fig. 5

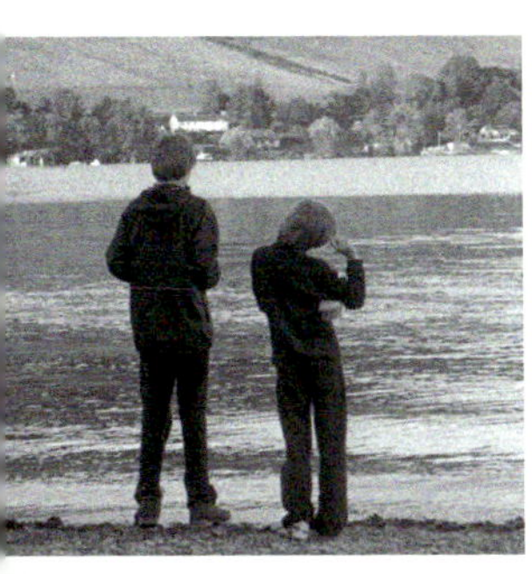

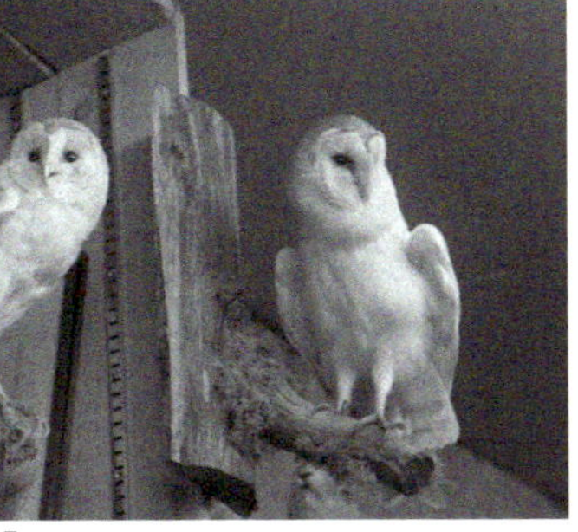

7

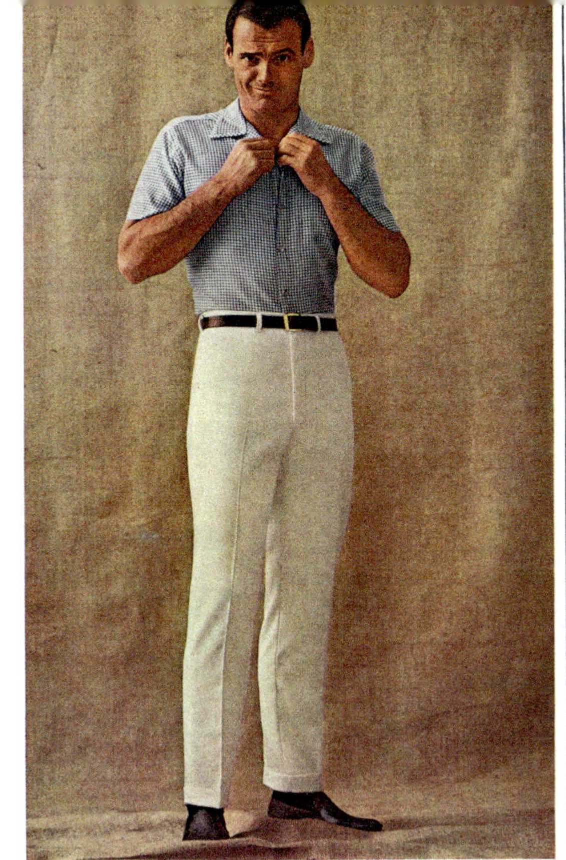

Fig. 8

explicitly direct the course of dream
your money back, and by low-vol
stimulae — safe for children — which w
emotions into soaring sonatas of se
tion. I have been drawing a close par
to show business because I am pos
that the next generation will greet t
titillations as yet another appendag
the entertainment world. Some nat
will establish state pleasure monop
while others will reaffirm their fait
the free-enterprise system with freel
pleasure technicians, performers,
ducers, directors, costumers, set desig
and scriptwriters under contract to n
moth pleasure-drug manufacturers
Hollywood "Feelie" studios.

PLAYBOY: You foresee, then, an explo
of technological developments and
coveries which promises to enlarge
— hopefully — enrich man's insight, i
lect, emotions, sensations and self-kn
edge. Do you anticipate similar scier
strides in his search for complete com
hension and mastery of the human
— and of all the ills to which flesh is l

SERLING: Well, this may be pretty s
potatoes in the technological worl
1984, but I envision a highly sopl
cated computing machine programe
analyze medical symptoms, conduct b
ingly fast chemical analyses of sar
cultures, and then dispense infal
diagnoses for every known disease.

ANDERSON: I think we can expect to
even more spectacular advances in
field of *curing* illnesses — such as m
breakthroughs in the transplantatio
whole organs, and less dramatic but r
important advances in the developr
of antivirus drugs, including, at l
long last, a cure for the common

BUDRYS: By the turn of the centu
anticipate that medical research will
progressed at a geometric rate which
have ushered *all* illnesses, from psyc
to heart disease, as well as *all* ser
aids such as glasses and hearing aids,
permanent extinction.

PLAYBOY: The elimination of dis
would seem to bode well for the pros
of lengthening the human lifespan
matically in years to come — if no
attaining man's immemorial drean
eternal life. What do you predict wi
the longevity of the average America
the year 2000?

BUDRYS: I think that the first man to

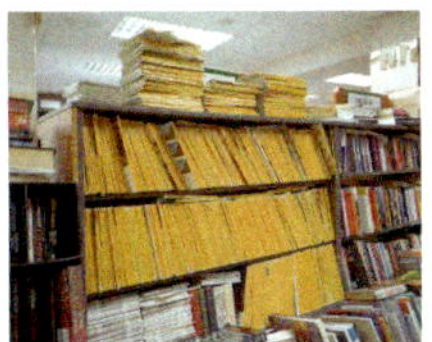

Fig. 9

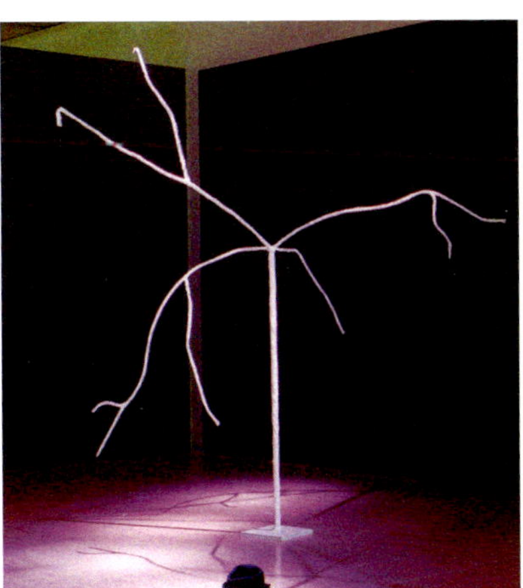

Fig. 10

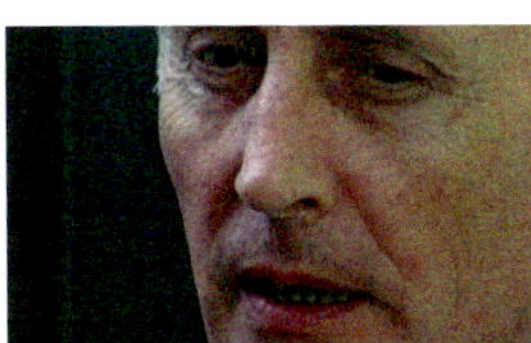

Fig. 11

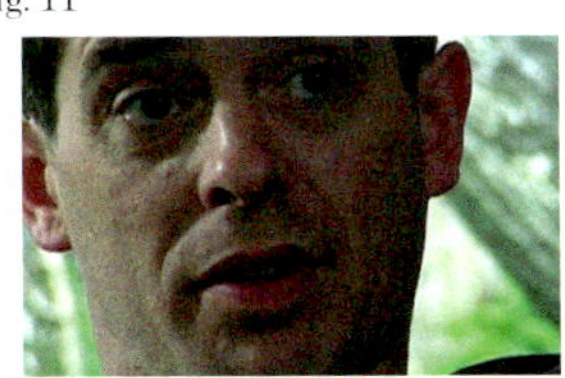

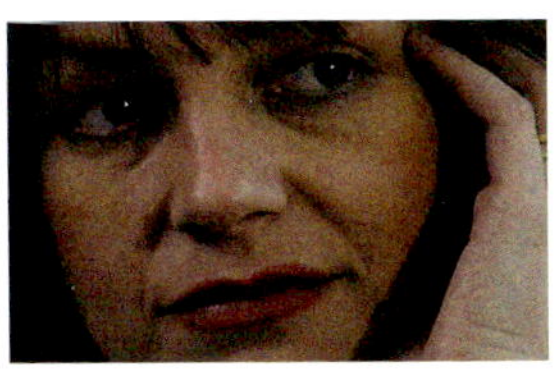

The Chairman of the Board tells "The Chairman of the Board" why it's time for Imperial.

Lee Iacocca talks to Frank Sinatra about the future of luxury cars in America.

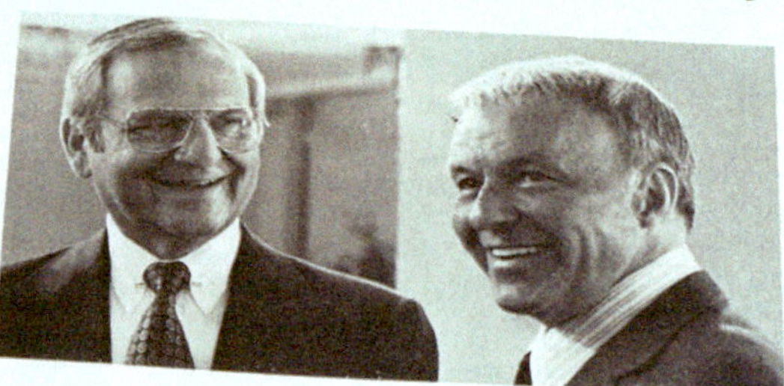

On July 18, 1980 Frank Sinatra, the entertainment industry's "Chairman of the Board," joined Lee A. Iacocca, Chairman of the Board of The New Chrysler Corporation, at the first public exhibition of America's newest luxury car, the 1981 Imperial.

This new Imperial is an unusually timely automobile. In price and size it is comparable to Cadillac's Eldorado and the Continental Mark VI. But it is a newer automobile than its competitors and, in significant ways, it is substantially different from either of them; it is these differences that make the Imperial the unique automobile it is.

After opening the exhibition and viewing the new Imperial, Sinatra and Iacocca spent some time discussing what America needs in a luxury car today and how this new Imperial fills those needs.

Sinatra: When you build a luxury car, where do you start? How do you lay down the specs for a new luxury car?

Iacocca: You try to build a luxury car that's better than the competition. Say you take your leading potential competitor and you might say, 'I'm going to give a customer 105 percent of this guy's riding comfort. Or 100 percent of his cornering ability.' You can set your sights on what the people are already buying.

Sinatra: Is that what you did with the new Imperial?

Iacocca: Sure. But our standards for this one were based more on what the people need today than on what the competition is giving them. You know, times have changed in the automobile business.

Sinatra: You mean the energy crunch.

Iacocca: Partly. That's why today you have to try to build a car that's the right kind of car for now and, hopefully, for tomorrow as well. Now, you've owned a lot of cars.

Sinatra: You'd better believe it.

Iacocca: What do you think today's luxury car should be.

Sinatra: I don't know where to start.

Iacocca: Start with the way it should look.

Sinatra: Well, first of all, I'd want it to look simple. I like a clean look. Because I believe that a lot of chrome looks dated. I think things are getting cleaner and simpler looking and that's how it should be.

Iacocca: Agreed. That's why we tried to keep the Imperial as uncluttered as possible.

Sinatra: It looks rich, Lee.

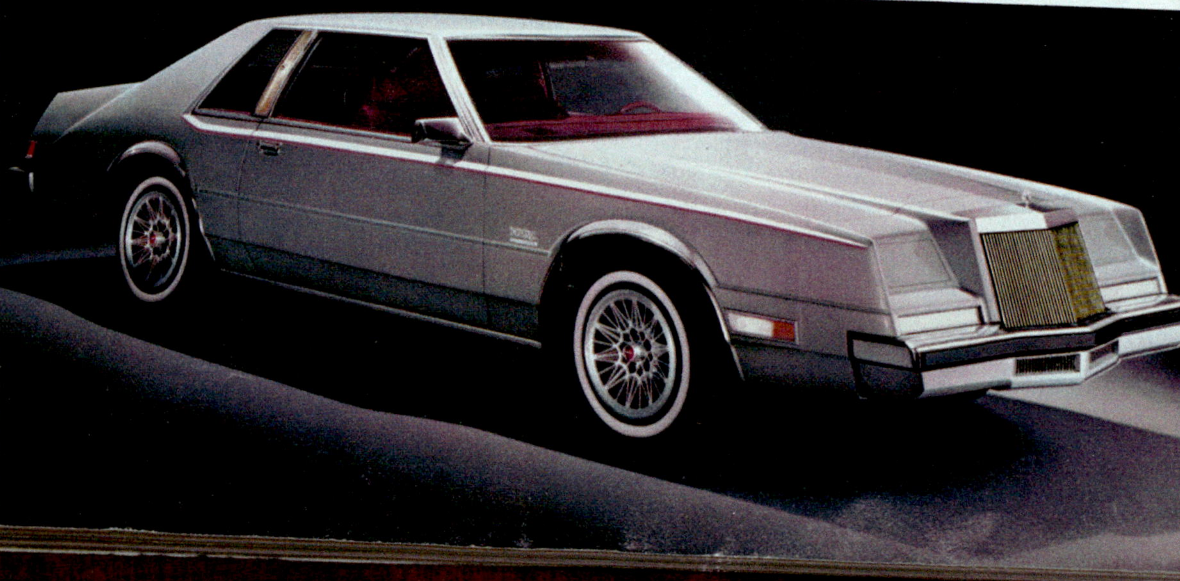

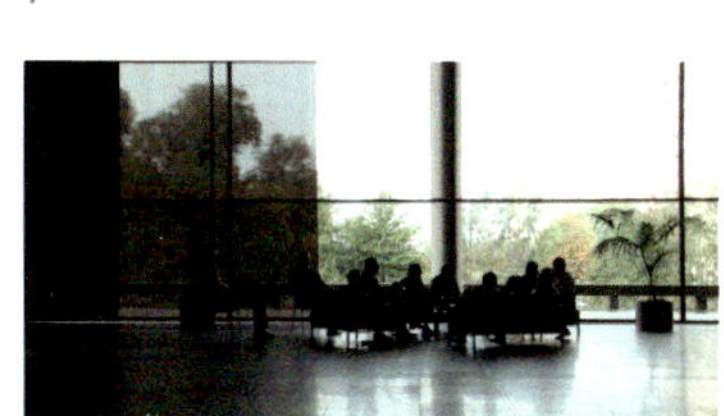

Fig. 13

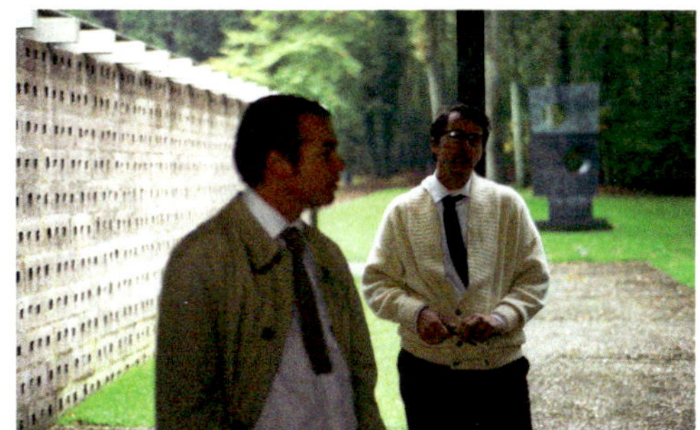

Fig. 14

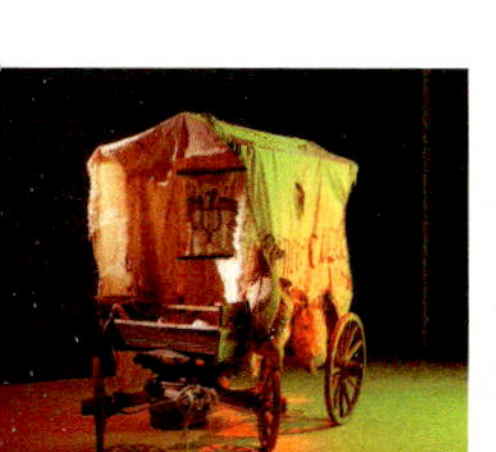

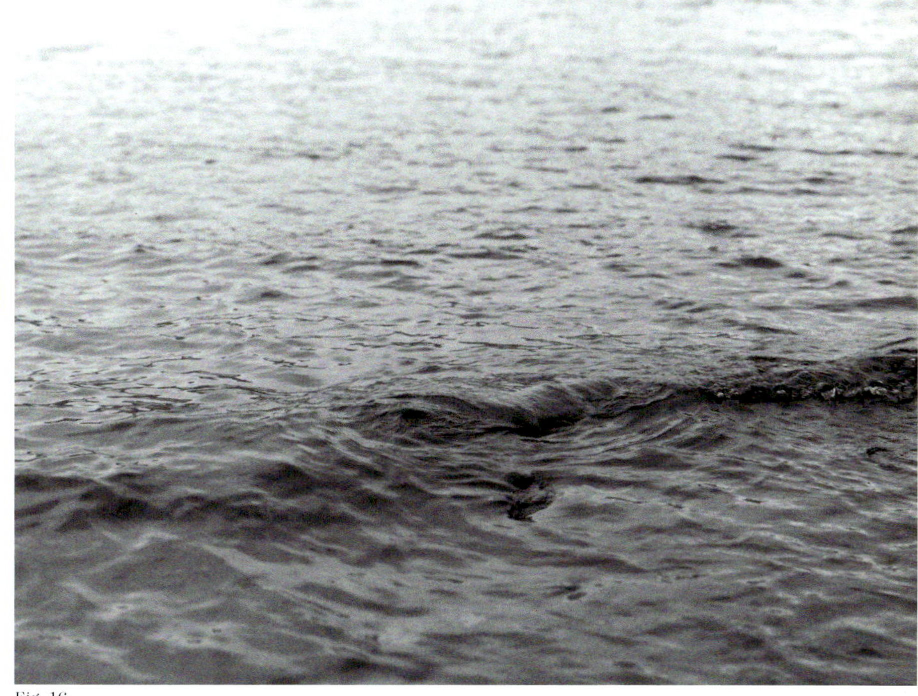

Fig. 16

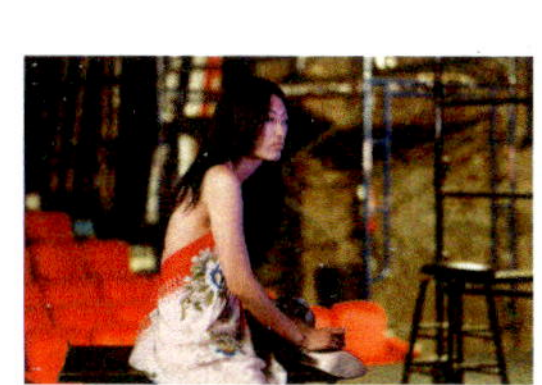

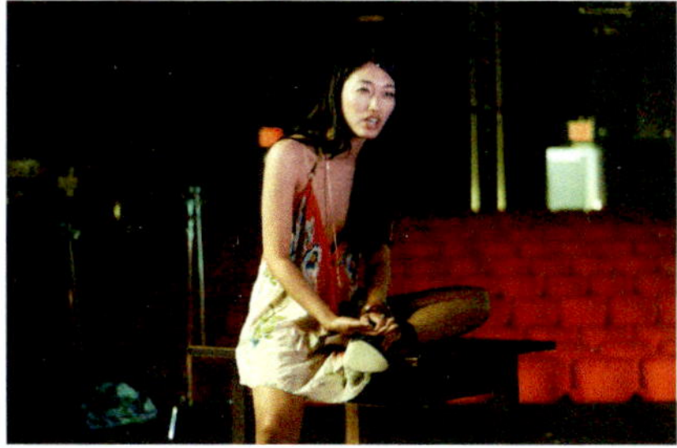

Fig. 17

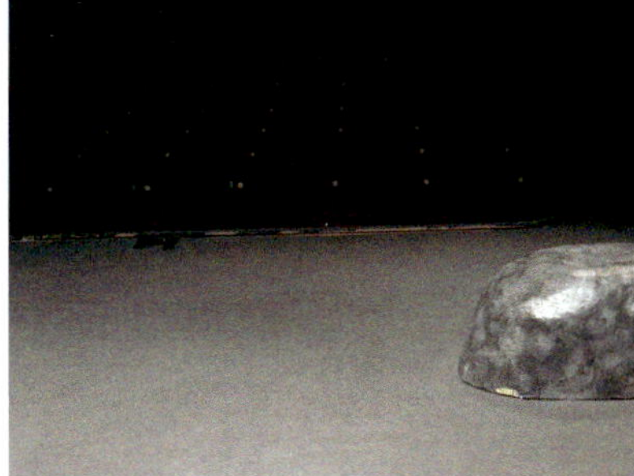

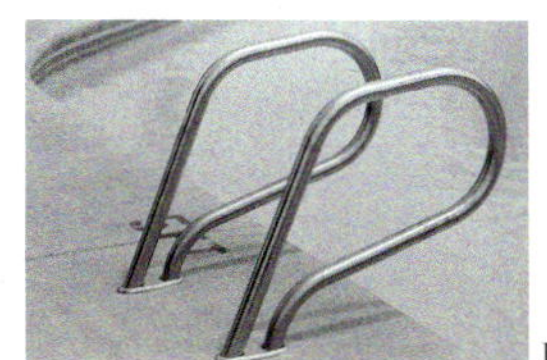

Fig. 18

Fig. 19

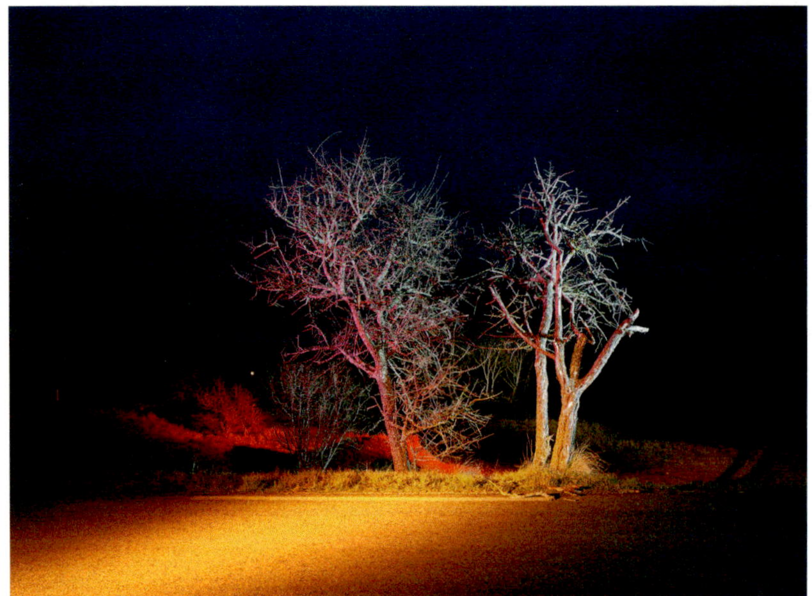

Fig. 20

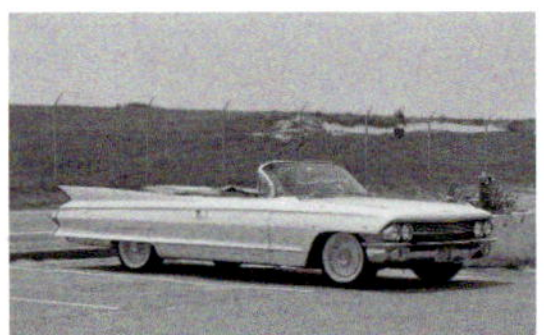

Fig. 21

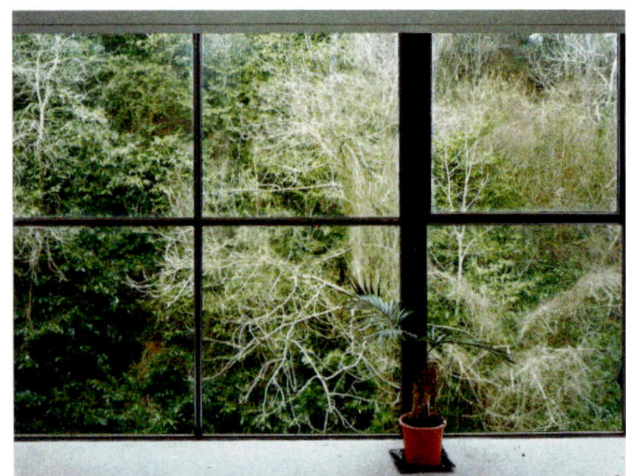

Fig. 23

Fig. 22

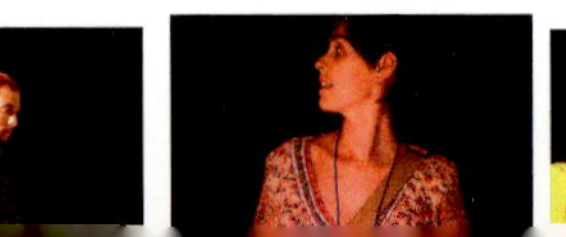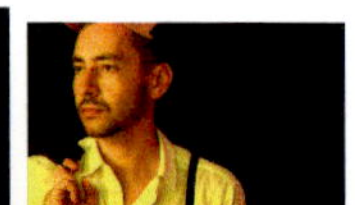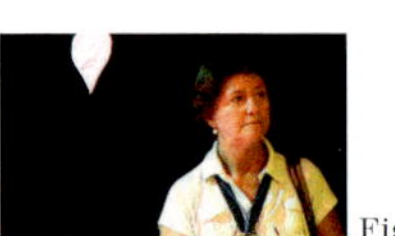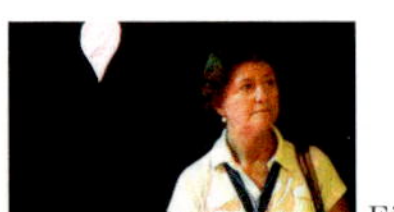

Fig. 24

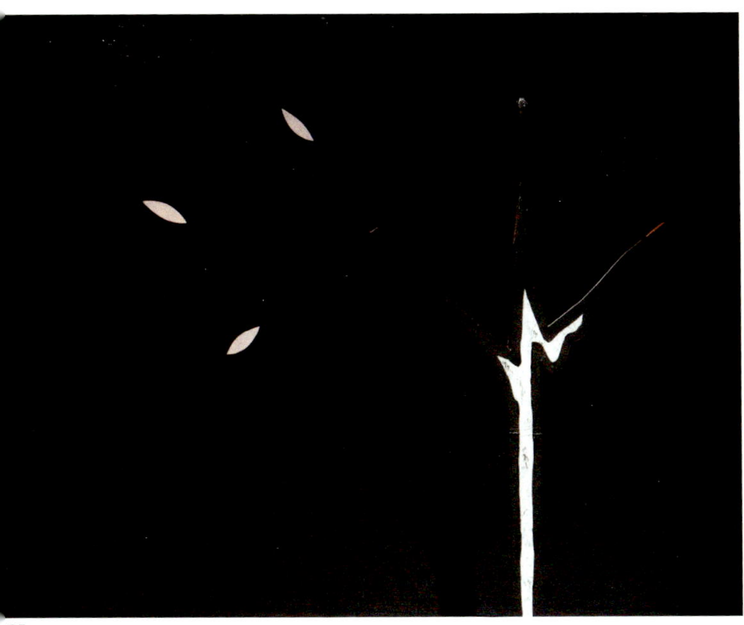

25

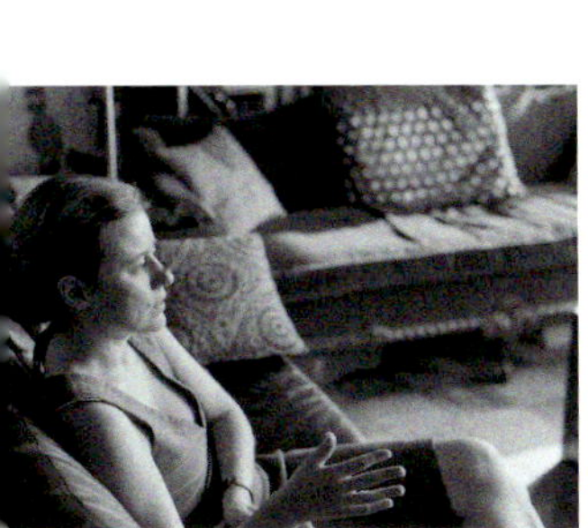

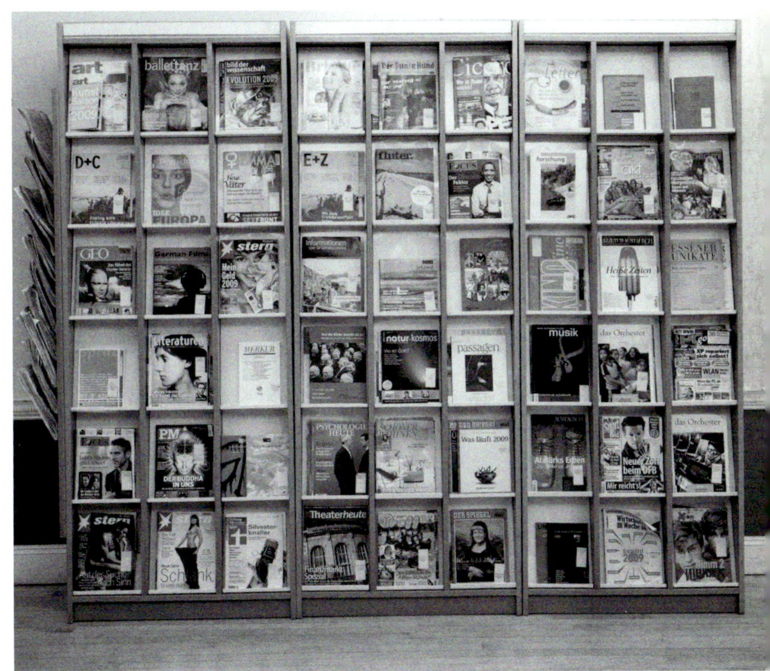

Fig. 26

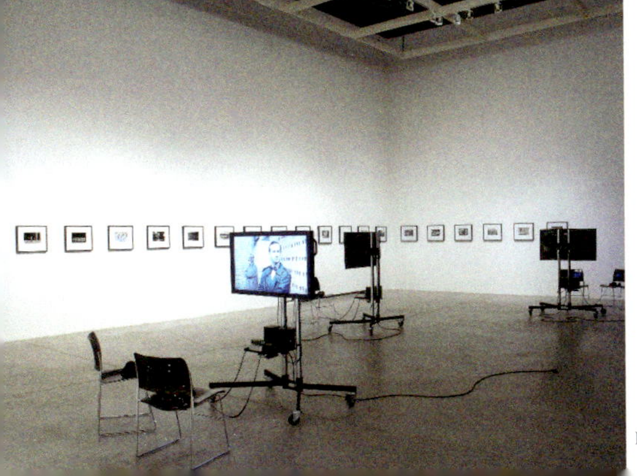

Fig. 28

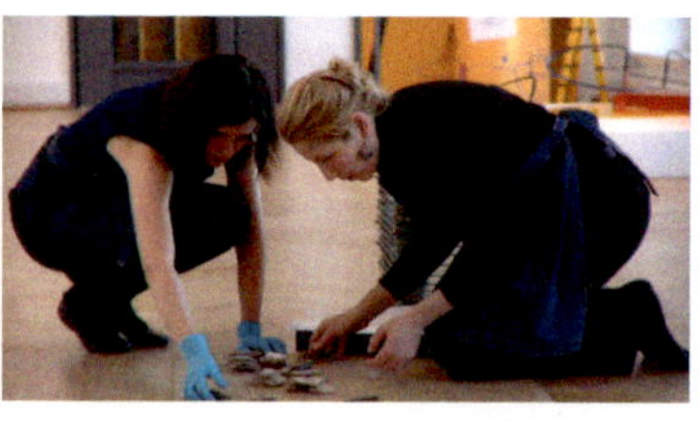

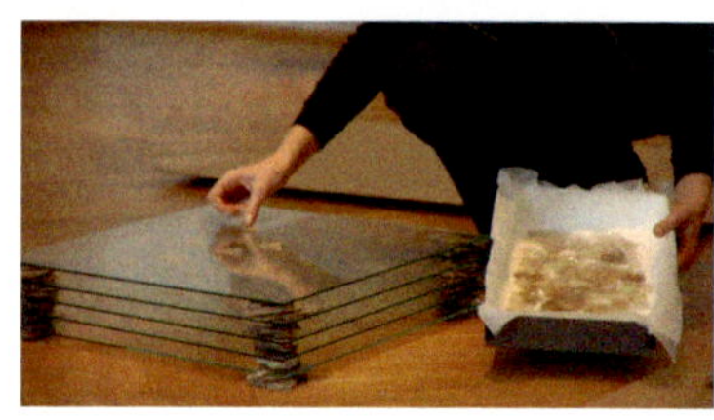

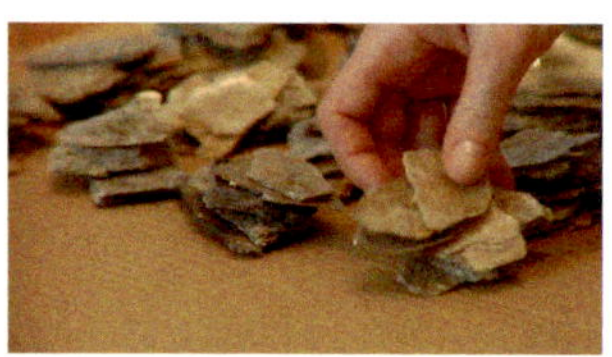

Fig. 29

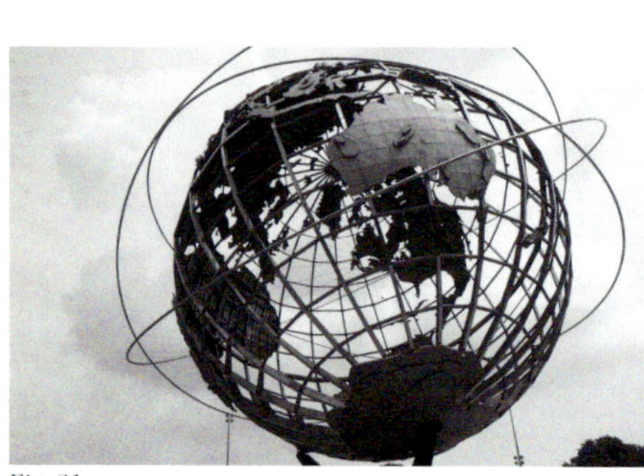

Fig. 31

of *Yale Marratt* (bigamy), *Thursday, My Love* (open marriage), *The Zolotov Affair* (sexual economics), *That Girl from Boston* (a comic novel), *You and I . . . Searching for Tomorrow* (another collection of letters) and, most recently, he has edited *Adventures in Loving*, a group of essays written by people living in alternate life styles.

WILLIAM SIMON, 43, holds a Ph.D. degree from the University of Chicago and for three years was a member of the Institute for Sex Research at Indiana University. Much in demand as an interpreter of the sexual frontier at universities and medical schools, as well as on the more erudite TV talk shows, Dr. Simon is currently program supervisor of sociology and anthropology at the Institute for Juvenile Research in Chicago, working in a U.S. Public Health Service–sponsored project focusing on youth and youth cultures. Dr. Simon, who participated in the *Playboy Panel* on homosexuality (April 1971), is the co-editor of *The Sexual Scene* and *Sexual Deviance* and the co-author (with John Gagnon) of *Sexual Conduct: The Sources of Human Sexuality*—which contains, says one scholar, "the most original thinking on sex since Freud."

ERNEST VAN DEN HAAG, 59, is a professor of social philosophy at New York University (where he earned his Ph.D.), a lecturer in sociology and psychology at the New School for Social Research and a practicing psychoanalyst. He has testified in nearly a dozen pornography trials, the most recent being New York's *Deep Throat* case, in which he spoke for the prosecution; and he has written extensively in *Harper's*, *Atlantic* and *Commentary* on sex education and political philosophy. Dr. van den Haag, who has lectured at the University of California at Berkeley, Columbia, Yale, Harvard, Colorado and Minnesota, is a senior fellow of the National Endowment for the Humanities. His books include *The Fabric of Society*, *Education as an Industry*, *Passion and Social Constraint*, *The Jewish Mystique* and the recently published *Political Violence and Civil Disobedience*.

PLAYBOY: In the 25 years since the publication of the first Kinsey report—and perhaps in part because of it—sex has become not merely respectable but almost unavoidable as a topic of conversation, magazine articles, how-to books, X-rated films, encounter therapy, even school "visual aids." And subsequent surveys indicate that Americans are simply talking more about it; they're practicing what's being preached in ever-increasing numbers, despite rear-guard actions still being waged by the thinning forces of sexual puritanism. According to reports in the press, these new patterns of behavior are developing into genuine life styles: mate-swinging, group and open marriage, communal living, self-proclaimed

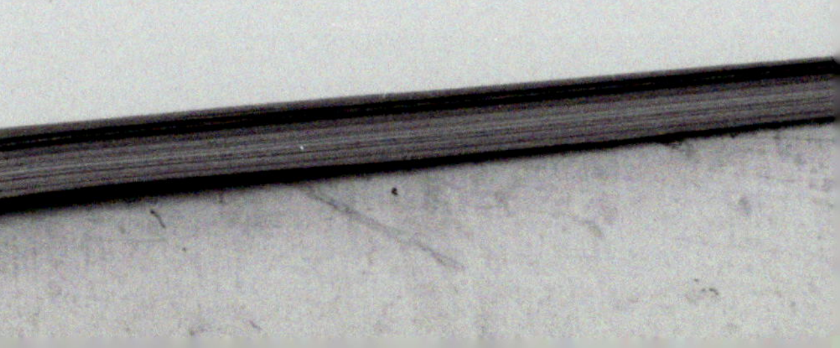

Fig. 30

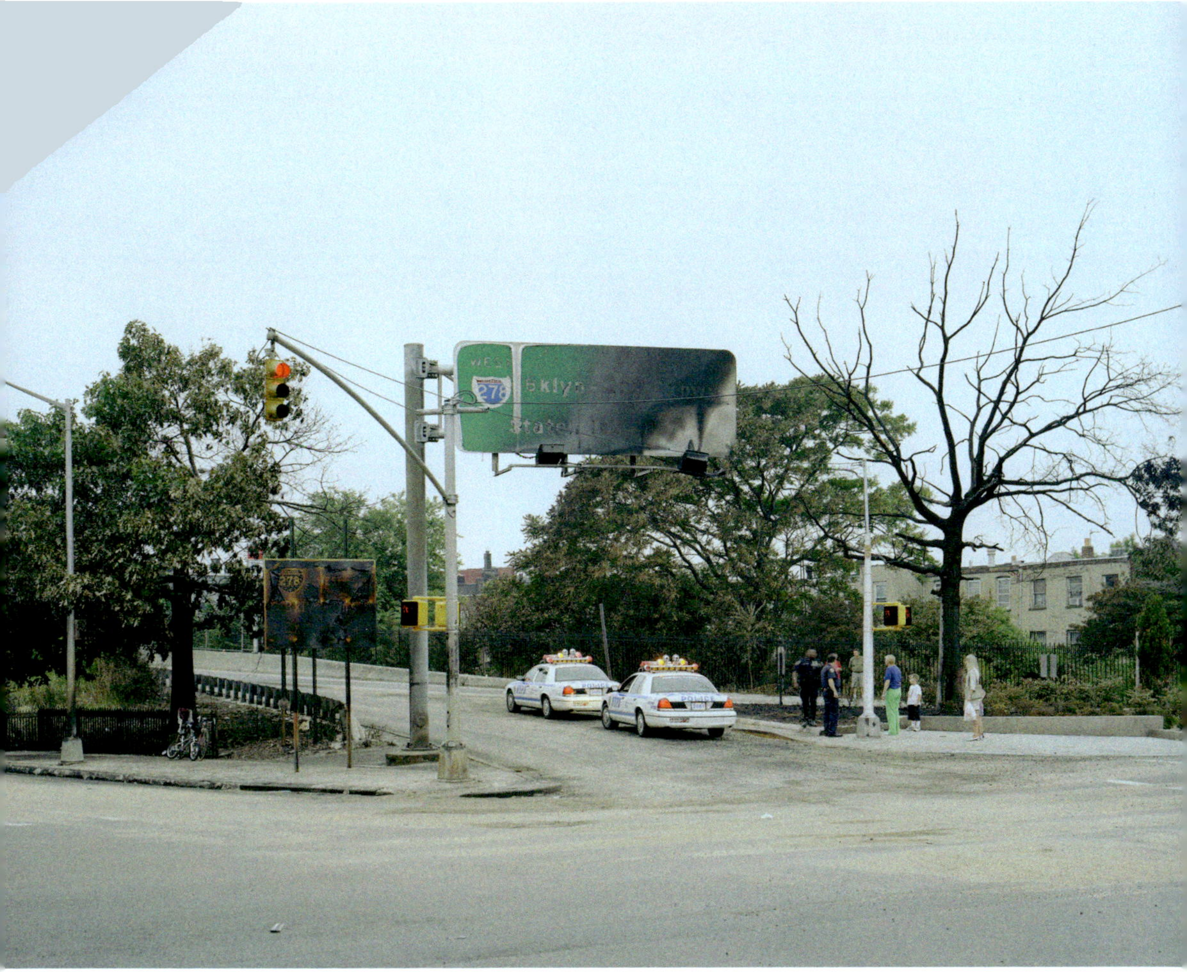

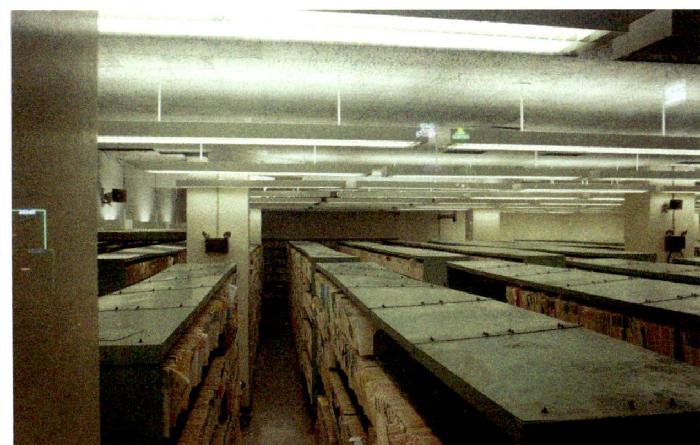

Fig. 32

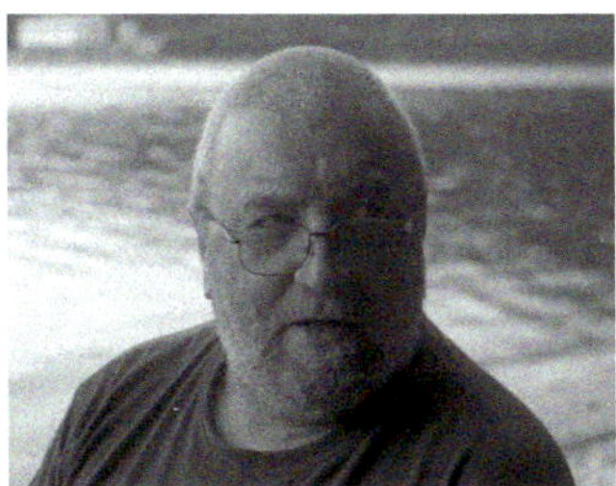

Fig. 33

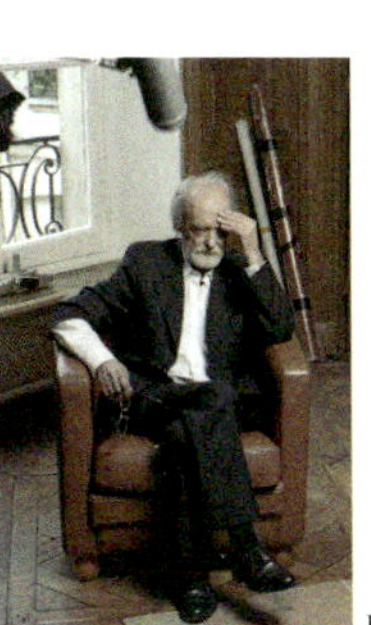

Fig. 34

Fig. 35

Jay Chung & Q Takeki Maeda

*Nikola **Dietrich***: *In your recently produced video work, you figure as the two singers Daryl Hall and John Oates and restage a strange, mysterious music clip of their song "She's Gone." Why did you choose this?*

*Jay **Chung** & Q Takeki **Maeda***: We only knew the original from YouTube, and we liked it so much that we remade it, shot-for-shot. What was mysterious was that when we showed an early version of it at an art fair, the original video was taken off YouTube immediately. It's a pretty obscure video, and we are not sure why it was taken down. When we found out, we felt a strange twinge of guilt and shame: It was as if by copying it we had somehow annihilated it.

ND: Popular culture is an omnipresent phenomenon in TV series, bestseller literature, or fashion and one occupation of yours. Its own standards of narration and rules are reflected in your work. How do you relate to this strategic, effective language that influences our social reality massively?

JC & QTM: When we think of popular culture, we think of it as the most immediate, unavoidable kind of culture. When an artist deals with a subculture (as opposed to popular culture), they choose to throw it in relief. In contrast, our work deals with popular culture with respect to the fact that one does not choose it—one has no choice but to deal with it, because it imposes itself.

ND: Yes, I agree. There is this need of relating to the things that one is surrounded with. You made the choice to handle it, to grab the heritage, and work with it—transform it. How do you add to it? What narrative line are you following?

JC & QTM: It probably doesn't always appear consistent from the outside.

We assume that an artistic identity is a privilege. That means that having a signature style, method, or narrative is the result of either endowment or struggle. What we do may seem random or contingent to a spectator, but we are certain that we have always been constant in our attitude and methodology.

ND: Besides the video work, you have chosen to show old-fashioned corner-closets that look like heavy antiques, but are basically worthless, rather useless pieces of furniture. Would you describe this work as significant for a throwaway mentality?

JC & QTM: Corners are often read as having a particular connotation. Especially in art, they can stand for the marginalized or the repressed. For us, there is a tension in the objects being so voluminous and intrusive, yet designed to be relegated to a corner. The objects also have a very specific significance for us, but it is probably best not to overdetermine them.

ND: Still, I would be interested to know what this specific significance of the objects is for you? The piece brings also the work Cornered *by Adrian Piper from 1988 into mind ... benches and tables squeezed into the corner and the woman on the TV trapped in this situation. Then there is also the domesticated aspect of this furniture when seen in a museum space where they become even more alienated objects. Do you agree?*

JC & QTM: Although we are running into trouble because an interview is supposed to clarify things, when we say specific significance, we actually mean that we put a lot of work and deliberation into making certain works ambiguous. The vitrines are approximately two meters high. That makes them anthropomorphic. They are

mostly late copies or cheaply made.
Yet, somehow, they persist. Sometimes,
they are miscast as heirlooms.

ND: *Your earlier performances have
been rather immaterial, and in some
way or another, about motion and
fiction, like the trip in 2005 where you,
together with ten other crew members,
set sail from the Port of Ushuaia in
Tierra del Fuego, Fin del Mundo, or
End of the World, southward. This
would mean that you would, indeed,
sail to the outside of the world. Or
Caducean City (2006), a drive in an
ambulance that moved through the
streets of the city center and suburbs
of Bologna, or the Frankfurt airport
work.*

JC & QTM: In addition to involving
motion and fiction, all the works
you mention are antisystemic. In the
Antarctica work, we purposely re-
frained from producing anything that
would depict its sublime or romantic
qualities. In *Caducean City,* we tried
to make a civic disruption that was
not only sanctioned, but also endorsed
and paid for by the state. In *Modus
Tollens,* which we made at the beginning of our collaboration, we tried to
depict the end of our friendship.

ND: *Can you describe the genealogy
of* Modus Tollens?

JC & QTM: We were convinced that
contemporary art was backgrounded
by the more general category of representation. Within representation, you
had different aspects and types. Each
had a surplus meaning that served
to distinguish it from the other types.
For example, we were thinking about
deception as a mode of representation
because, at the time, that seemed to
have a lot of currency in the overall
climate of ideas. When we started
Modus Tollens, we approached the idea
of self-deception, actually, self-deception

and the formation of subjectivity.
From there, we depicted the end of
our friendship by insisting on it as
scenario. Making the pictures in-
volved in a psychological game, almost
like a neurotic Avedon. The outcome,
however, was so much richer than
we had imagined: It had all these
layers in the way it was put together.
It opened up many issues for us—what
the terms of performance could be,
how language could enclose a work,
how repetition sets up a multivalency,
and so forth. And we think that
helped to solidify our working process.

ND: *Talking about friendship/part-
nership, I guess this is an important
part of many of your works, which
possibly would be very different in
their physical outcome if you would
work on your own. One senses, especially with the work* Artxanda, 2007,
*in the deserted fun park in Spain, a
strong companionship.*

JC & QTM: In our work, the idea of
friendship is explicitly articulated. We
use the term in a literary and philo-
sophical sense. Think about narrative
film, where friendship is practically a
genre in its own right—*Modus Tollens*
is linked to that convention, but because it is what it is, the narrative is
unstable. Friendship is also a good
entry into ethics: It can function as an
assumption that provides a recurring
context for our work. We're probably
the only artists who regularly treat it
like that, although it took a friend to
point this out.

ND: *Would you consider working as a
team a generally safer mode, as you
are able to refer to the partner as a
kind of backup or responding person?*

JC & QTM: You mean in the day-to-day
sense?

ND: *Yes, in your day-to-day collaboration.*

JC & QTM: We often get asked about collaboration. We think that the term has been overloaded: It's as if it inherently implies a countercultural ethos. Let's set the record straight—collaboration, literally "working together" is a euphemism. In one sense, it means joint accreditation, in another, exploitation. That goes for just about anyone, in any industry. Everyone works together; the term just becomes a truism. What we do in our case, however, is to resolutely abide by certain values. When we work together, it is not an optimization. What people project into the term collaboration should actually be attributed to the consideration we have put into our pieces.
ND: Do you believe in magic?
JC & QTM: No. We're more into magicians. It's not at all the same thing.

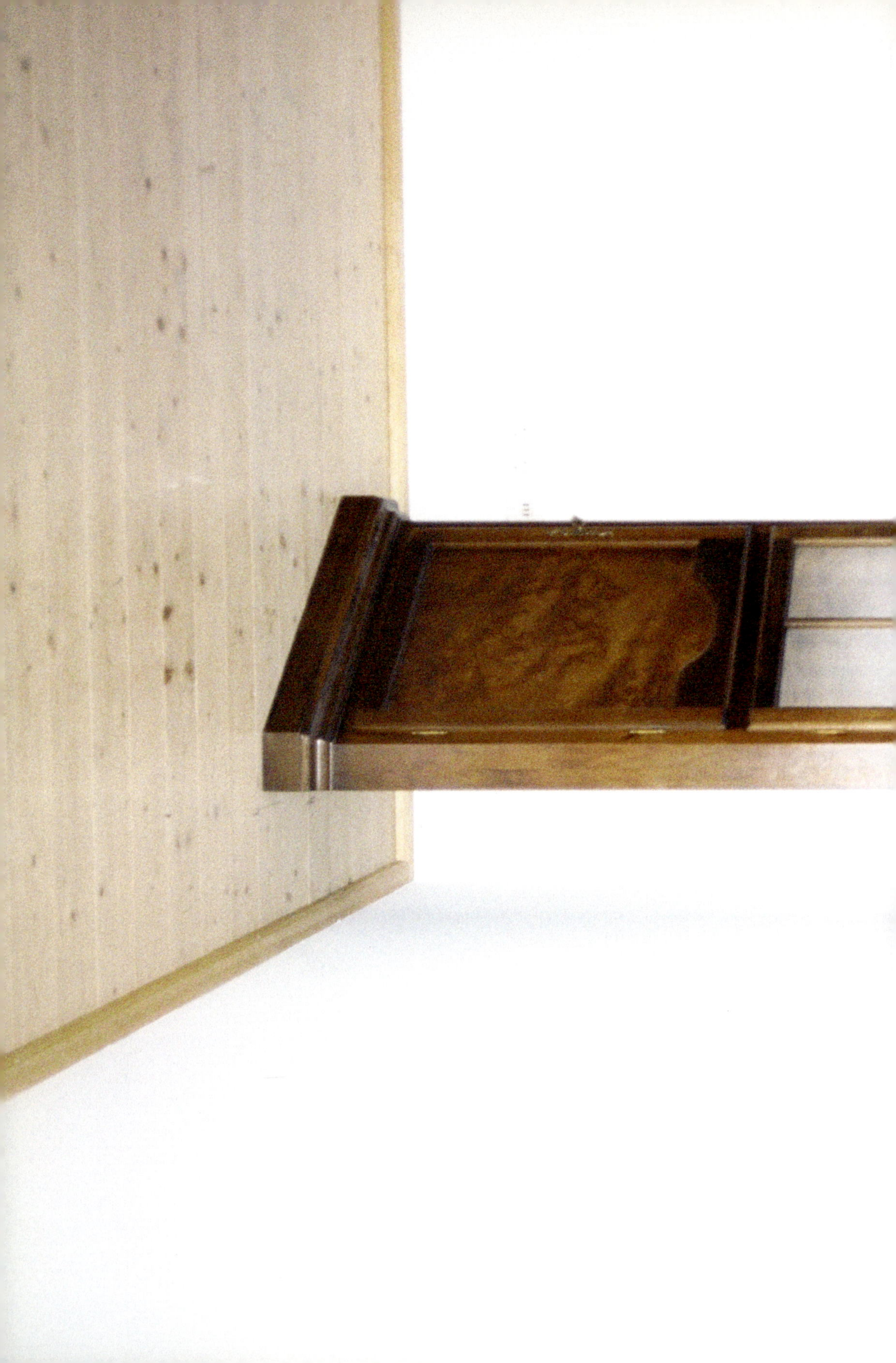

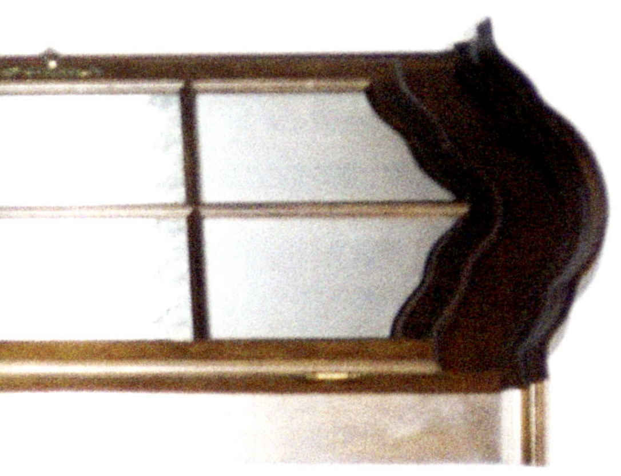

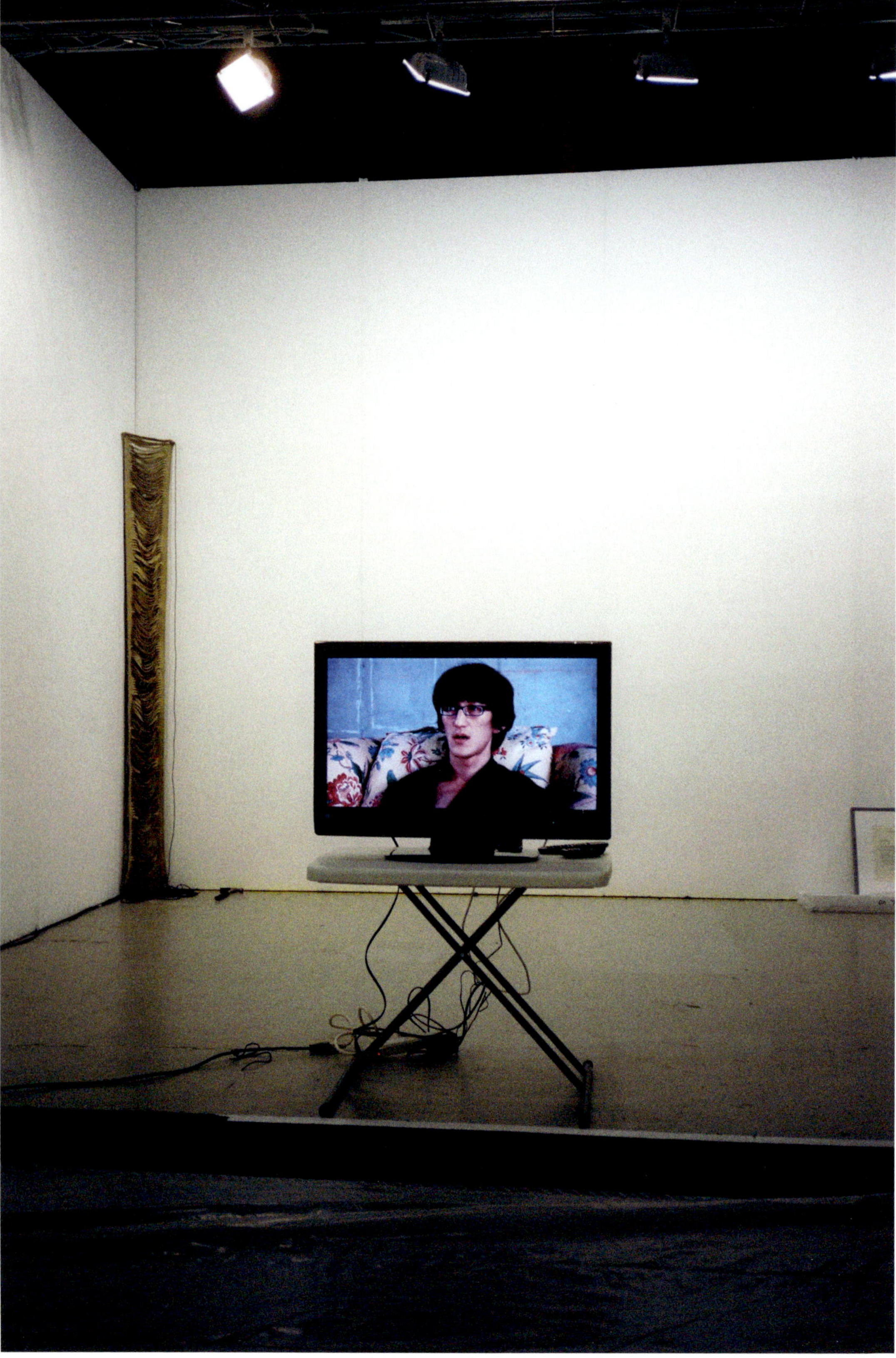

PS: The real hero of neoliberalism is Harry Potter.

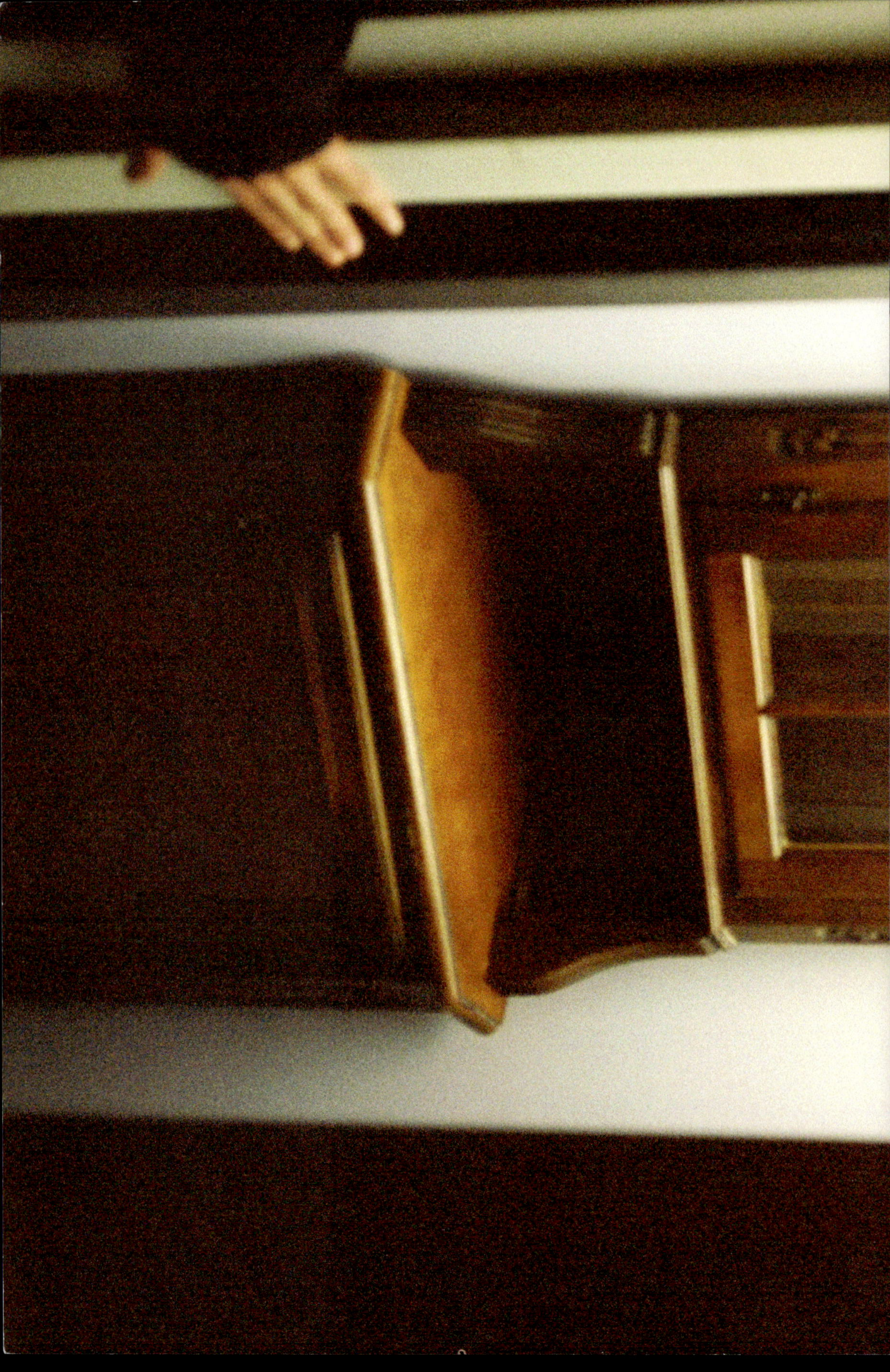

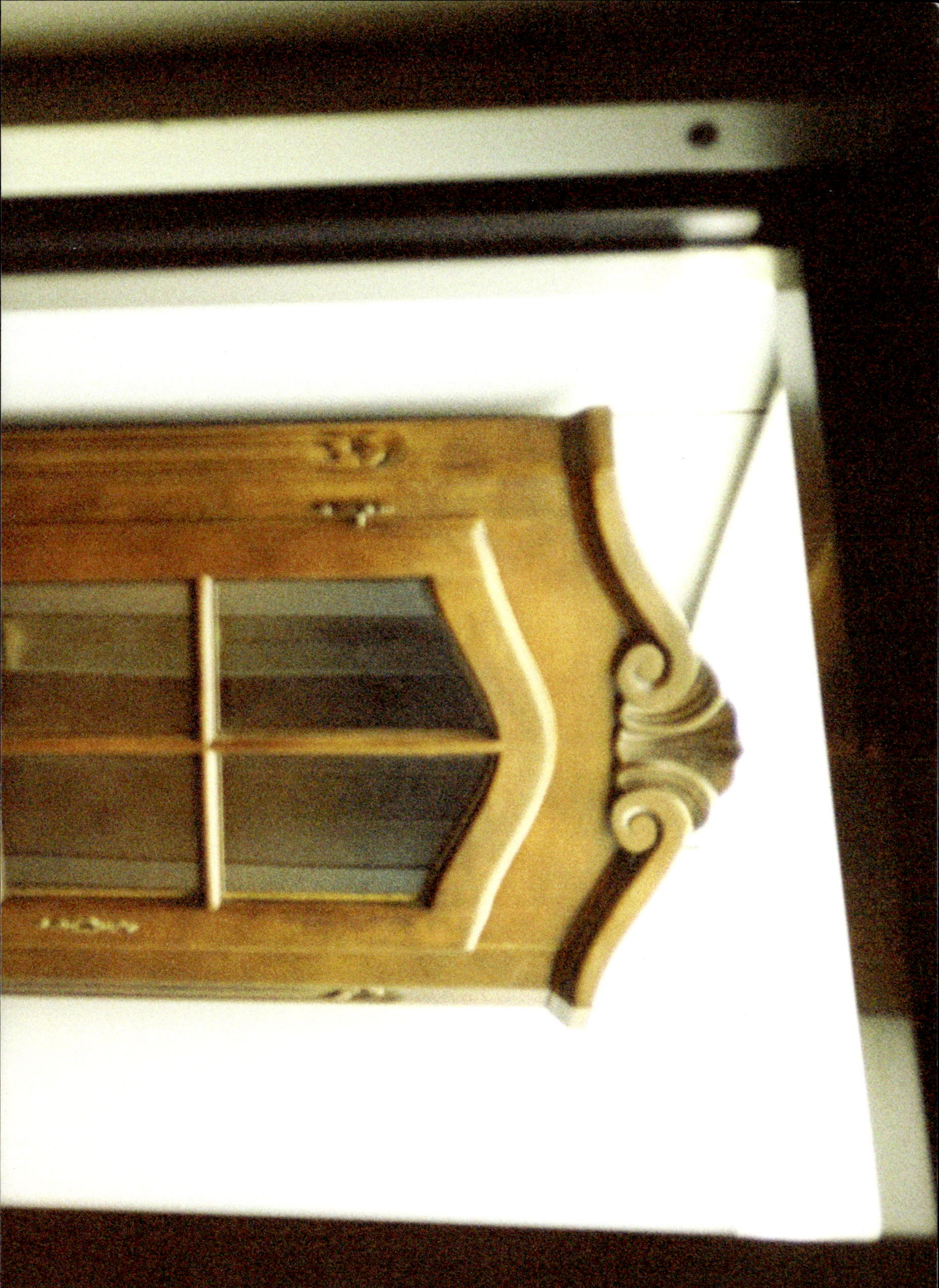

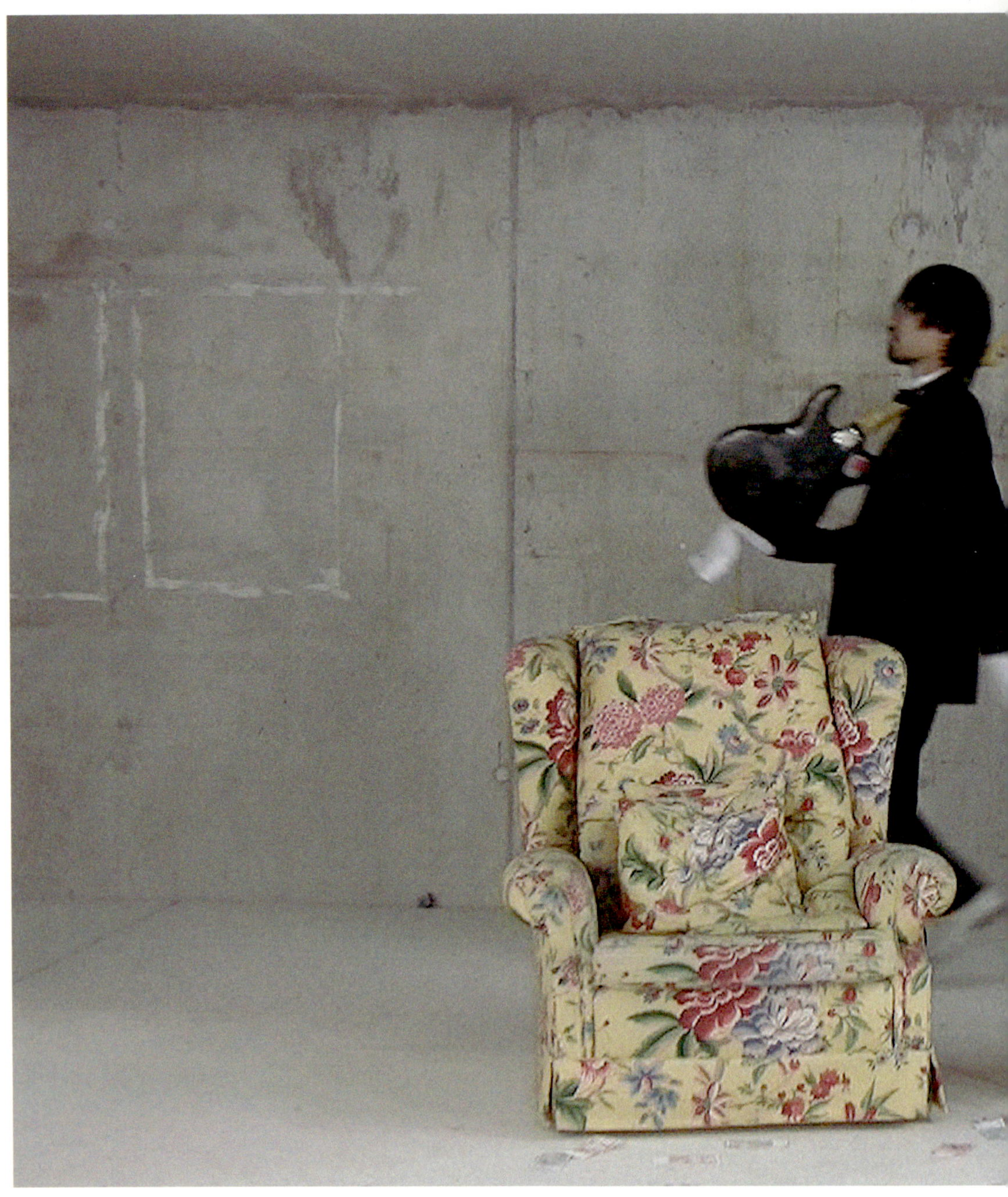

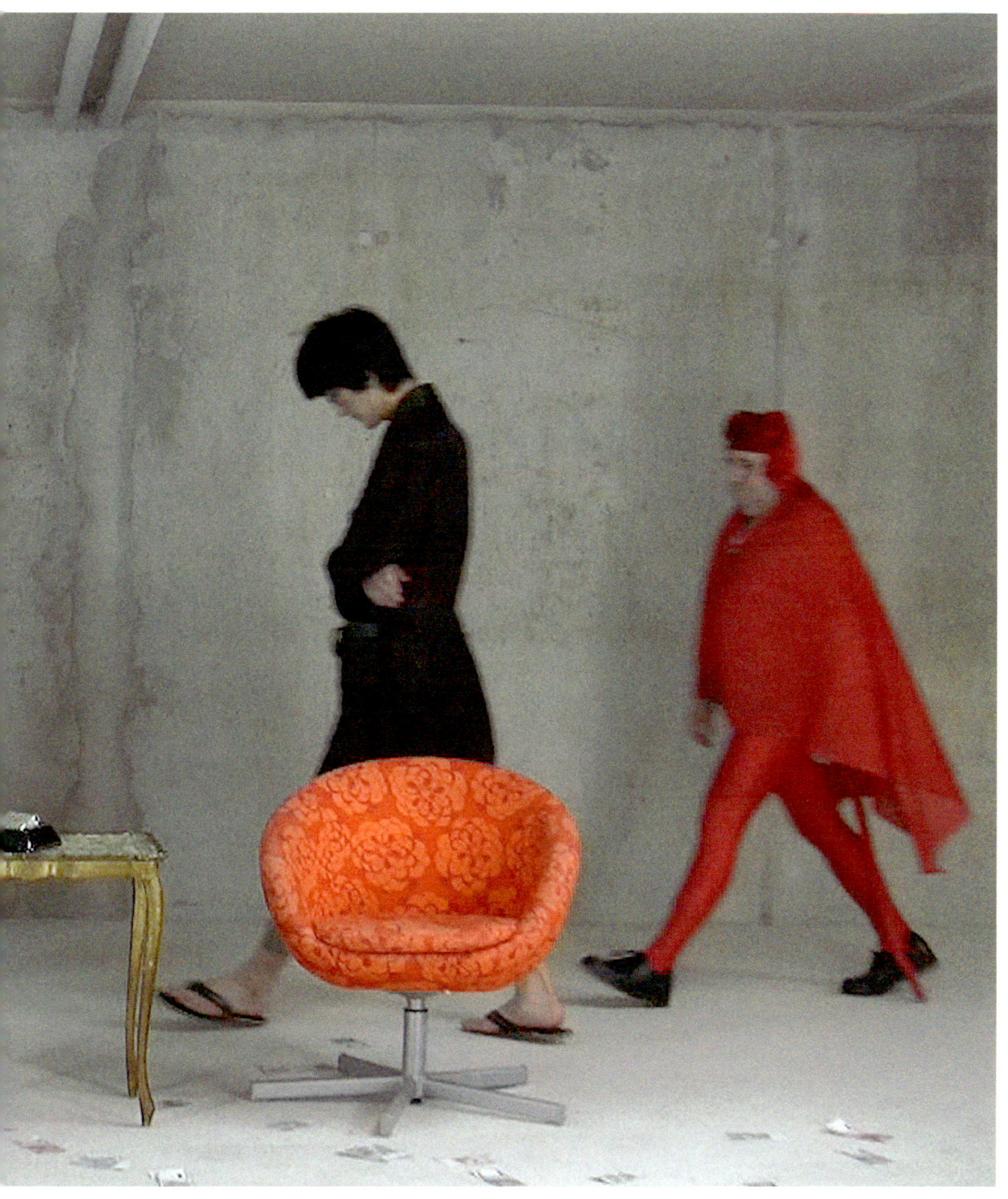

SZ: How do you mean?

PS: Because the Harry Potter novels tell fables in which reality has no limits. They convinced a whole generation to find the magician in themselves. The potter is someone who makes vessels. Today only losers believe in work, the rest believe in magical pottery and making their structured products fly.

SZ: Because they have no content?

PS: No, they must have content, just not as an end in itself. Vessels are a means to receive and dispense. Martin Heidegger, in a profound meditation on the being of things, used the example of a jar; he showed how being hollow, it only fulfilled its function upon being filled. What it then contained could be let out in the gesture of giving. Modern man has plugged up the spout; nothing more comes out. This isn't good in the long term.

SZ: What's the best way for us to quit magic?

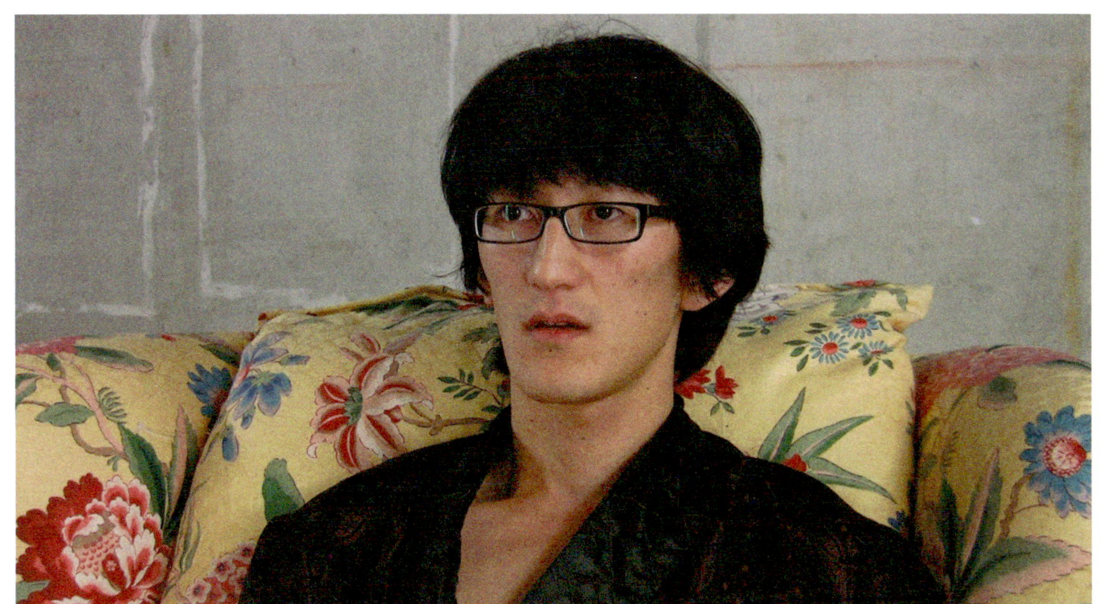

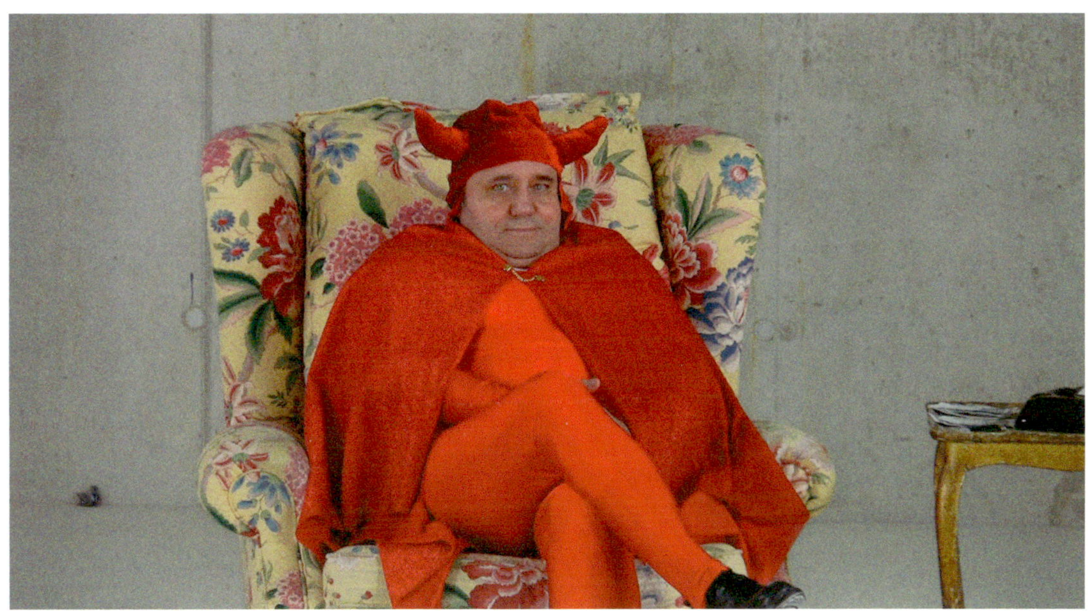

Rodney Graham

Nikola **Dietrich**: *With your exhibition, Picasso, My Master (2005) you turn your practice toward painting for the first time; painting seems to be the medium that is consistently afflicted with the cliché of an art practice that legitimates the artist to be an artist. Artists do what artists have to do?*
Rodney **Graham**: Well, I always felt bad that I could not draw and that I had no training in that area. I felt less of an artist, it's true. My friends and teachers, like Ian Wallace and Jeff Wall, came out of painting, and I always envied them for that. I guess I entered into the educational system just a couple of years later, when everybody was moving away from painting and, of course, I was inspired by the possibilities of conceptual art, which did not require the same skill set, and which was closer to literature, where I had a bit of a background.
*N**D**: In a Night School program at the New Museum in New York (March 1, 2009), the main question was, "why are conceptual artists painting again?" That is answered with "because they think it's a good idea." What is your answer to this question?*
*R**G**: I don't know if my painting is very conceptual. It's more of a reaction formation in relation to conceptualism, with which I had become quite bored. At least I'd seen and done so much of that sort of thing. It was interesting to approach the making of something with no preconceived idea as to what it will look like, instead of taking an idea and watching it go through a series of successive compromises and distortions in the process of becoming a reality. This is kind of simplifying things, of course. I know, I was probably trying to recapture a studio practice I never had in my youth. That's why my *Wet on Wet* show at the Lisson

Gallery in 2007, which included paintings, was subtitled *My Late Early Works (Part 1 the Middle Period)*.
*N**D**: In an earlier interview of yours with Matthew Higgs (in* Rodney Graham, *exh. cat. Whitechapel Art Gallery, London, K21 Kunstsammlung Nordrhein-Westfalen, Düsseldorf (2003)) you were talking about your songwriting practice as a kind of hobby. Would you see your practice of painting from a similar point of view?*
*R**G**: Painting is different, really. Playing music could only ever be a distracting sideline because the music does not engage art issues at all—say, in the same way that Martin Creed's musical project does, insofar as it can be related to performance art, and it seems to be in harmony with his other work. I find it difficult to connect my music to my art practice—I feel like it's being done by a different person really, and I don't think this is a good thing. I would prefer to have a well-integrated personality.
*N**D**: Would you agree that your paintings could be seen as a result of a kind of performative action, even if it happens in private—the performance of the artist painting in his studio?*
*R**G**: Not really. I am just trying to make a painting that looks like a painting, and I only stop painting when the work completely resembles a finished painting. For this reason, I have been painting over the same paintings for a couple of years now. It's terrible. Even ones that have been documented and exhibited. They are getting very thick and heavy. I like heavy impasto painting insofar as the grooves and ridges of the previous painting offer pathways for further exploration. I started painting assuming that I could think about other

things when I worked (multitasking) but I found out that painting is absorbing to a frightening degree.

ND: Would you see your painting practice in any way related to work of yours that emerged from your research into Freud?

*R*G: My "research" into Freud was an "allotrion" that was, itself, very Freudian, I suppose. Freud used the word to describe an all-absorbing hobby that sidetracked one from one's main aim in life and he applied it to himself, calling his work on dreams an allotrion that took him away from his "serious" work as a doctor. In his dreams, this goes back to criticism from his father who reproached him for spending too much money on schoolbooks. My research subject was Freud's allotrion really, and the whole idea of being sidetracked, which I was, since I didn't make any art for two years or so while I pursued this subject. There are lofty artistic precedents in Leonardo's botanizing, etc. The only thing this experience taught me is that if you stick with something long and hard enough you do get results, and maybe this insight has helped me with my painting.

ND: I like this notion of allotrion—an altered path. I see your gesture of painting as another way to remove your self from yourself, as an almost hallucinatory act or a gesture out of the subconscious. Was it a decision to launch painting in your art with a figure like Picasso, whose work can be considered as commonplace in the pictorial world, a way to clarify your intentions, or were you ending automatically up in his style?

*R*G: All my work as a so-called conceptual artist goes back to Duchamp's critique of stupid-as-a-painter "retinality," which, I guess, I questioned when I really looked at and was shocked by Picasso's paintings of the analytic Cubist period of 1911–12. So I became a convert. As a songwriter, I liked the rhythm and sound of "Picasso, my master," and the mild hint of provocation in it.

ND: In other works, you were staging yourself in specific roles, such as that of a castaway, cowboy, or prisoner. Did you put on the costume of the painter?

*R*G: Yes, the humble mantle of the disciple.

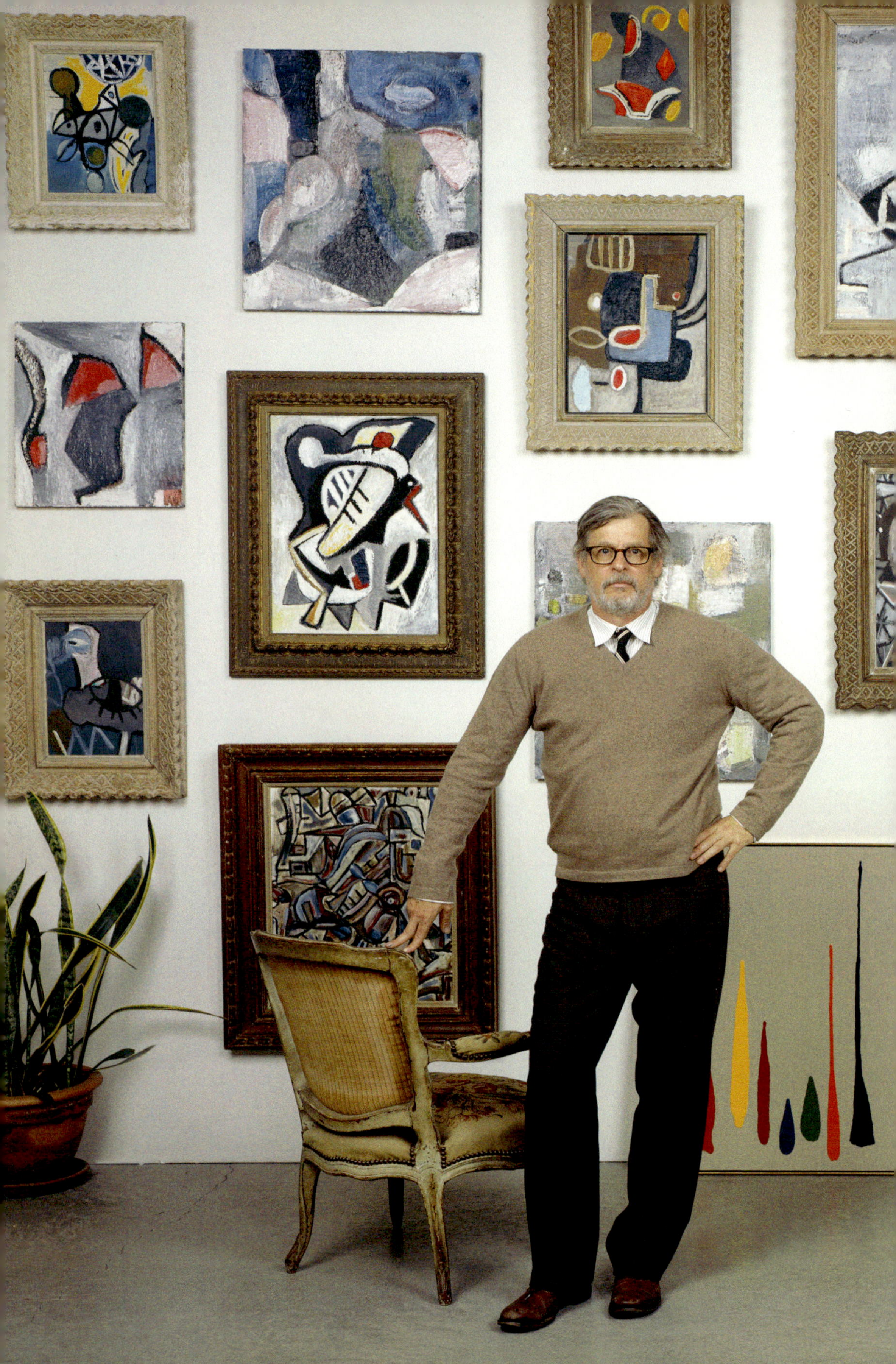

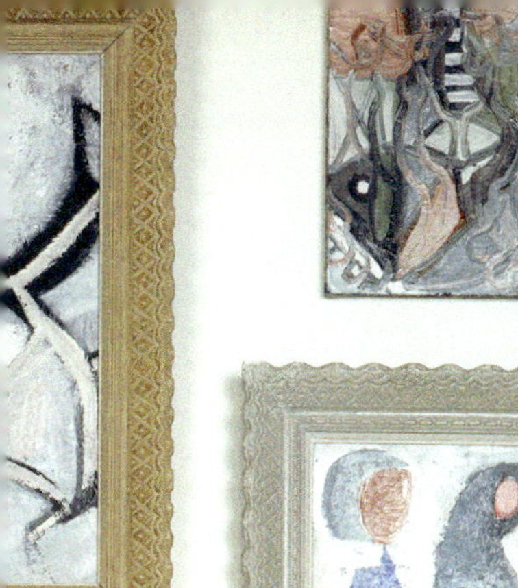
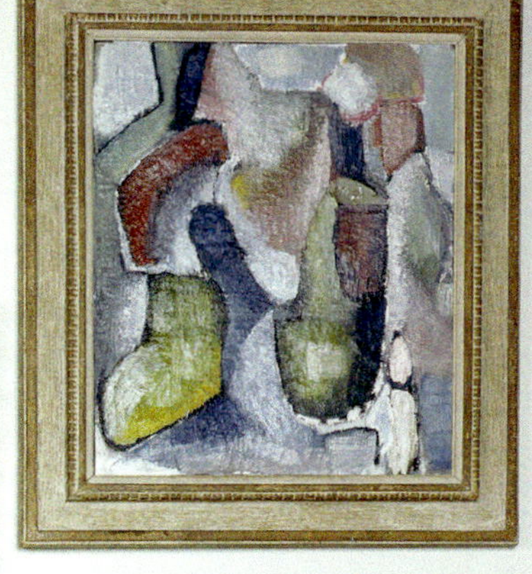
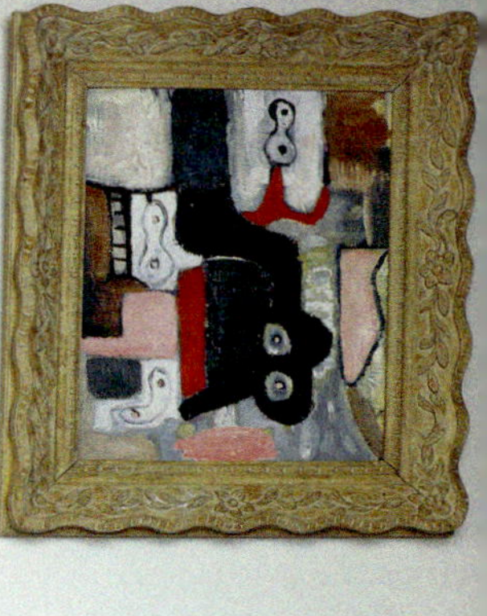
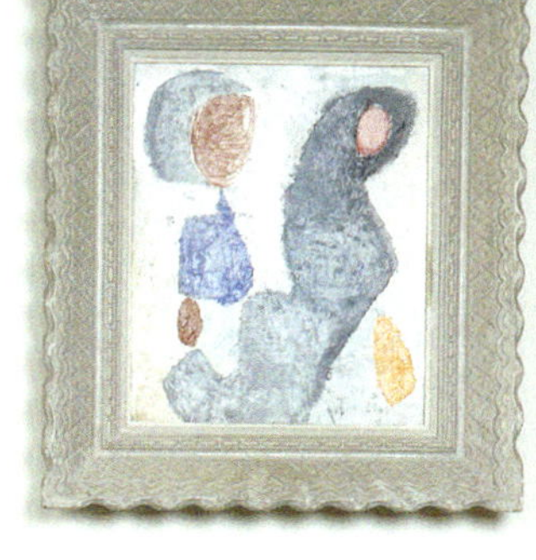
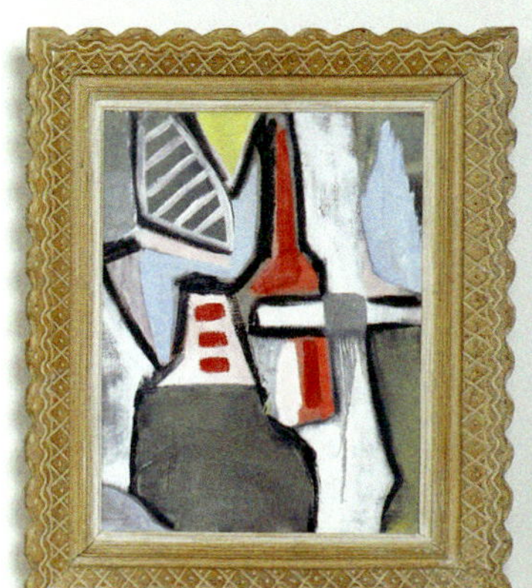
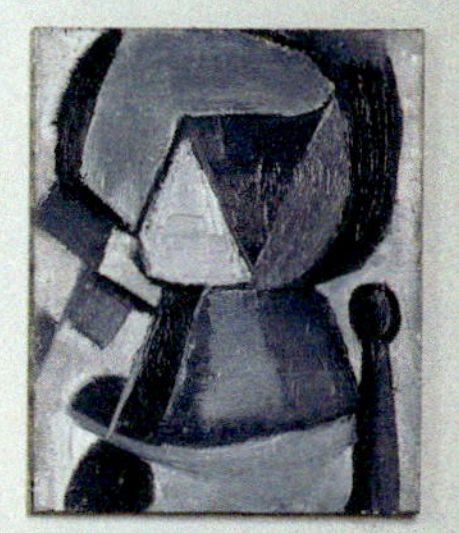
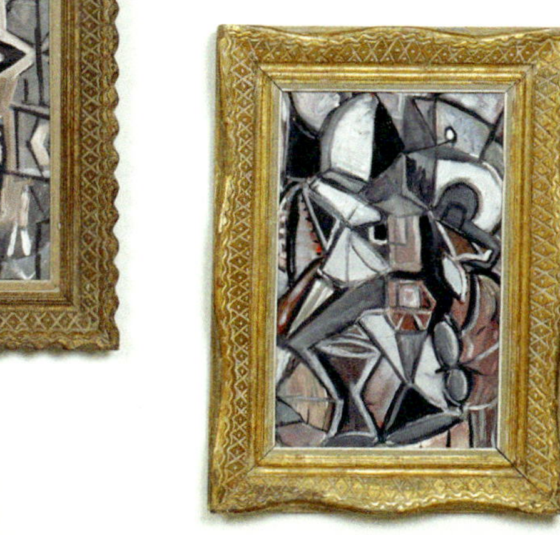
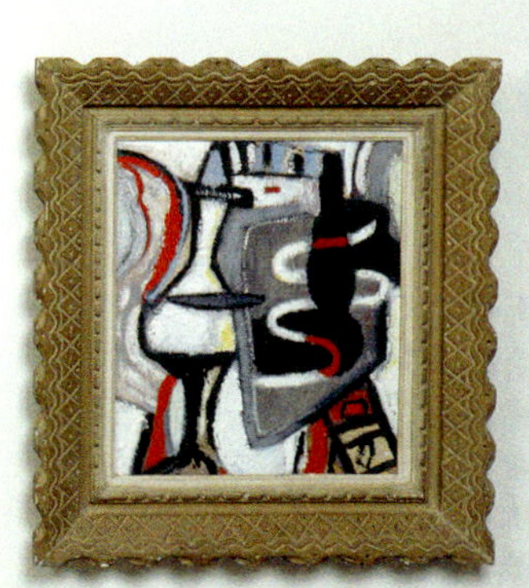
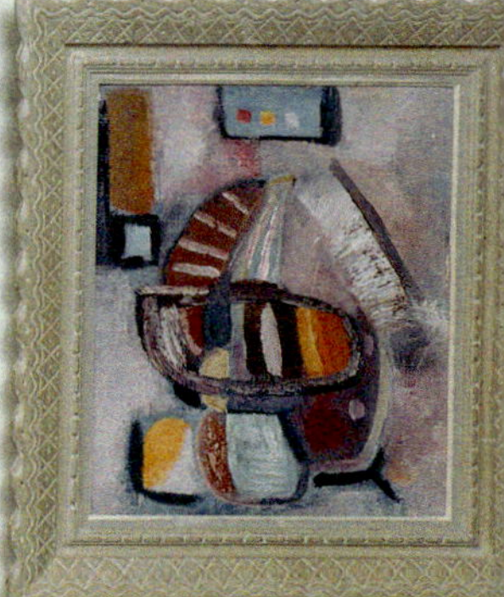
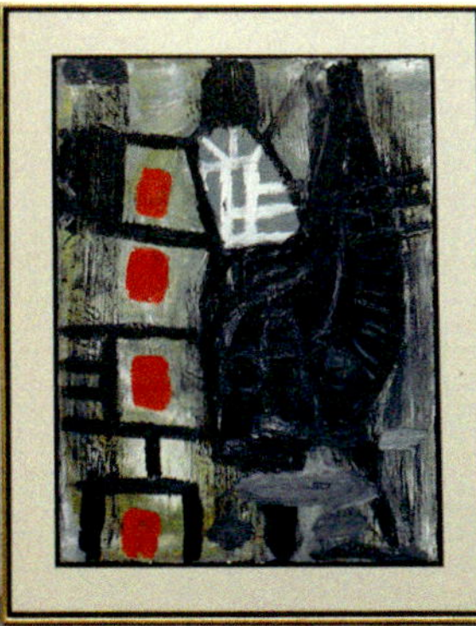
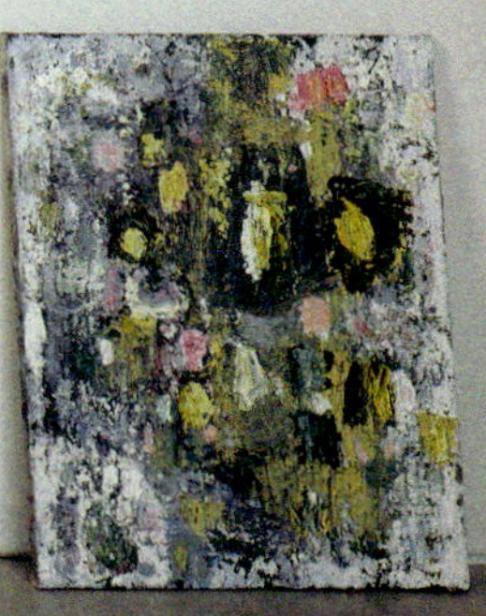

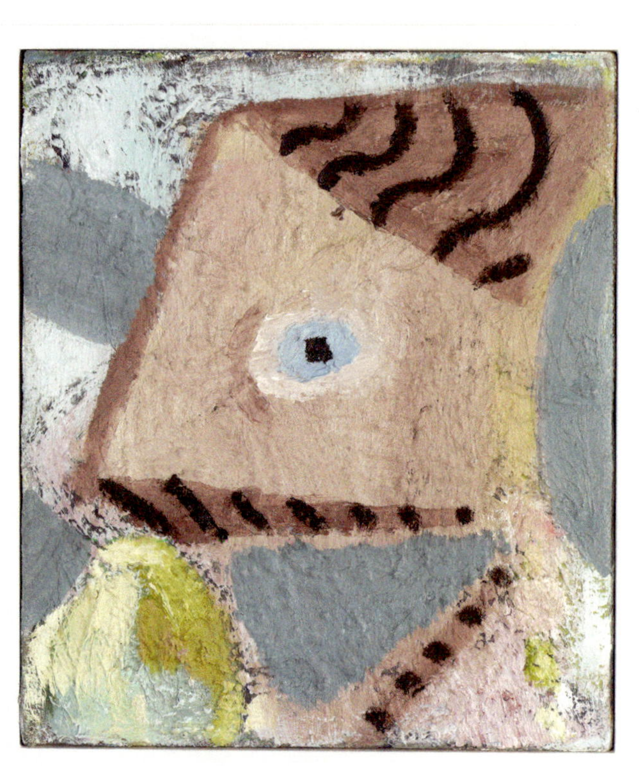

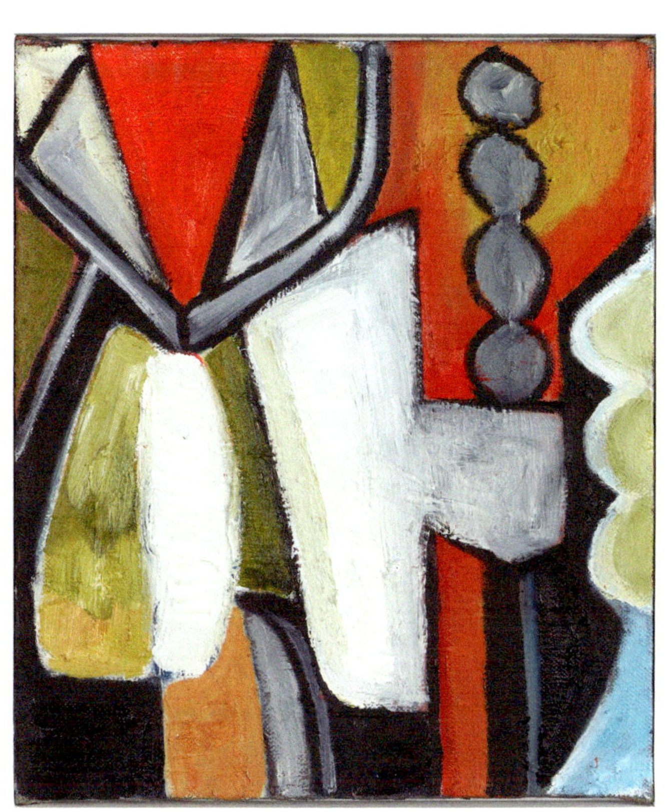

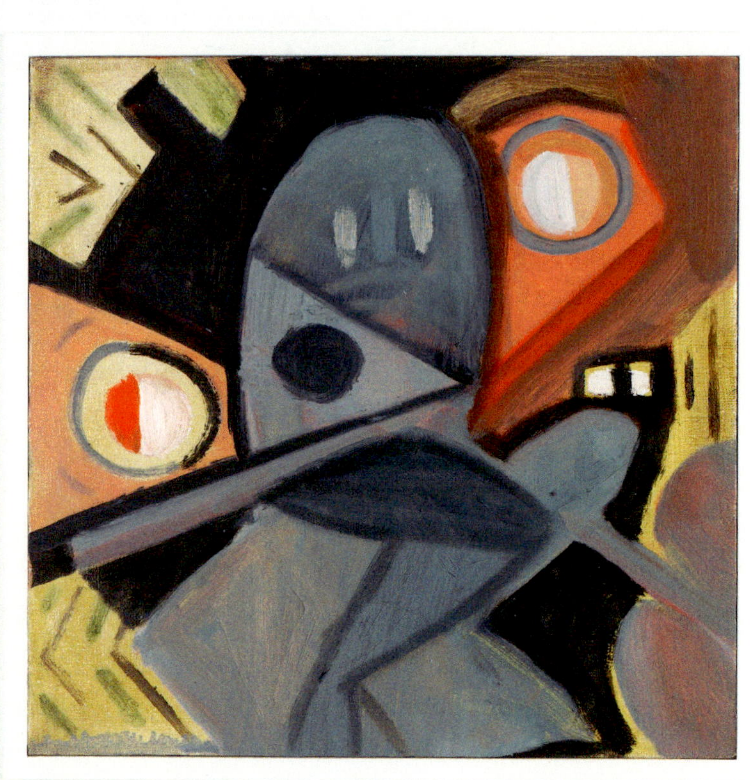

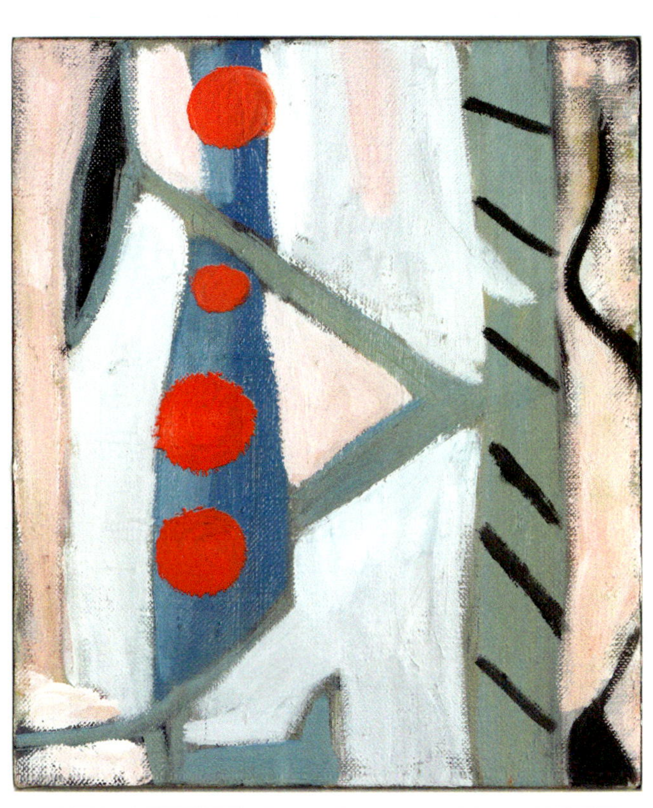

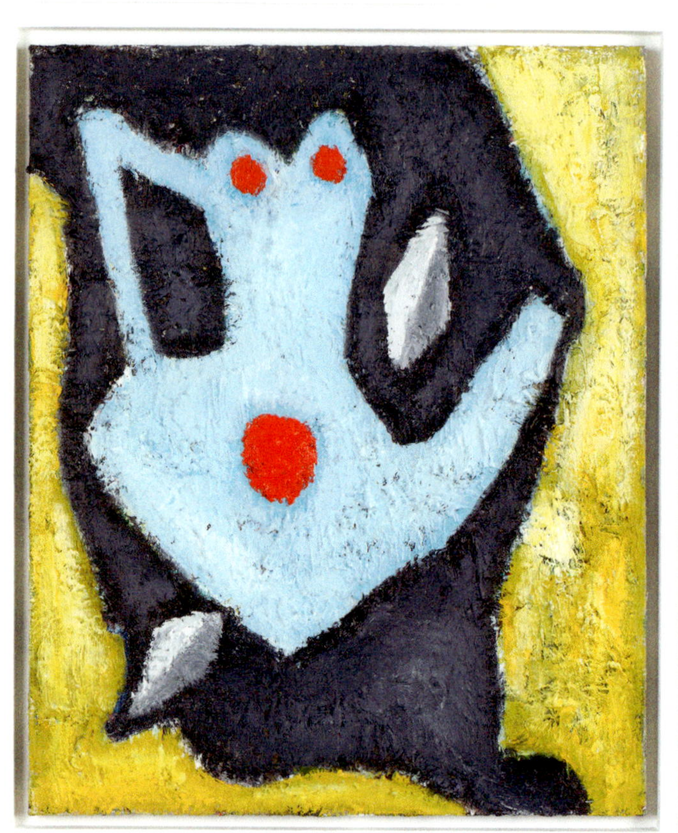

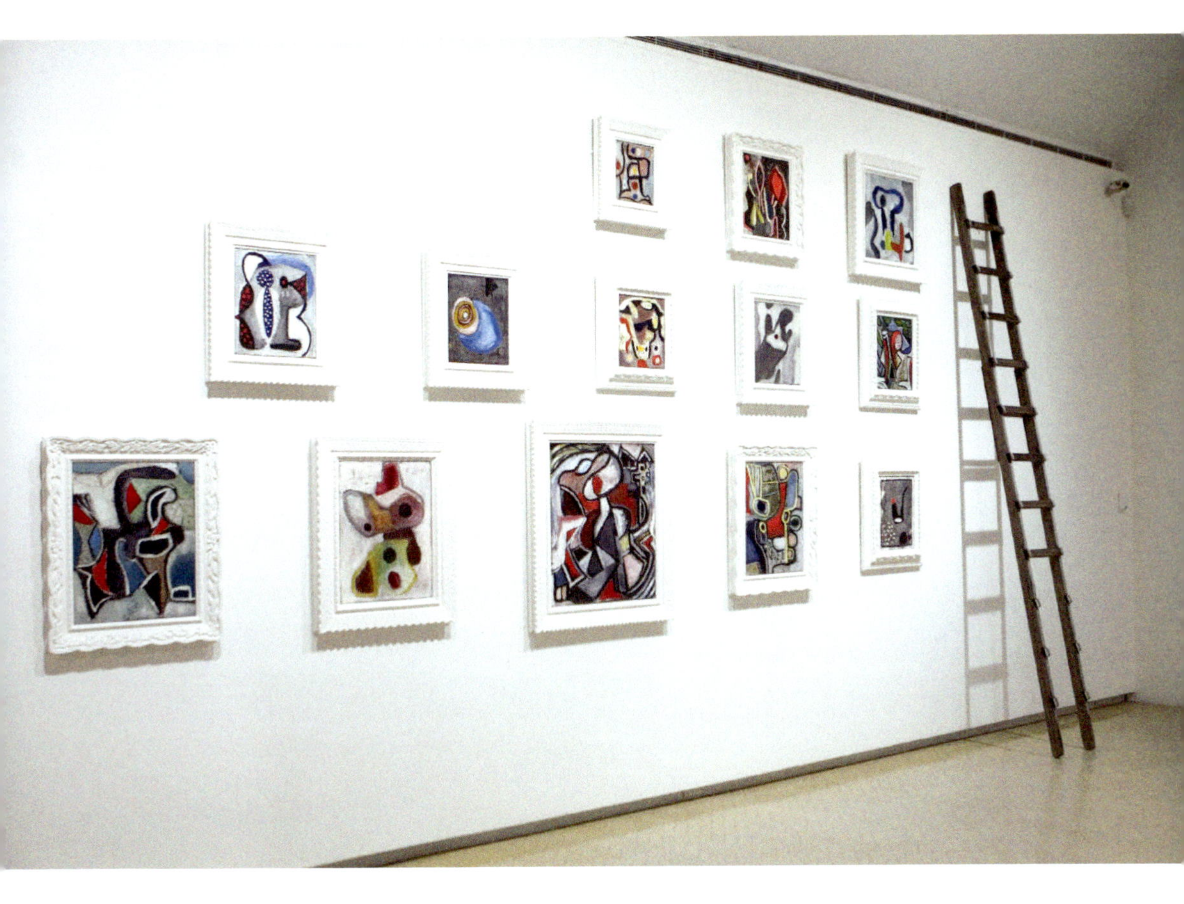

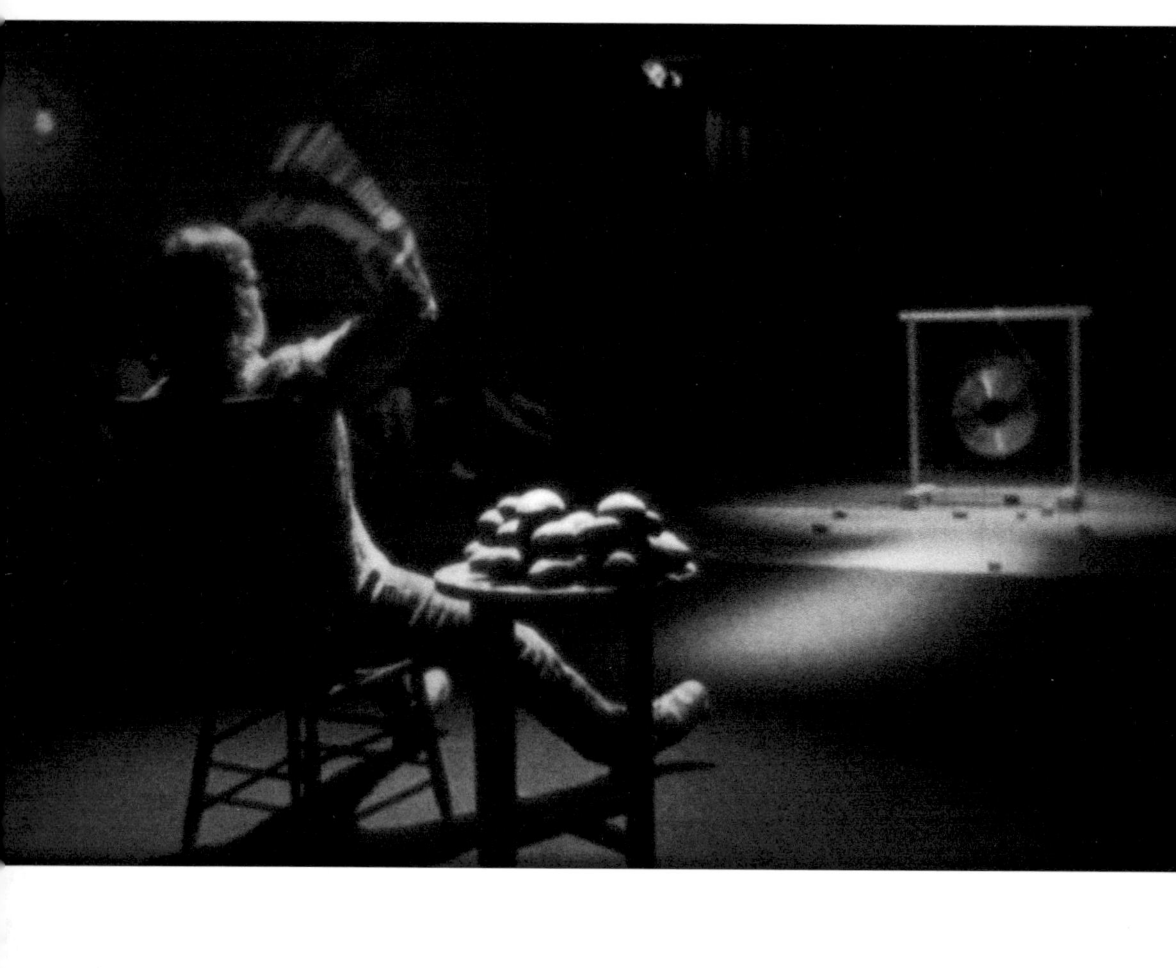

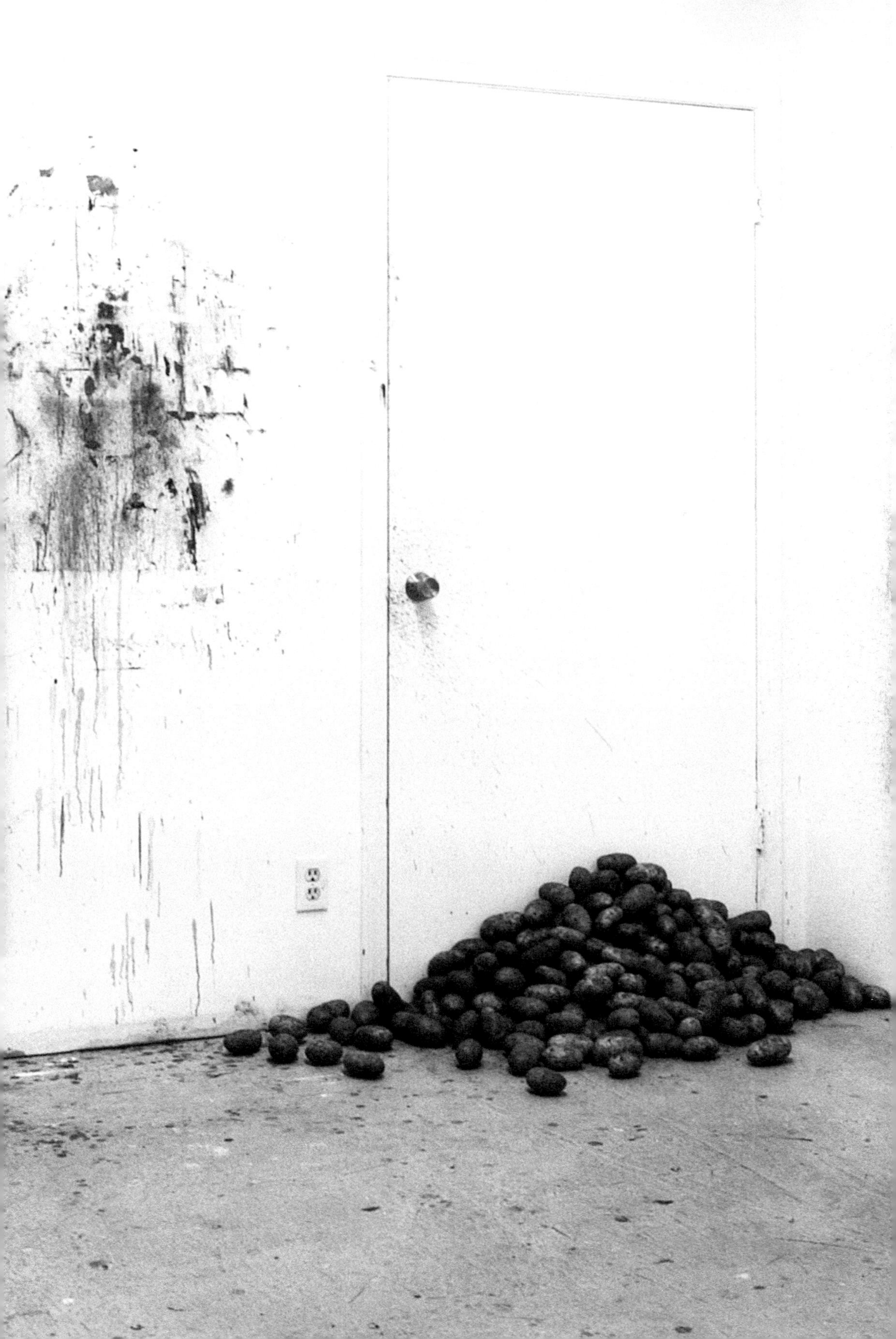

Hilary Lloyd

Jacob **Fabricius***: In November, I was at a Kenneth Anger event, a night of film screenings, interviews, and a live performance by Anger himself. I didn't think of a connection before, but his film* Scorpio Rising *and his interest for leather, chrome, and crotch-shots made me think of your way of documenting details and performances. Can you relate to Anger's films and the way he works?*

Hilary **Lloyd***:* I love leather, chrome, and have a passing interest in crotches. I'm also interested in whether it's possible to make work out of something so facile as cut-out pictures of men's crotches from fashion magazines.

JF: The installation Car Wash *(2005) shows 320 slides of men washing cars, a job that many see as a typical blue-collar male job, but here, it is turned into an almost feminine ballet performed in the street. You focus on the men's movements and muscles, almost like you follow the muscles in* Motorcycles *(2008). What triggers your interest in these different engines?*

HL: "Different engines"—love the sound of that.

JF: What interests you in the car and motorcycle visuals?

HL: The skill, the efficiency, the repetition, the waiting, and the unpredictability of the movement.

JF: Would you describe yourself as a voyeuree?

HL: No.

JF: In some of your earlier works, you have included both voyeurism and being looked at. How would you describe your project/book E1 *(1994) and the situation of being looked at?*

HL: It was a document of the conversations I was having with men in the street around where I lived. I was fascinated by the kind of things they were saying. These men, they were funny, conceited, arrogant, desperate, bored, stupid, wretched, brilliant, everything.

JF: The other day I was thinking about how Rei Kawakubo, designer and creator of Comme des Garçons, *uses non-traditional notes to create new scents and perfumes such as Dry Clean, Garage, Skai, Soda, and Tar. The* Comme des Garçons *series isolate things from the everyday and focuses on something in our near surroundings. How do you choose and isolate your structural features?*

HL: Well, I come across things or places in the city that I find exciting. It takes a lot of investigation before I finally work out how to translate exactly what I find exciting into a work.

JF: Are there potential theatrical performances everywhere?

HL: Yes, maybe. I thought the motorcycles were great performers.

JF: Just out of curiousity, have you ever considered recording performers at a theater, concert ... , a stage event? If so, what would be the ideal event?

HL: Yes, I've thought about it. Maybe I would prefer to direct something that could develop into a stage event, theater, concert, etc., rather than film an event. I don't find the idea of documenting an existing work interesting, but who knows. I filmed a DJ in a club, but I think, perhaps, that was different. It was a back-to-back monitor work where the DJ, Ewan, was practicing his set in his bedroom and then playing the exact same set in a club in Brighton.

JF: There are also the more minimal works, where you look at floors in such a way they become like abstract paintings. Could you tell me about

Daisies *(2004) and the painterly ges-*
tures and aspects of these slide works?
*H**L**: Daisies* is very slow and there
is nothing else to see except daisies.
What do you mean by painterly gestures in this context?
*J**F**:* Studio *(2007) and* Untitled *(2005)*
are quite painterly, don't you think?
It seems like there are references to
Abstract Expressionism in your slide
work Studio *and to Minimalist, hard-*
edge painting in Untitled. *You photo-*
graph the floors and blow them up on
the wall and they seem to have refer-
ences to the tradition of painting with-
out having one brush stroke, without
being paintings. Do you see these
works in relation to painting?
*H**L**: Studio* is projected floor to ceiling,
so, in effect, the floor is on the wall.
I wanted the movement of the camera
to be controlled and fluid, to shoot the
two videos simultaneously and in one
go. They needed to be planned, timed,
choreographed, and then rehearsed,
a lot. I was thinking about different
movements in painting, individual
painters, what painting is, what's exciting about it, and my relationship
with it. It's not so much the idea of
floors that I'm interested in, but the
act of investigating how I can make
something from the things I find spectacular, like a field of daisies, a studio
floor, or colored sheets of card laid out
in a geometric pattern.
*J**F**: What are you working on at the*
moment?
*H**L**:* The psychedelic and the chaotic.

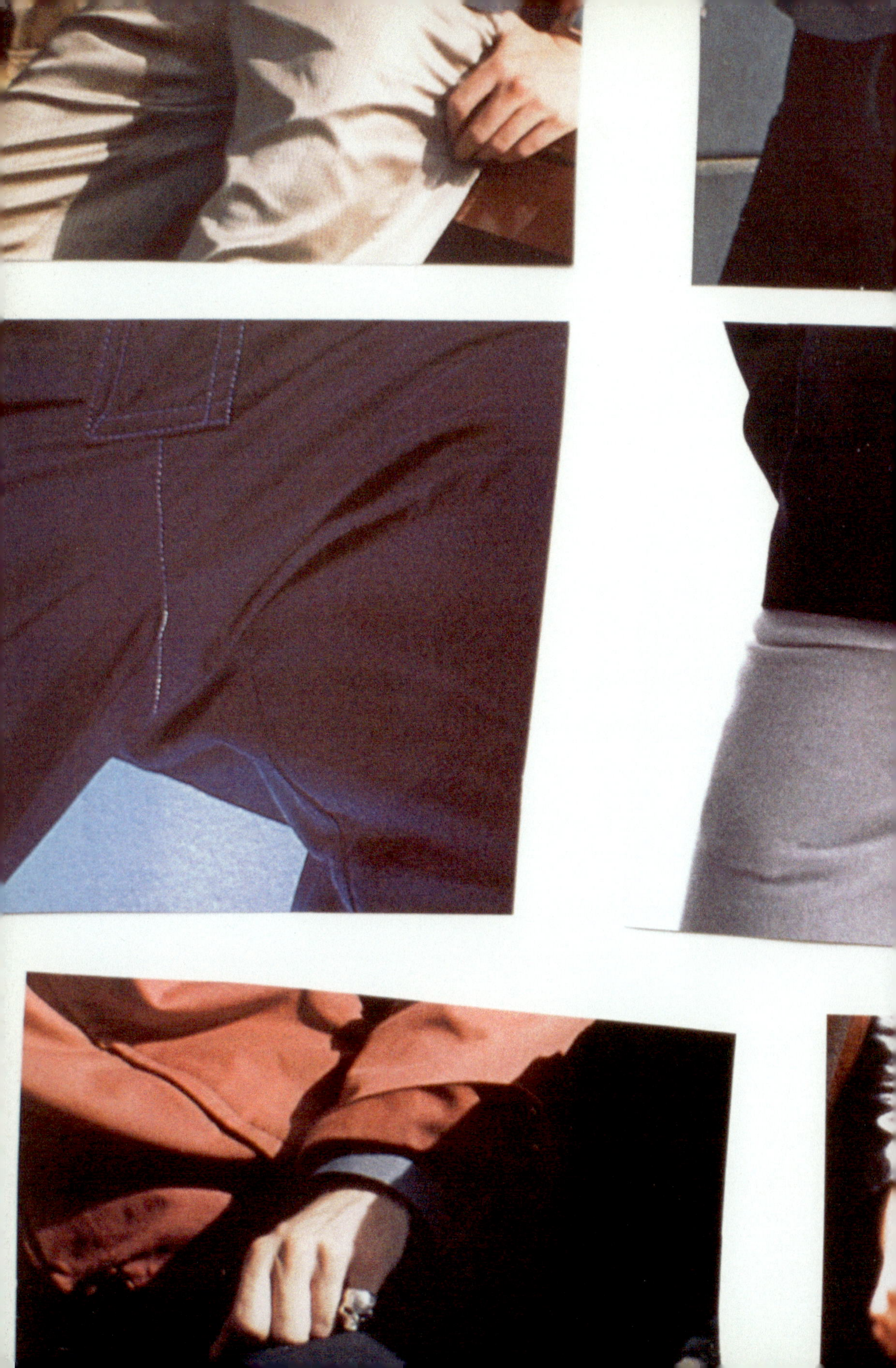

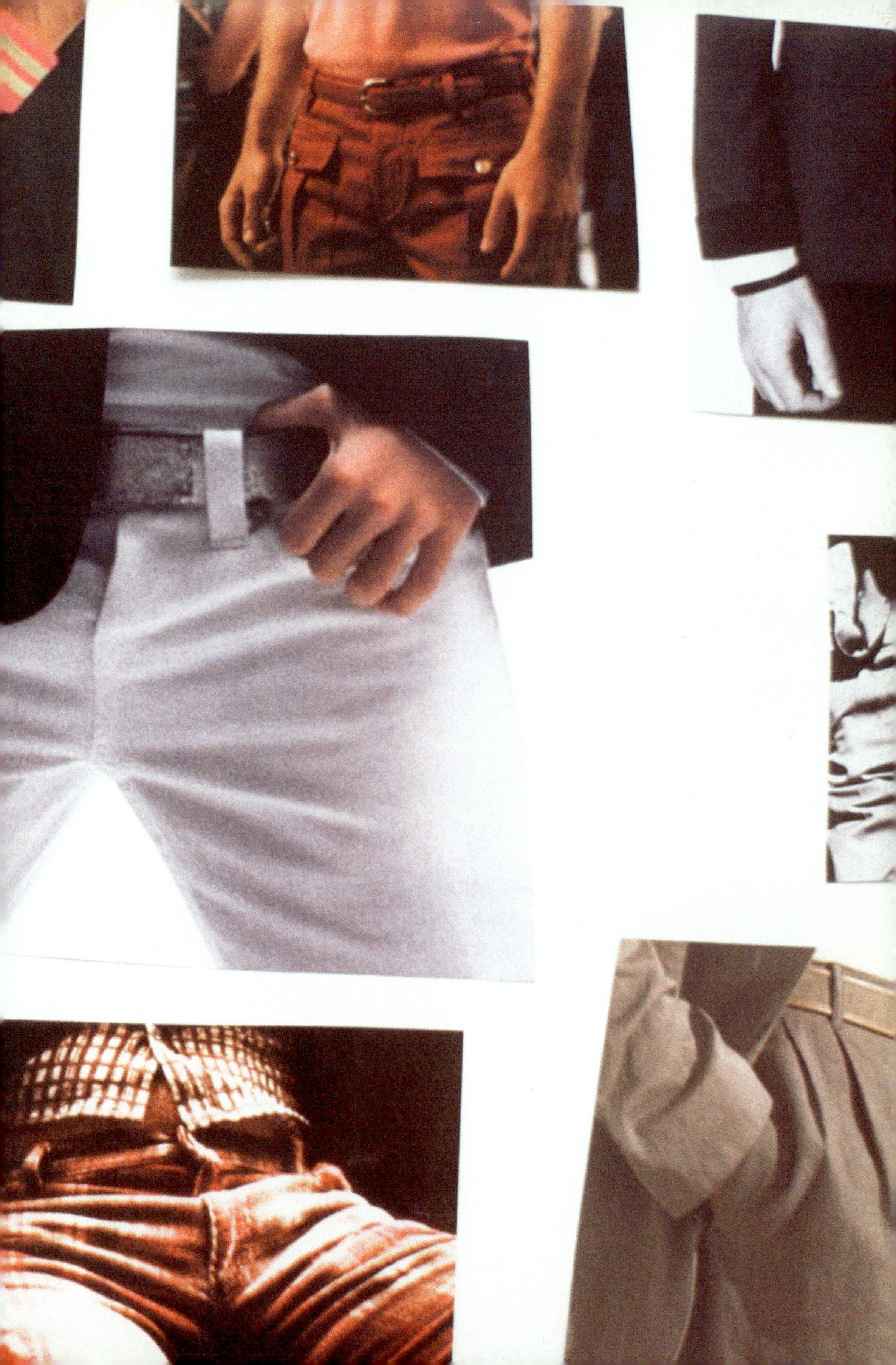

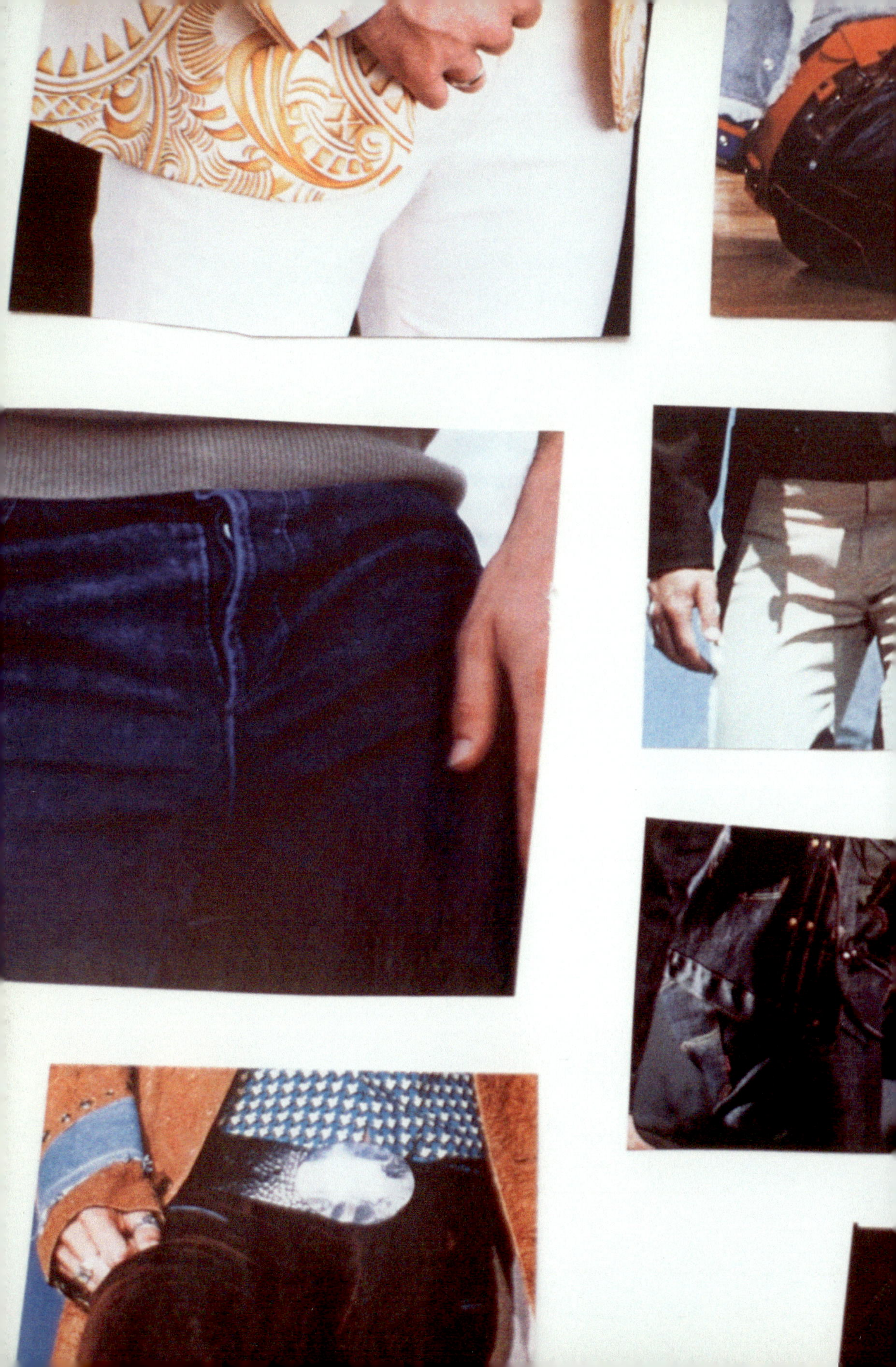

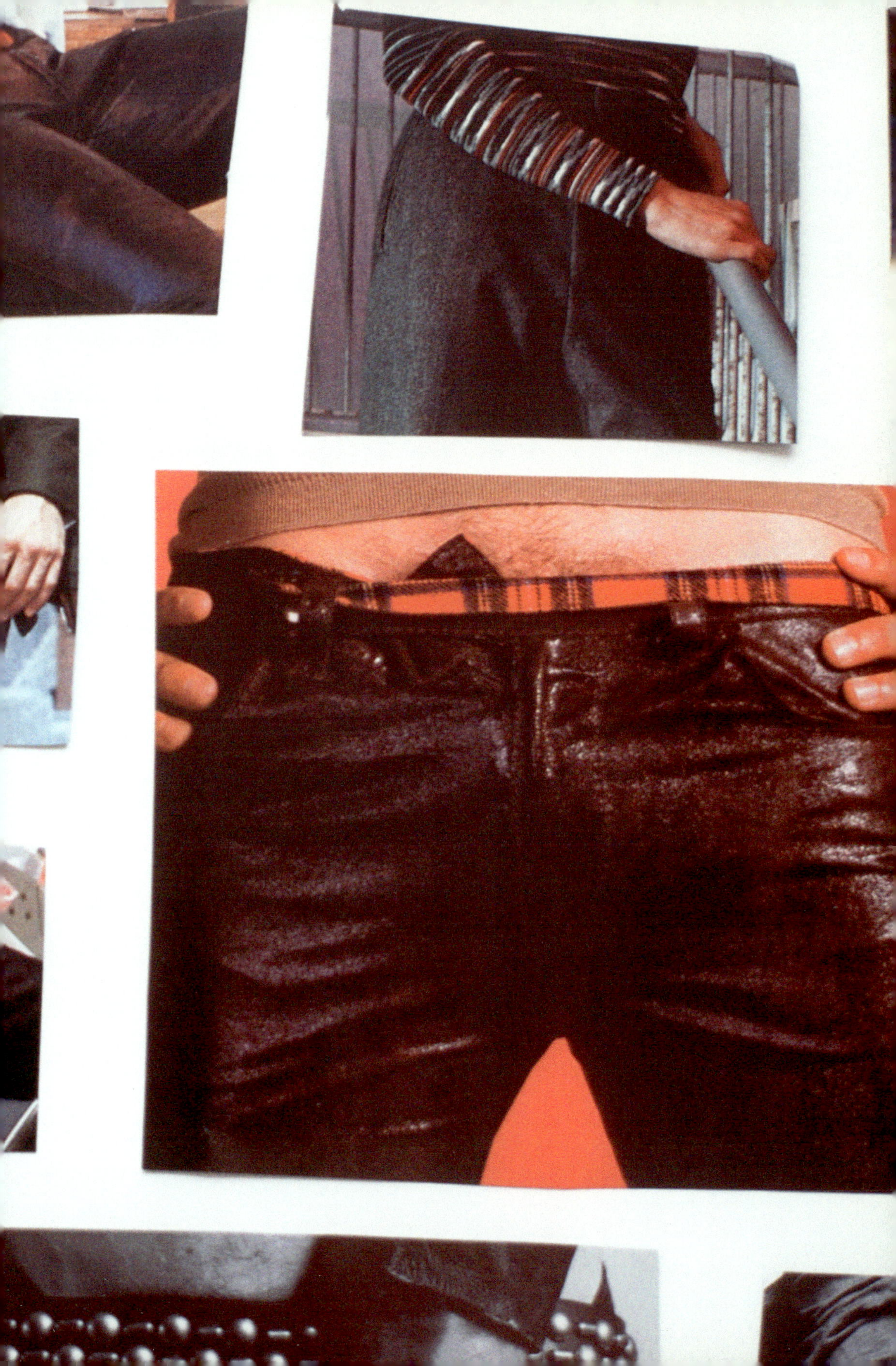

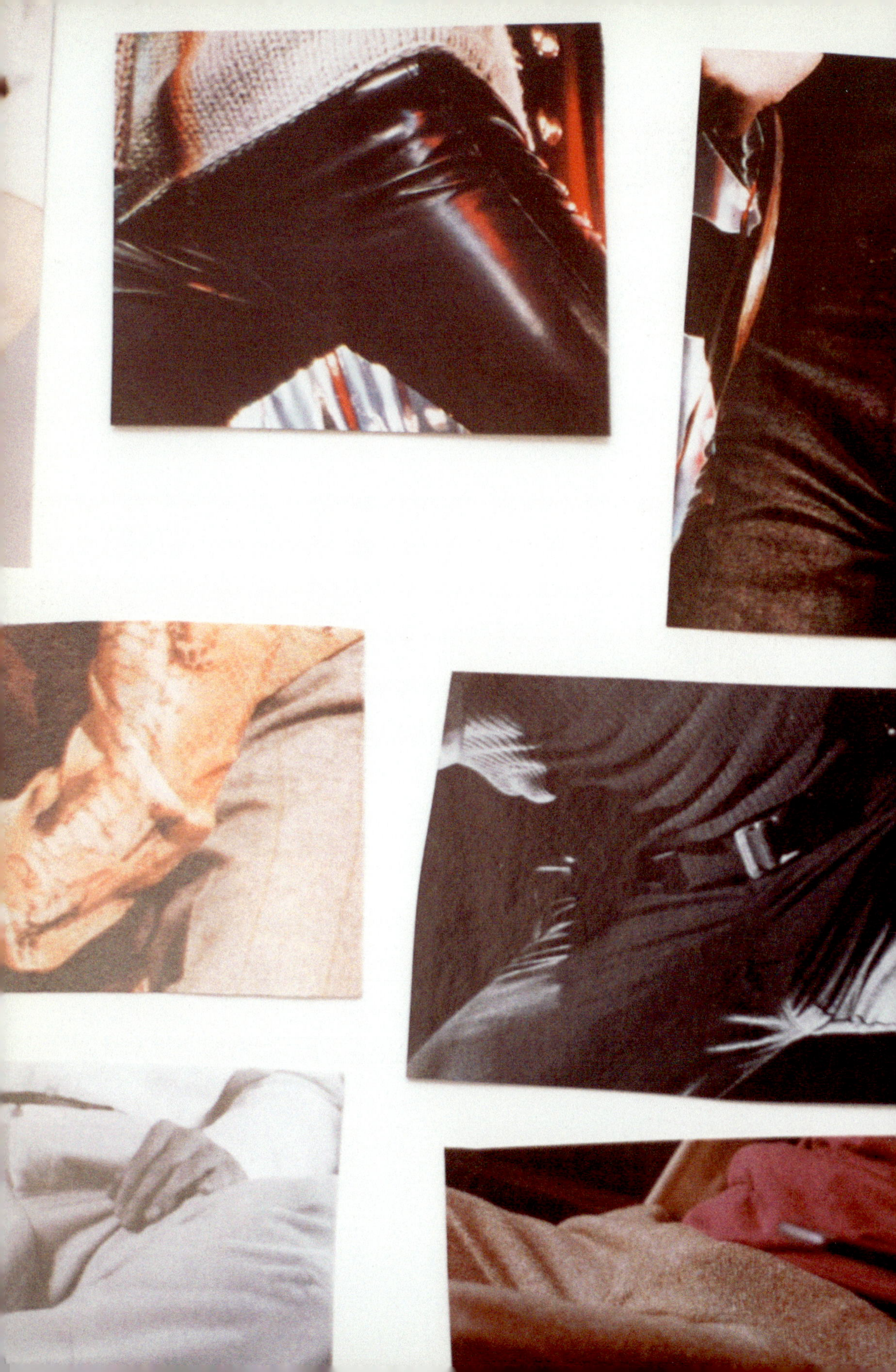

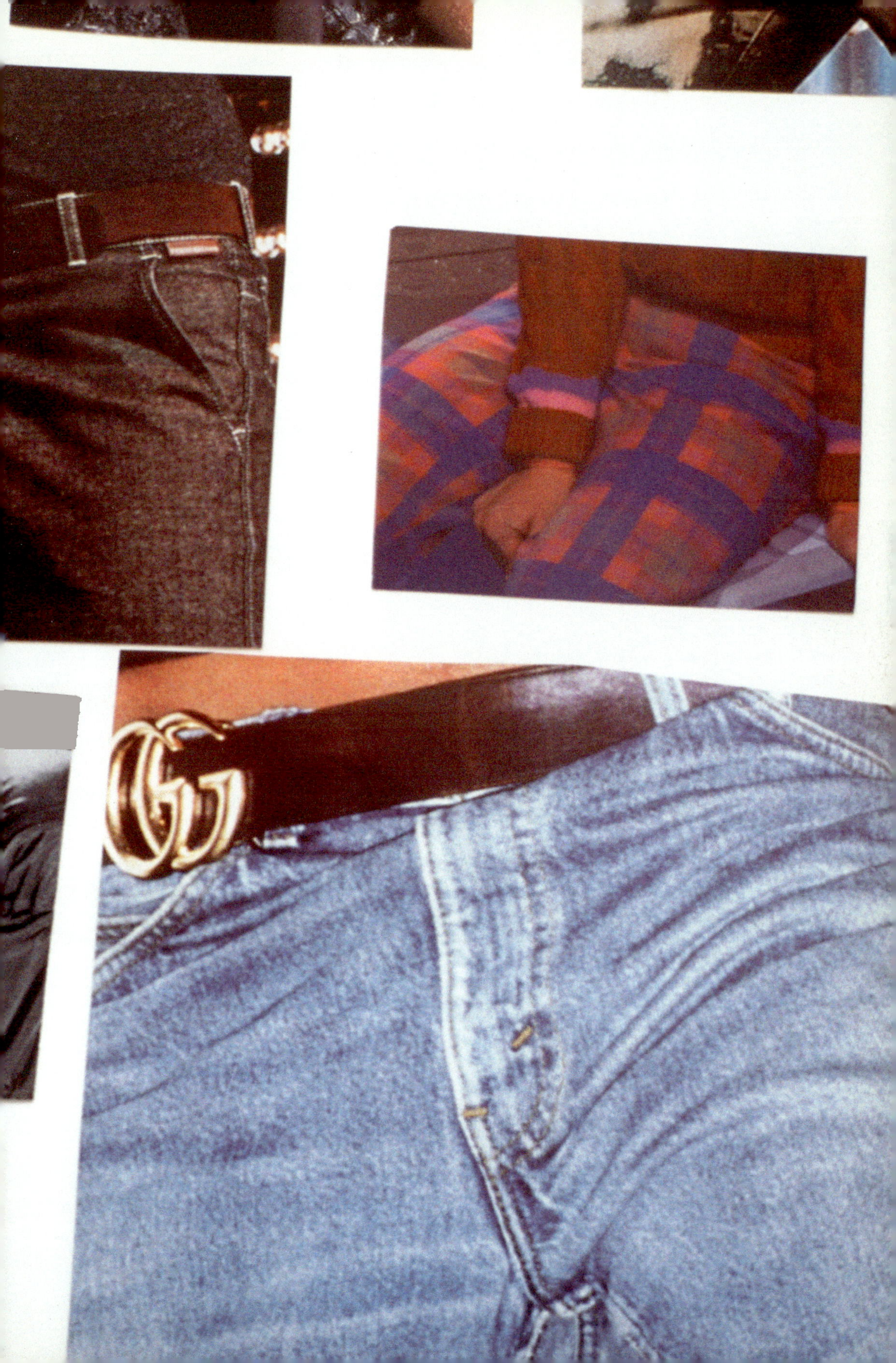

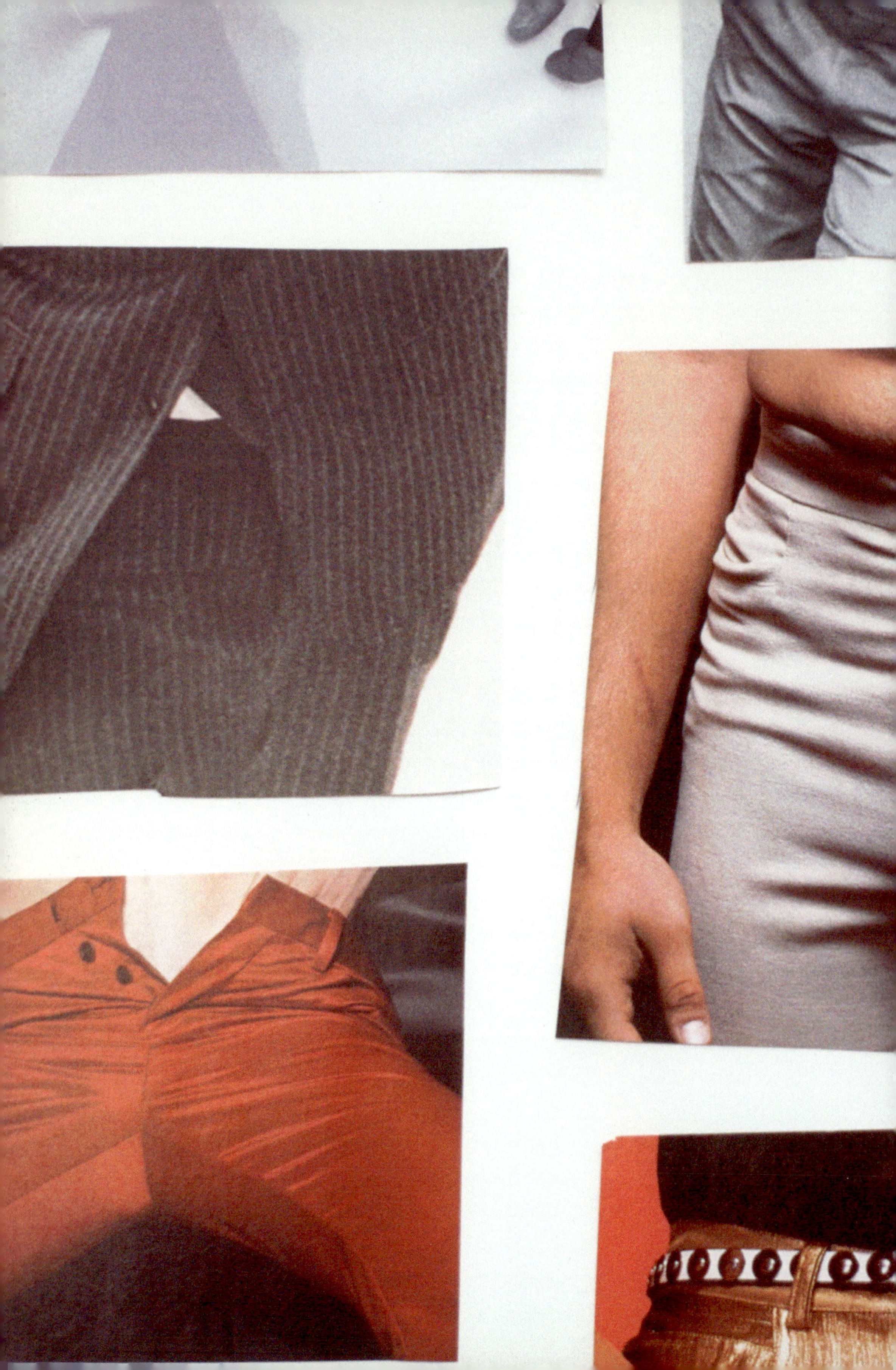

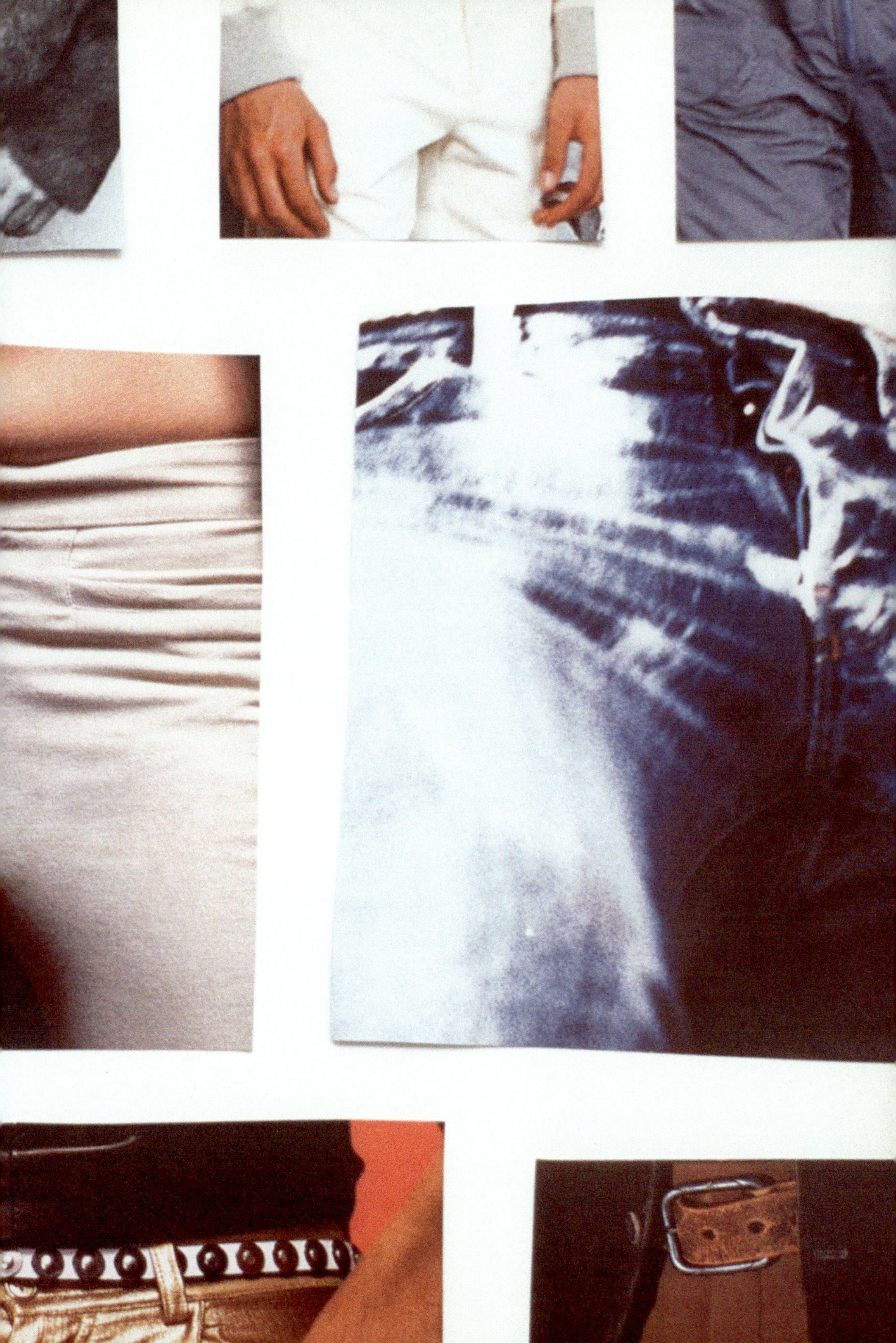

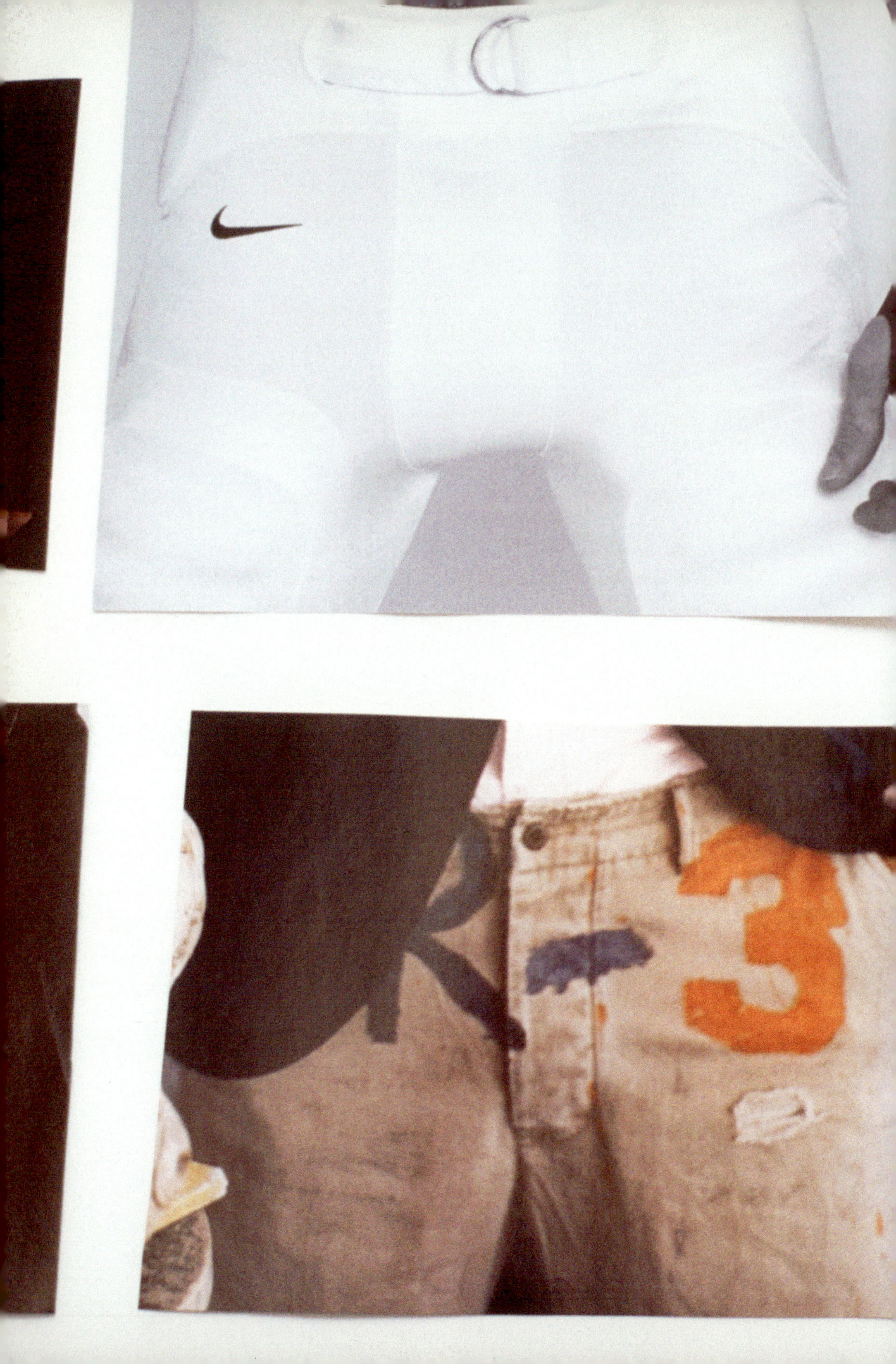

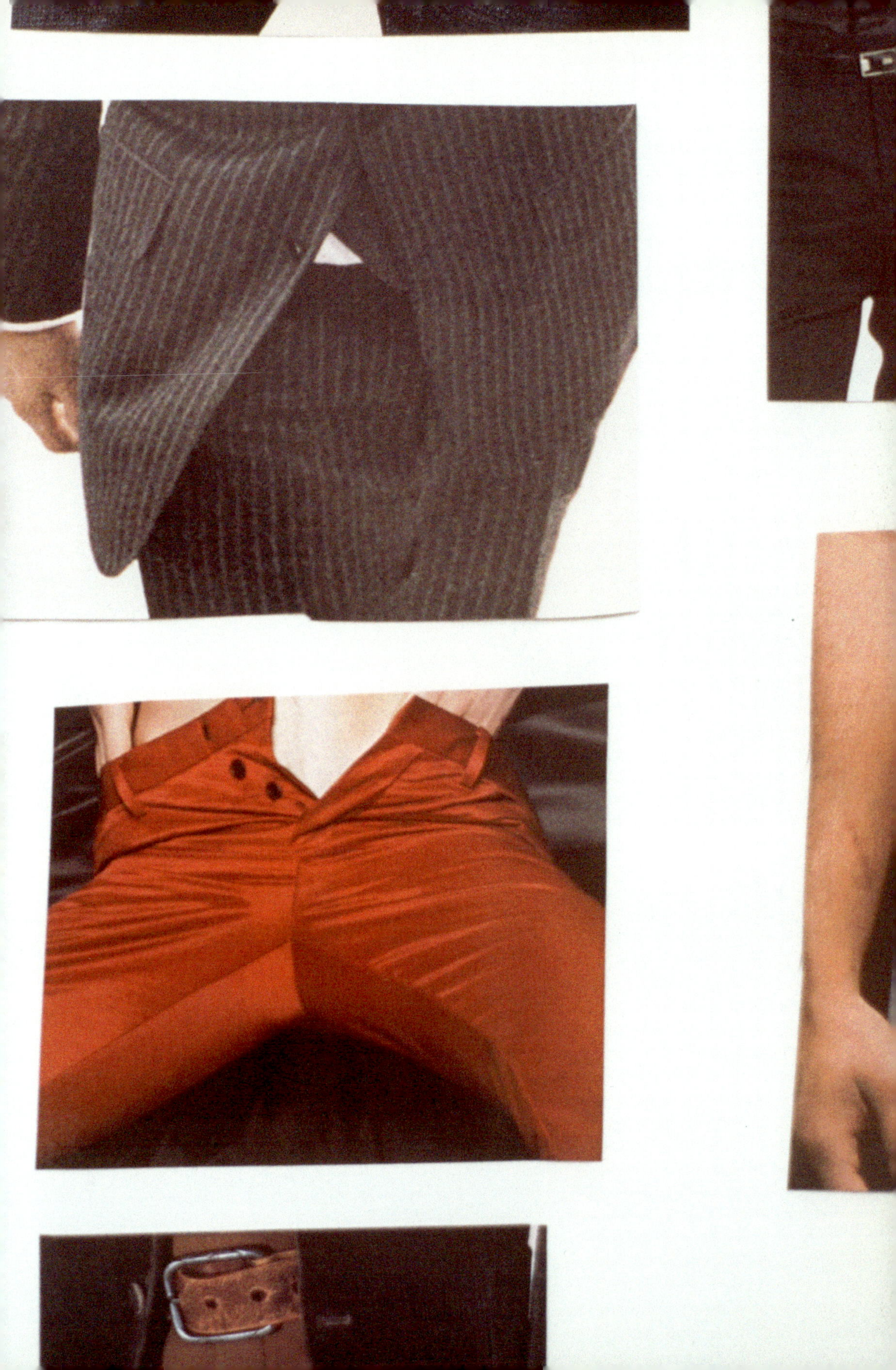

Kirsten Pieroth

*Jacob **Fabricius**: Loan (2007) has a twist of institutional play ... a process, performance and play between the original context and the context you put the object into. It is still the same "sign" but the placing and reading is disconnected from its original setting. Could you reflect on the idea of being out of place?*

*Kirsten **Pieroth**:* I had the idea when I was working on a piece for a group show at Tate Modern called *Learn to Read*. I wanted to borrow a museum label from another institution and hang it on a wall at the Tate. Just as institutions do when loaning paintings to other institutions or museums. The museum that I had asked to borrow the label from also took it as if it was a normal request. They made a proper loan contract for it, with an insurance value of twenty-five Euros and everything. Maybe this was because I had asked to borrow the wall label of the *Mona Lisa* ... The funny thing was that the curator at the Louvre demounted it with his bare hands but once it arrived at the Tate they used gloves to put it up on the wall. As if it was a precious painting. I like this transition. It looked like a normal guideline, just as any wall label in an institution looks like. Sort of disguised. But of course it became something different to the visitors ... looking at the wall label they also must have felt out of place ...

JF: I can only imagine how much security and how many policemen would protect the actual work in the transport and process ... compared to how the label was protected.

KP: You know, the *Mona Lisa* had its own first class cabin in 1963 when it was shipped to the States, with both the neighboring cabins occupied by twenty-four hour body-guards. And a police escort on the way from and to the museum. A bit like a diplomat. The label had a "personal" courier as well, one of the curators of the show.

JF: Incredible! Did you know that the number of visitors at the Louvre increased when the painting was stolen right off the wall in 1911. Apparently, it wasn't even noticed missing until the following day. The missing painting attracted more visitors than the work itself.

KP: That's funny.

JF: Transport is part of many of your projects. In Trophy (2008) you hired a bicycle courier to deliver a wooden box in Sheffield. He drove all the way from Manchester and when the bicycle courier arrived, he received a trophy, the wooden box that he had just transported 44 miles ...

KP: ... well, it wasn't only a box. It contained a bicycle pump with his name, the route and the distance engraved on it.

JF: The bicycle courier is the actor, the messenger, the receiver, the accomplice, and the viewer. The bicycle courier joins the dots ... How did he react to this rather absurd and irrational act, tour, performance, and artwork?

KP: I had contacted several bicycle messenger companies in Manchester and they were mostly wondering why I didn't just hire a car messenger for the trip. From their perspective it seemed of course inefficient and too strenuous to cycle over the Pennine mountains. But this was just what I was interested in, that moment of personal endurance in a culture that is all about speed.

JF: You have dealt with emptiness, voids, and loss of time in other works. Do you deliberately stage time in different ways?

KP: It's not that I sit there thinking how I can make work about time. It's

not my starting point. For instance,
I just did this piece with an accordion
player, who is inflating a rubber
dinghy with an accordion, which is
connected with a hose to the boat.
Usually inflating a rubber dinghy is
quite a monotonous job, very repetitive and unpleasant, until you finally
get the pleasure after it's inflated.
But he sits there playing music, as
he would normally do, while the boat
next to him gains its volume from
the air released by the instrument.
It turns work into leisure, in a certain
way.
*JF: What would you like the viewer to
obtain from your cultural mappings
and altered objects?*
KP: I like the idea of the viewer as a
sort of accomplice in the work, maybe
almost in the same way as I see the
connections I make within a work as
sort of accomplices to each other. It's
like the connections tell a different
story by being joined into one idea.
*JF: You often work with ready-made
objects. How do you consider enigmas
within the objects?*
KP: These moments where you won-
der as a viewer what happened or what
is going on, that's exciting for me ...
like a car driver's bewilderment when
passing a bicycle messenger seeming-
ly lost in the backdrop of the country-
side. It makes you reconsider the way
things go.

TATE

Exhibition Loan-in Agreement - Tate and Tour Venues

This loan agreement sets out the terms and conditions upon which a work of art is lent to Tate for a particular exhibition. This loan agreement sets out the terms and conditions upon which a work of art is lent to Tate and other Tour Venues for a particular exhibition and covers display of the work of art at Tate and any subsequent exhibition venues.

The lender is asked to fill in the details on the front of this Agreement, sign the Agreement and take note of the terms and conditions attached.

THIS AGREEMENT is made the 6 day of June 2007

1. BORROWER The Board of Trustees of the Tate Gallery Tate Gallery Millbank London SW1P 4RG England	**2. LENDER** **Musée du Louvre (Paris, France)** Entrée des Lions Paris 75058 Cedex 01 France
Contact: Nicholas Cullinan **Tel:** +44 (0) 20 7401 5216 **Email:** nicholas.cullinan@tate.org.uk	**Lender Contact Details (please provide):**

3. PLEASE RETURN COMPLETED FORM TO
Nicholas Cullinan
Tate Modern
Bankside
London
SE1 9TG
England

LOAN PERIOD
Approximate date of collection from Lender: 08/06/2007
Approximate date of return to Lender: 14/09/2007

EXHIBITION Learn to Read : Level 2 Gallery / Tate Modern

TOUR VENUES AND DATES
Tate Modern (London, UK)
19/06/2007 – 02/09/2007

ADDRESS FOR COLLECTION of Work of Art (please complete if different from Lender's address):

ADDRESS FOR RETURN of Work of Art (see clause 18):

tel: fax: tel: fax:

WORKS:

Artist:
Title: _Léonard de Vinci : Portrait de Lisa Gherardini dite Monna Lisa, la Gioconda ou la Joconde_

Date:
Medium: _Exhibition label (metal)_

Inventory Number: ________________ Tate Object Number: X21559

Dimensions un-framed/mounted
Height (mm) _____135_____   Depth (mm) _____4_____
Width (mm) _____175_____   Weight (kgs) _____0,2_____

		YES		NO	
Is work framed?		YES	☐	NO	☒
Does the frame have glass?		YES	☐	NO	☒
Does the frame have plexiglass?		YES	☐	NO	☒
Can the Borrower remove existing fittings?		YES	☐	NO	☒
Are you aware of any third party entitlement to ownership of the work of art?		YES	☐	NO	☒

If "Yes" please provide details:

Has the Work of Art been accepted in lieu of tax by the Inland Revenue?   YES ☐   NO ☒

If "Yes" please state the amount of tax that was satisfied ________________

VALUE OF THE WORK OF ART FOR INDEMNITY/INSURANCE PURPOSES (see clause 7 for details):

Value: _25,00 Euro_

CREDIT LINE: please provide details of how the Lender wishes to be named in the catalogue and on the Exhibition label:

Credit Line: _On loan from the Musée du Louvre, Paris_

REPRODUCTION (see Definitions and clause 8):

Is the Lender the copyright holder?   YES ☒   NO ☐

If no please supply deatils of the copyright holder ________________

Does the Lender grant the Borrower and Tour Venues permission for reproduction of the Work(s) of Art:

a) In media coverage for the Exhibition?   YES ☒   NO ☐

b) Displaying an image on the Borrower and Tour Venue's websites at low resolution?   YES ☒   NO ☐

c) In the Exhibition catalogue?   YES ☒   NO ☐

d) For talks and other educational activities?   YES ☒   NO ☐

e) Does the Lender consent to new photography of the Work of Art if required?   YES ☒   NO ☐

Can the Lender supply a colour transparency/digital file?   YES ☐   NO ☒

PLEASE SUPPLY CONTACT DETAILS FOR THE PERSON RESPONSIBLE FOR SUPPLYING AN IMAGE:

____

IMAGE CREDIT LINE: please provide details of how the Lender wishes to be named:

Credit Line: ________________

If the Borrower wishes to reproduce the Work of Art for commercial purposes or merchandise the Lender will be contacted separately by Tate Enterprises Ltd (a wholly owned subsidiary of Tate). If the Tour Venues wish to reproduce the Work of Art for such purposes, then they will be contacted separately.

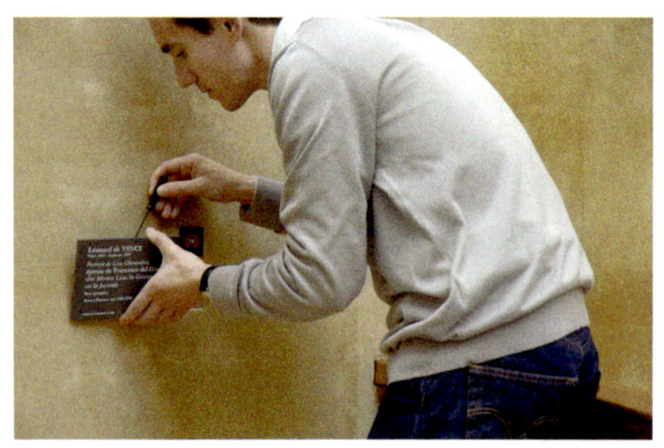

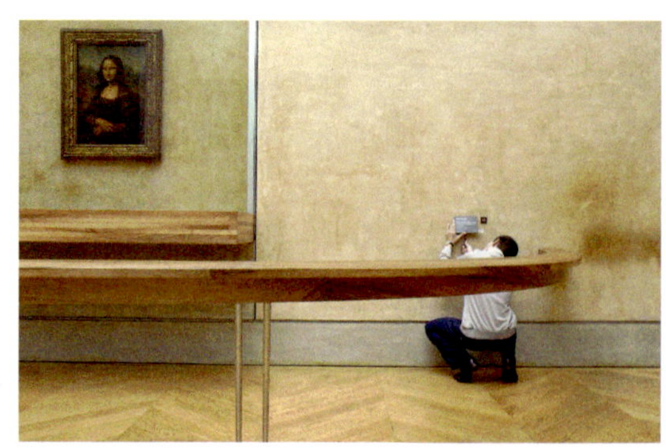

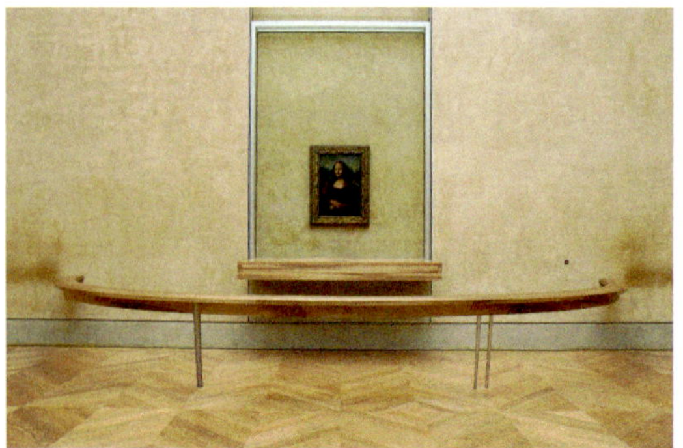

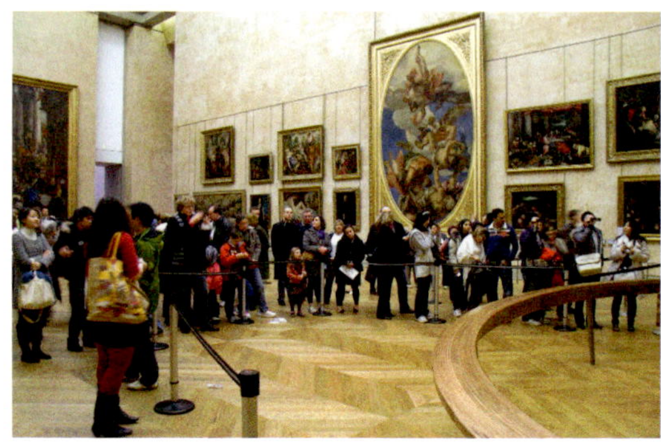

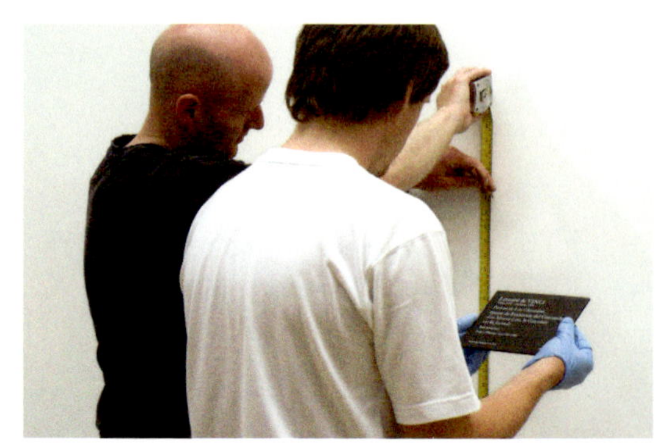

Léonard de VINCI
Vinci, 1452 - Amboise, 1519
Portrait de Lisa Gherardini,
épouse de Francesco del Giocondo,
dite Monna Lisa, la Gioconda
ou la Joconde
Bois (peuplier)
Peint à Florence vers 1503-1506

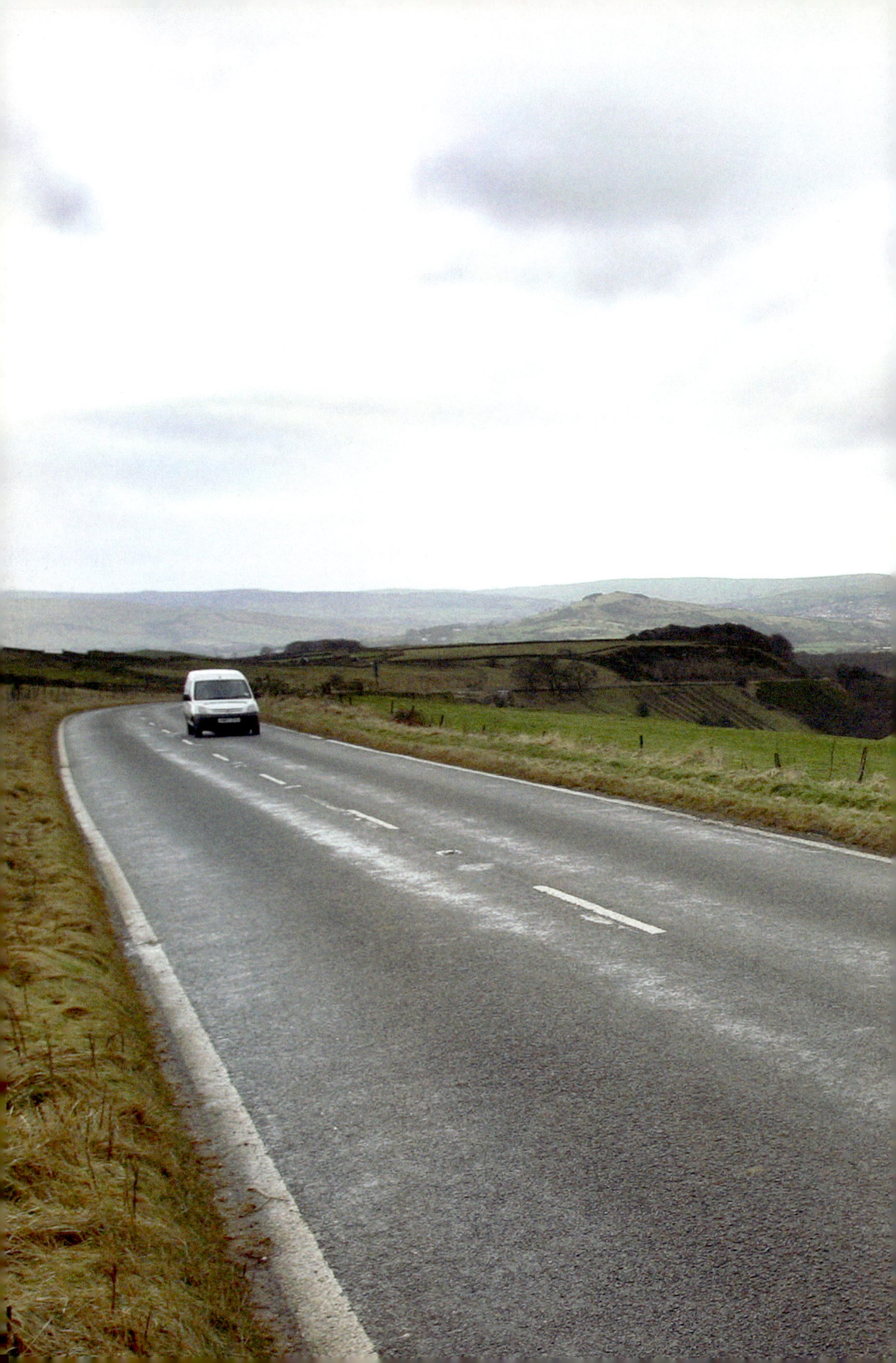

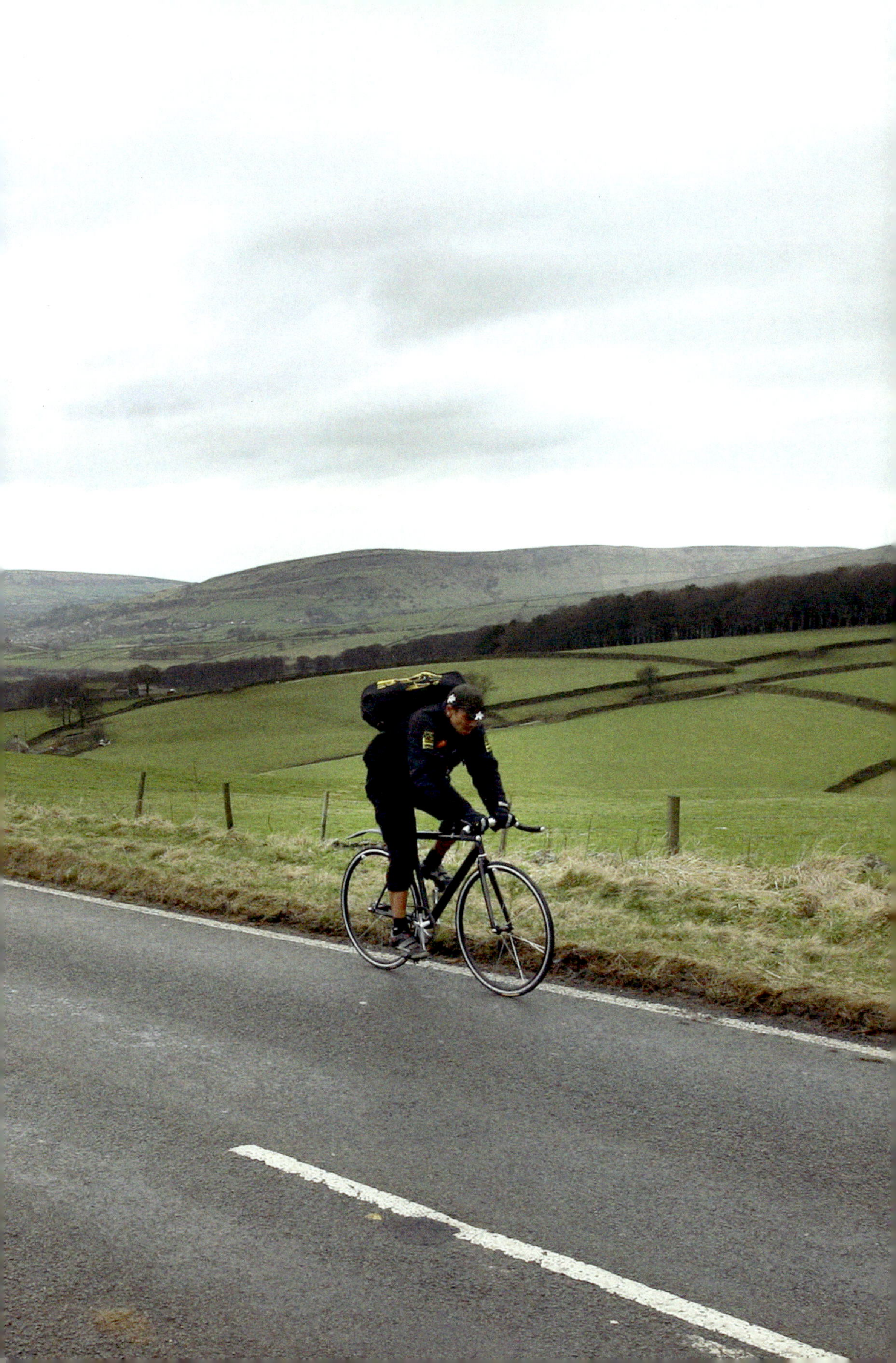

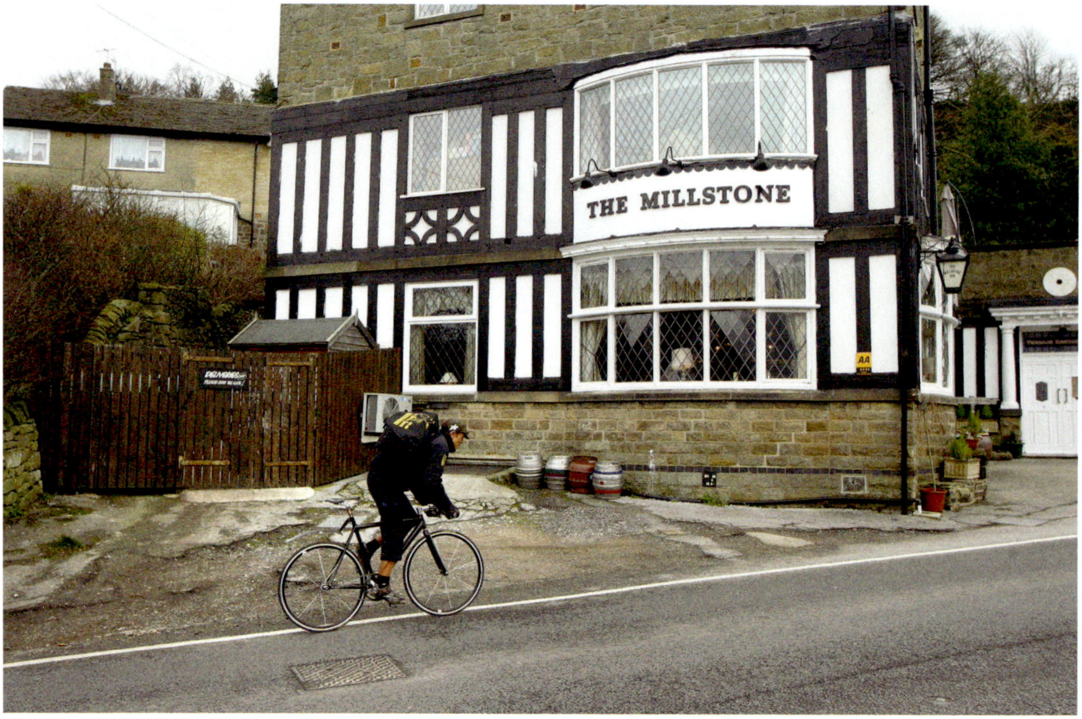

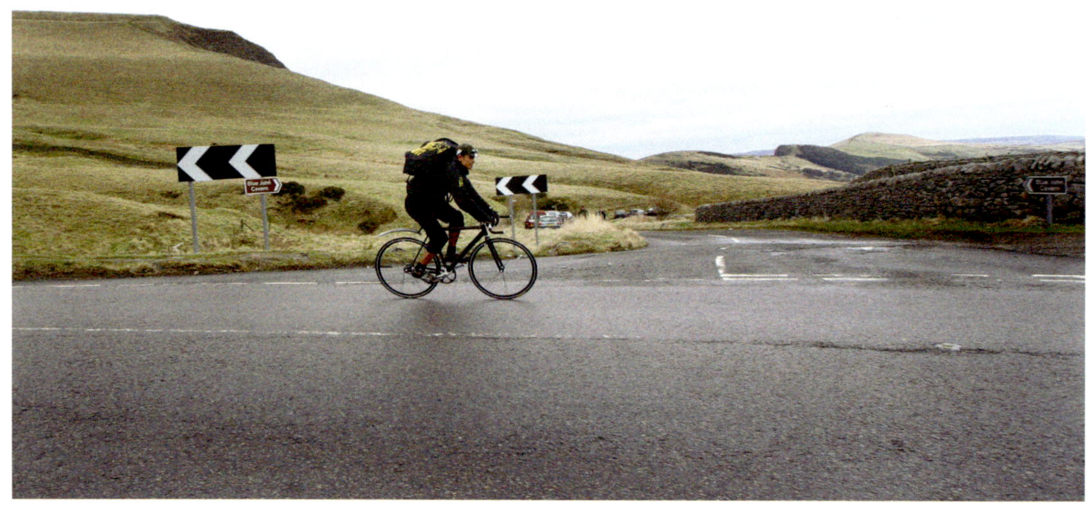

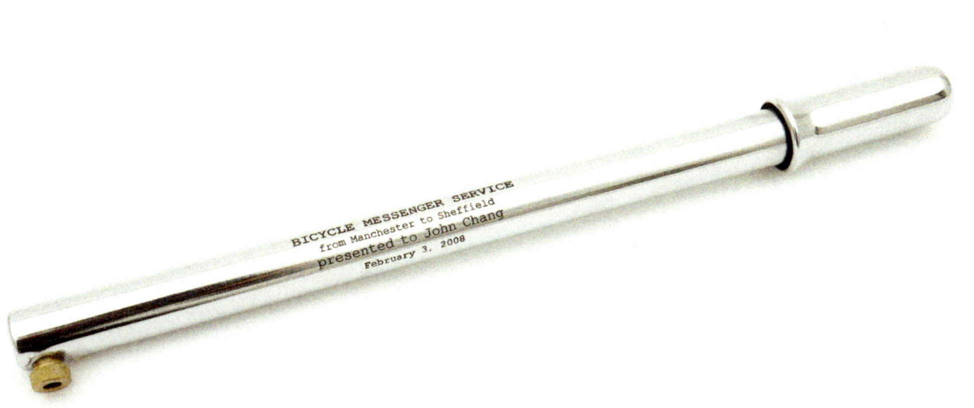
BICYCLE MESSENGER SERVICE
from Manchester to Sheffield
presented to John Chang
February 3, 2008

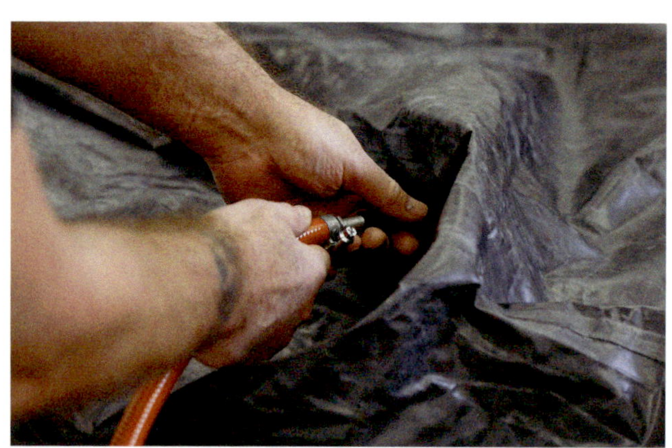

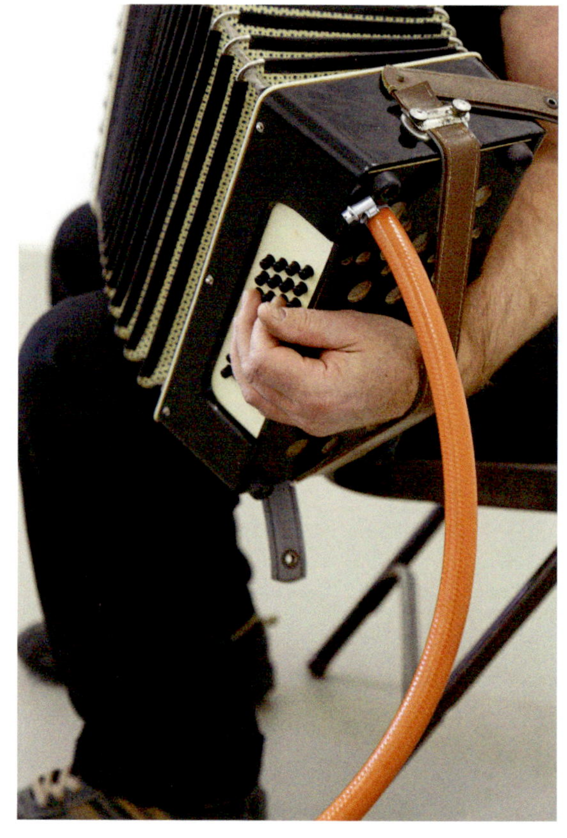

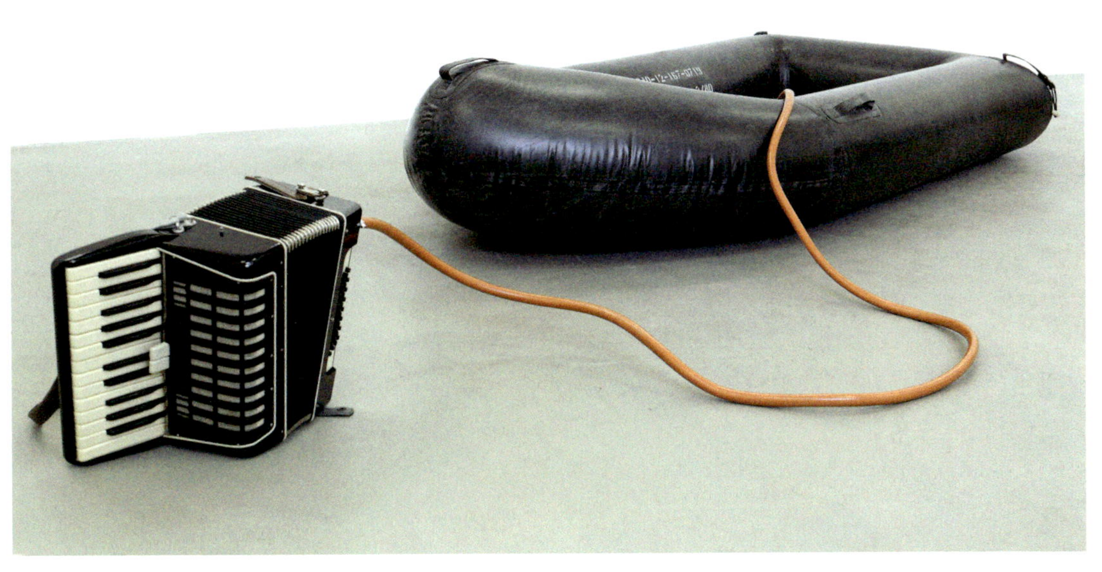

Susanne M.
Winterling

Jacob **Fabricius***: How would you say the feminine is portrayed and staged in your work?*

Susanne M. **Winterling***:* Oh, that is a big question. Just recognized that while I am reading this very intense play by Elfriede Jelinek, this question becomes like a monster. That sounds very heavy to me although I am certainly fascinated by whatever it might be one calls the feminine. And approaching it, one recognizes that it's tough to face all the stereotypes while trying to pay tribute to a sensuality and rationality that seems to be there maybe in the same way as when I watch my niece (she is eight) or films with my favorite actress Tilda Swinton.

JF: The women you portray in your work are individual (autonomous) and strong. Would you say that the feminine in your work is portrayed through layering images of a desired will or power ... so it's power rather than powerlessness that is portrayed in your work? You know what I mean?

*SM***W***:* Actually no, or maybe it's the power of imagination ... But this answer needs two parts: one is that the layering technique I use was an idea and experiment that evolved out of the dissolved. It is used in film mostly for a change of perspective, and I also recognized that it's a dynamic between the still and the moving image, which is something that is very fascinating to me. So piling up different layers allows different ways of reading for each individual viewer and an invitation to involve your own mental images as they also decide what you see like in the Wittgenstein duck-rabbit example. Secondly, power as such, in relation to personality, is not the democratic power to the people, but it has a more negative connotation, and I like to analyze power structures, let's say between the "third" world and the "first" (they are horrible terms, but that's why they explain the point) or like in the story of David and Goliath. But thanks to Freud, Lacan, as well as all the dictators, power, as such, is not a very interesting topic if it does not open up another dimension. Power to the Ego is a bit boring. I am sorry, but maybe other artists can talk about this. Anyway, now we could start talking about all the women and characters that are portrayed in my work themselves, but I guess this is already too much? Just to mention, they are anonymous single mothers in Russia selling liquid to make bubbles on the street as well as the Queen of independent cinema, or maybe the girl in *Mirror's Edge*.

JF: Could you tell me about your interest in the Swiss writer and photographer Annemarie Schwarzenbach? Maybe you could reflect on how Schwarzenbach poses in relation to how she presents women and identity in the early twentieth century?

SMW: It's interesting as she was kind of underestimated for a long time due to being in the shadows of Erika and Klaus Mann, and kind of digged out of the attic by a feminist/lesbian audience in the nineteen-eighties. But apart from a feeling of friendship and personal attachment to her way of writing and taking photos, I think her struggle as an artist, in times of conflicts (and with conflicts, I refer to personal, due to family and lovers, as well as political and economical) is very contemporary or could be of contemporary value.

Facing failure, she has been independent minded and passionate. And surely, in Hollywood terms an anti hero. But I think there are more people then just me, sick and tired of heroes on the surface as reality is just not like that. So, it is amazing how rich and stunning her experience of the world was, although Klaus Mann portrayed her as the "Angel of the Dispossessed."

JF: Often you use film stills—like

142

Caspar and Kes *(from* Kes *by Ken Loach) or* Porcellanpferd *(from* Effi Briest *by Rainer Werner Fassbinder) in the installation* I'll Be Your Mirror but I'll Dissolve ... *(2007)—so I would like to talk a little about icons and the way you make use of them in your works. They seem to represent social, political, and gender issues. Could you talk about how you choose, and use the cinematographic stills, characters, and elements of fictions in your works?*

*SM**W**:* Cultural productions and stories are part of the world of phenomena that surrounds us and I see them as material in a way. Especially film and film history, but also literature and music make up a huge part of the world how I perceive it. On the bottom of that might be the questions of representation and its dynamics, but the interesting feature is also that it relates to identity, individual as well as to the cultural. Therefore, it can combine an aspect that's very personal, let's say, for me, with something that does affect a lot of people, and it does that with means of identification or its opposite, creating an awareness and sensitivity. Like Caspar and the story of his relationship with the bird, it is not just interesting to me as I always thought my pony might be more important than the rest of the world when I was a kid. But it actually became a metaphor for a struggle with adolescence, not just for my generation. The icons as you call them are very often antiheros I guess, or there is a lot of failure and a very human aspect to them. Effi Briest was a character I hated when I read Fontane for the first time, and all the talk about the development of the character being so special seemed so hollow to me. But with Fassbinder's eyes in between, this figure became a symbol of the impossibility of the individual following her own ideas in certain structures of society; that is very contempo-rary in a lot of contexts. And it does not allow so easily for stereotyping or marginalization, which would be the case if I would refer to the story of my best teenage friend, a gay Turkish working-class boy, who was expelled from Bavaria and had to go back to Turkey.

*J**F**: In the installation* All Tomorrow's Parties: Stage *(2008), staging is imbedded in the title and the works. A bowler hat (with a bit of fur) is placed on a mirror pedestal, a tea cup with a gold rim is photographed enface, a scrambled Rubik's Cube is photographed from above so three sides are revealed ... and so on. What is the common thread between the objects and images in the installation?*

*SM**W**:* On one side, the ready-made is something that seems very magnetic, but on the other, it's the fact that the world and its materials as well as the cultural products are so rich that the challenge, for me, is more to work with the arrangement, which is very often a kind of staging, or perception, which is the side of camera mechanisms, eyes and light, illusion, and perspective. Maybe also the idea of recycling is more interesting than the idea of consumption. And surely, it's something about the glamor or magic of the everyday object that fascinates me as it involves "another" way of seeing it. But it comes from a mixture of playfulness and research when I start to think how. The cup is actually made by a part of my family before the business petered out, and as my father's attic is full of all this stuff and I did not have money, and also did not want to go to IKEA, I ended up having all this china, which, if you turn it around, has my name on it ... So maybe the beginning was a sort of tribute to Broodthaers and Duchamp. Of course, nobody can really see this story as a melancholic view of a fucked up bourgeois who goes bankrupt in a certain part of the family, but it might be some reason for treating the cup as a piece in a sci-fi lab. And the bowler is less a gimmick on art history, but more a reflection on devices of coding, and a *trompe-l'œil* in three-dimensionality, when you approach the installation, you see your whole body in the mirror, but the head is a bowler. And then again, there is the personal in the back, as this was my bowler for dressage when I was still seriously into that sport, and I always liked it as it might have been my beginning of cross-dressing.

JF: The installation is minimal, but the objects or photographs representing objects are somewhat theatrical in the way they are installed. It is as if there are narcissistic gestures within each object, as if they are posing. Would you agree?

SMW: Oh, yeah! I like the way you describe it, not because there might be a pantheistic aspect, but because it gives them a life on their own, at least in our way of perceiving, and that involves a lot of respect and attention to details. And there is a hidden desire to be Alice in Wonderland or Alice through the looking glass. It might sound idealistic, but this is not because the world is so fancy and full of fantasy, but the opposite. However, as an artist, I think you have to choose certain ways of communication, whatever that is, and in which ever way it works. Otherwise, nobody listens, like my friend recently accused me of being too extremely realistic when we spoke about politics in the art world, and since then, I have not heard a word from her. So maybe it's better to stage a little play where, in the end, you have a lot of respect for the "other," whatever it is, instead of accusing power structures and their string holders immediately, as not only can you get smashed, but all is turned ineffective as well. But I don't want this to sound too idealistic. This was only

meant to illustrate that it's not only about creating a certain smile or recognition of beauty or smartness and pleasure in the viewer. And the awareness of a pose gives you the attention to a gap between the stage and real life, and a consciousness. I always like the sci-fi voice in the London underground saying, "mind the gap," and the philosophy of difference.

JF: This leads me to think of our exhibition Little Theatre of Gestures. *So, I would like to hear your thoughts behind the work in the show and how you have approached this exhibition?*

SMW: It's a very beautiful title and, somehow, even too much to the point for me. In my portraits and videos, I have always been working on the extraction and abstraction of gestures, because they seemed to me like a microcosmos of psychology, human relations, and conditions, like the shy gesture of a teenage girl throwing her hair to the back or the handing over of a coat as a caring gesture. So, I guess my first association was with these real gestures and precious moments which can be between the staged and the documentary, because that's the way I have worked a lot. But, as I work more and more on this idea, and also the space for the exhibition, I think there is more of a Beckett aspect and a post-punk approach that I find seductive.

JF: How do you choose your exhibition titles? They refer to literature, songs, and films, but in relation to the work, they have a mysterious sweet oblivion to them.

SMW: Somehow, I want to say that the title always appears with the work, but surely, that sounds funny. However, I guess it's a mixture out of things that influence and also a kind of trigger for the viewer. And I like to offer possibilities of associations, dreams, and collected images without forcing a narration or certain way of reading.

Susanne M. **Winterling**

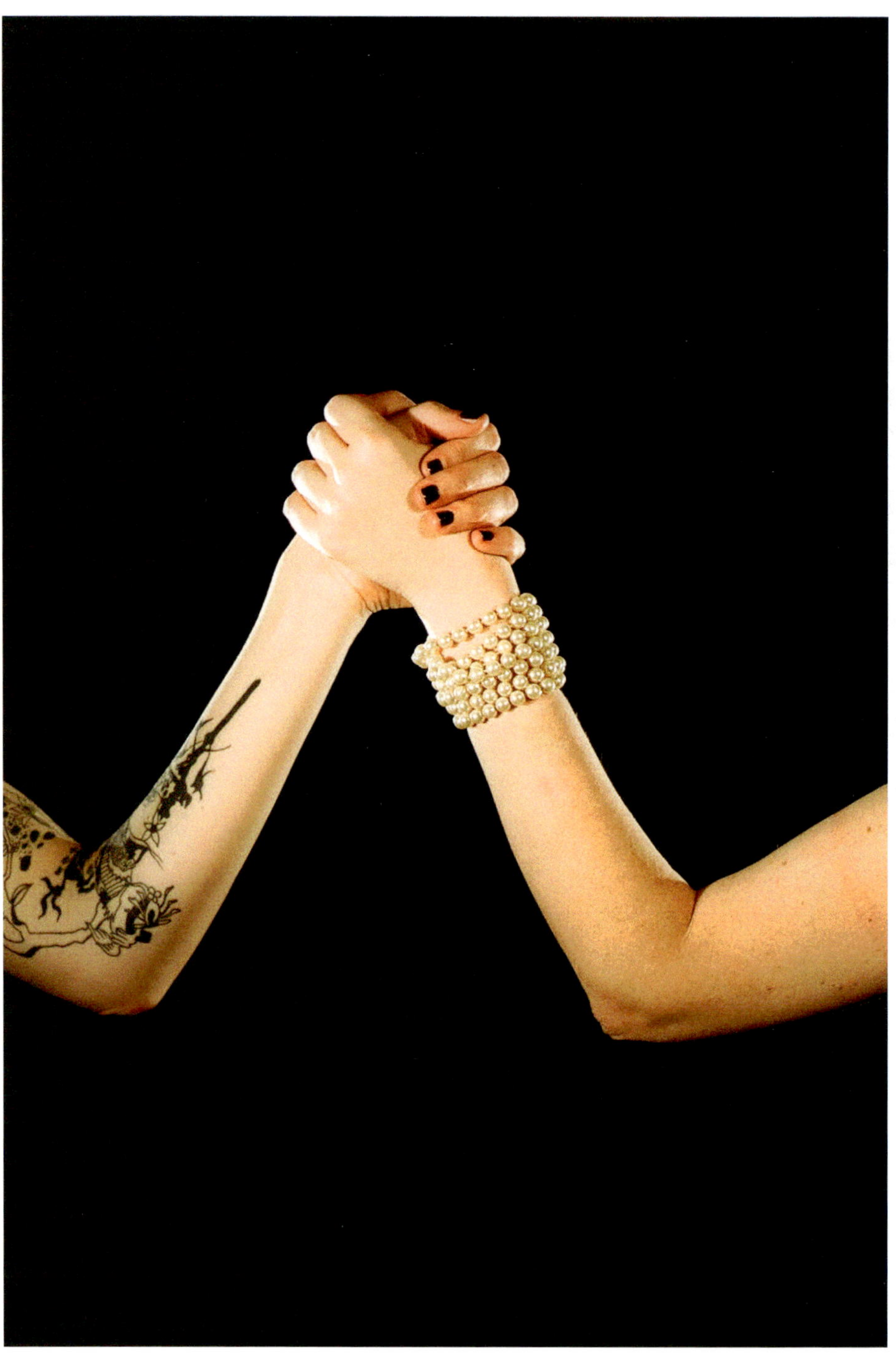

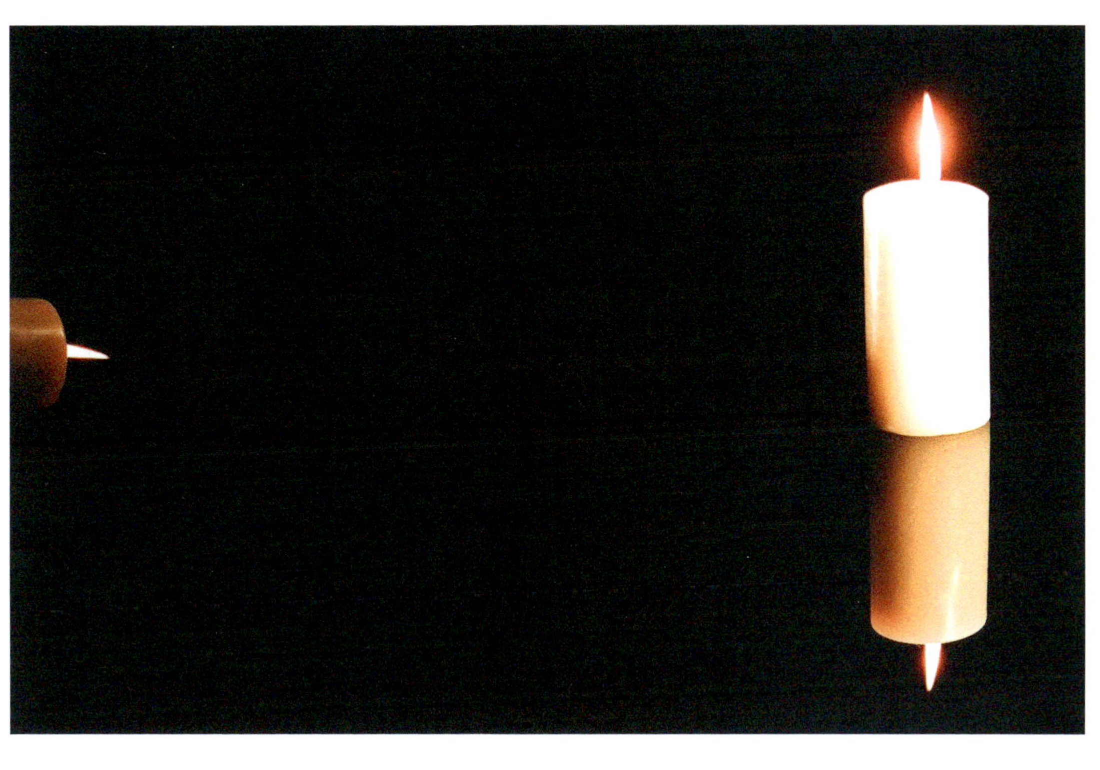

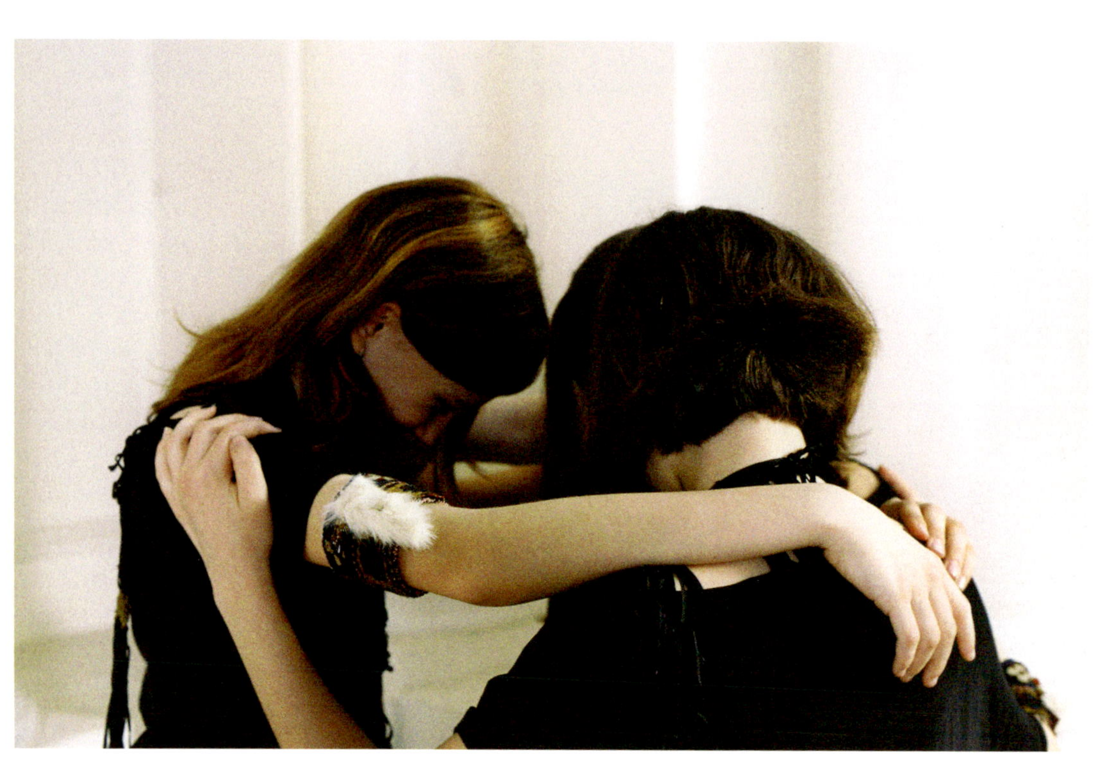

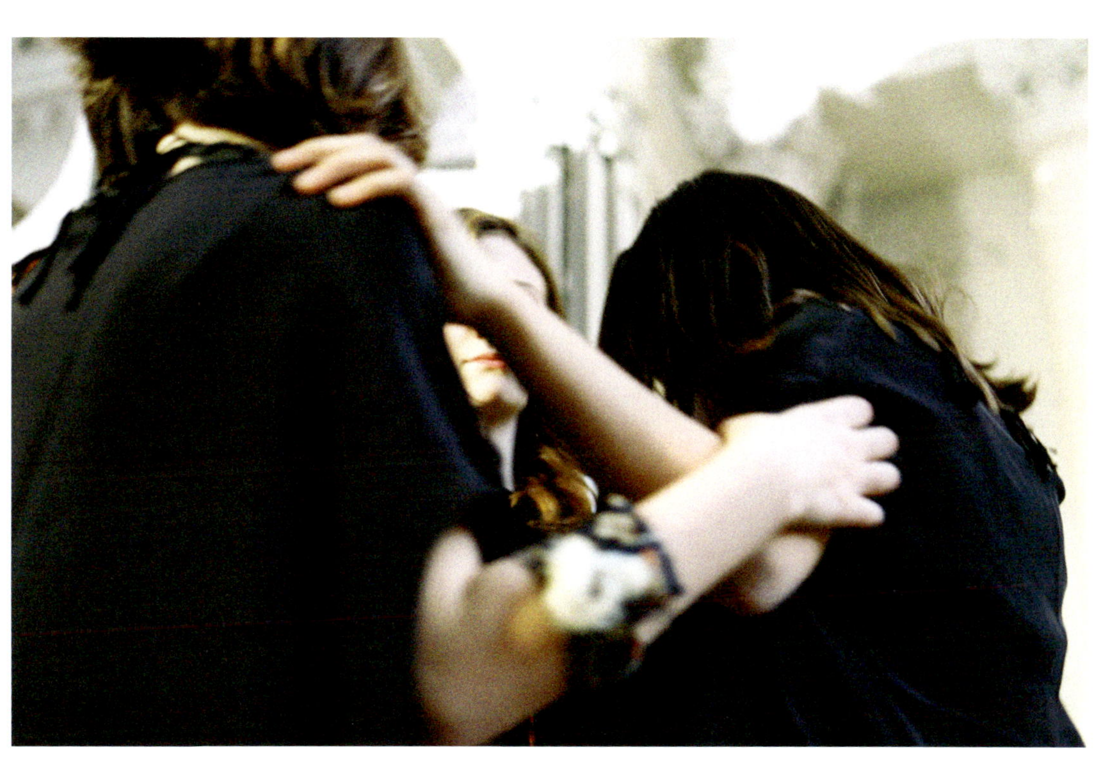

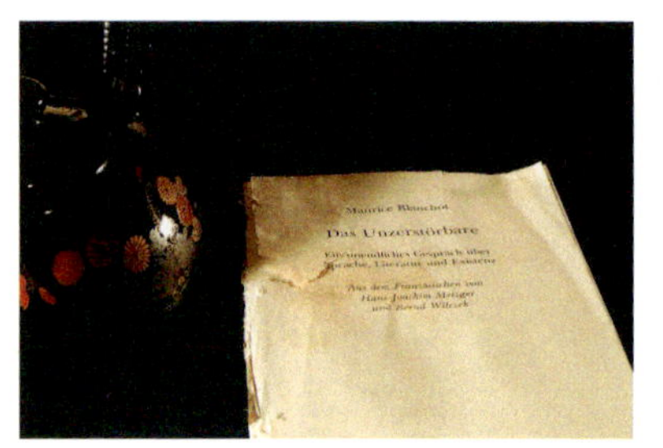

Maurice Blanchot
Das Unzerstörbare

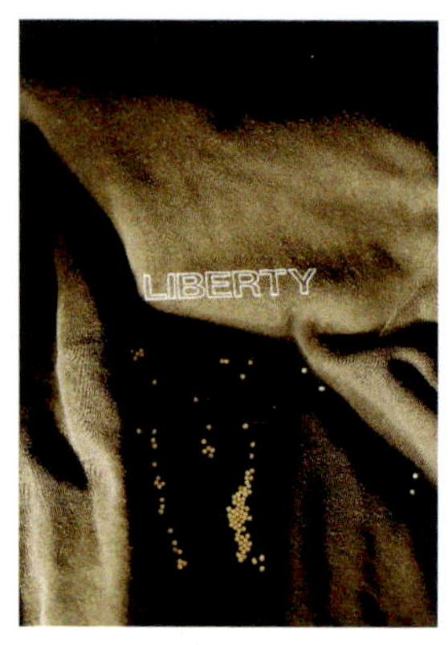

LIBERTY

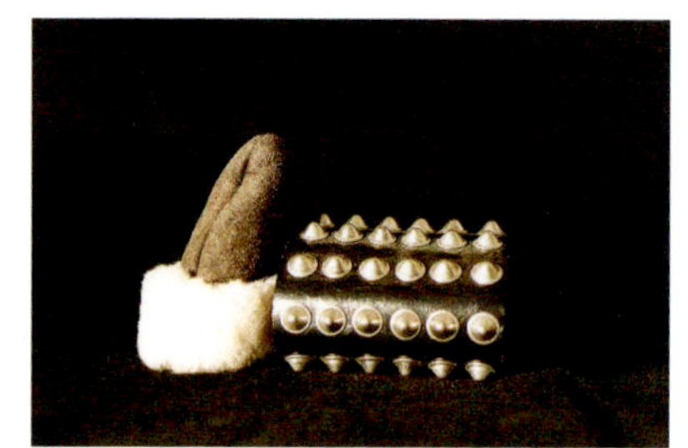

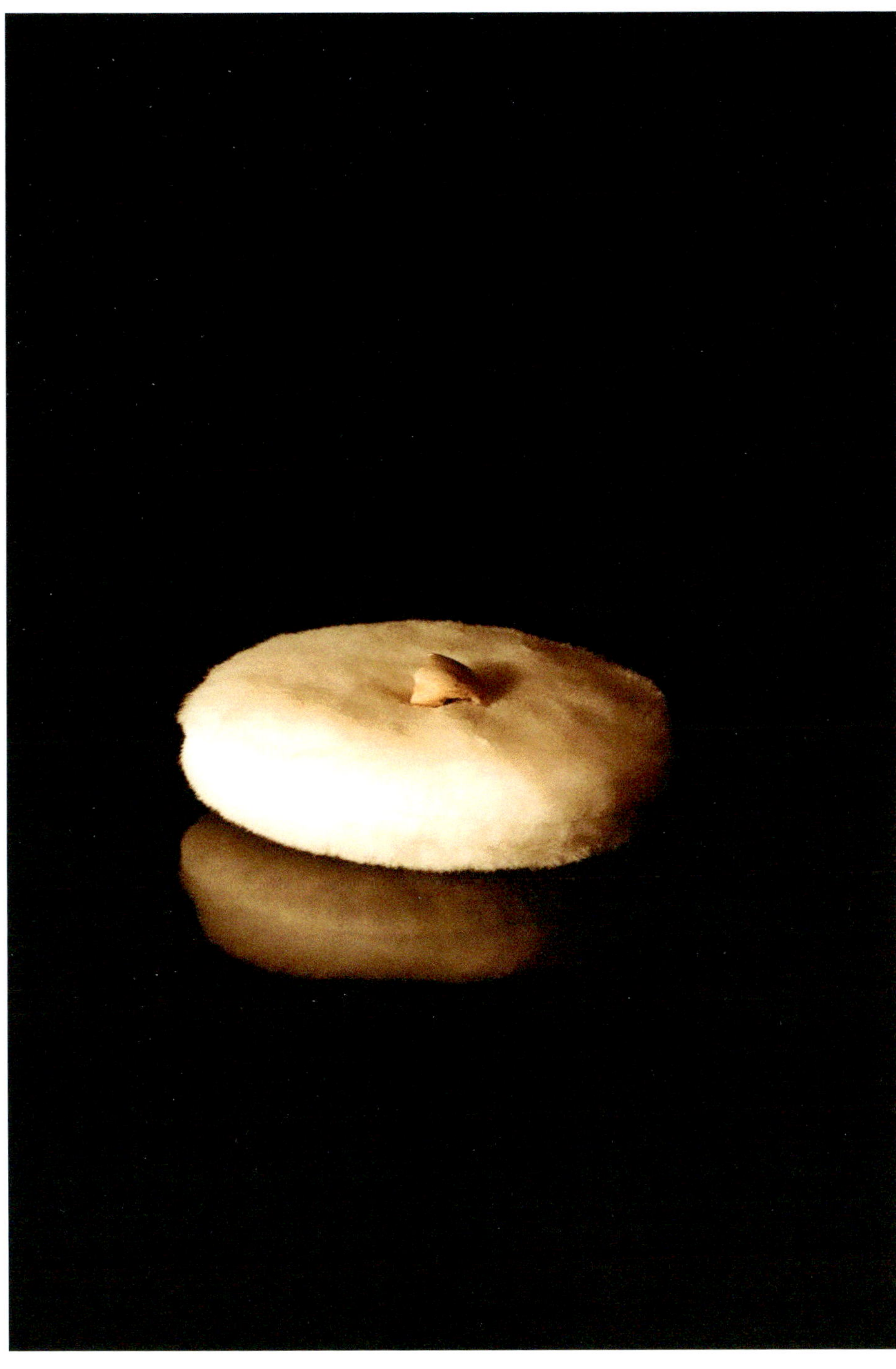

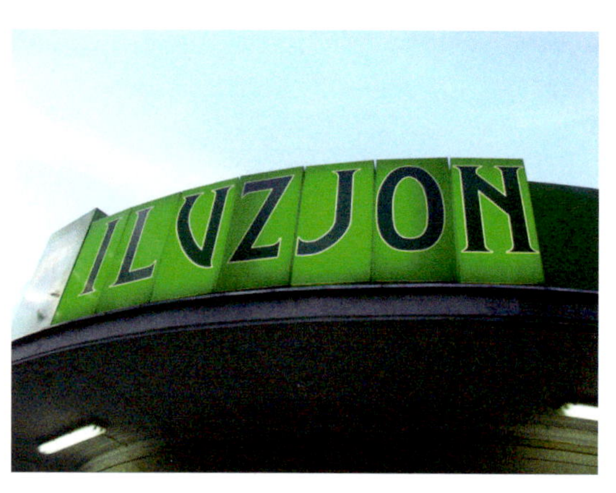

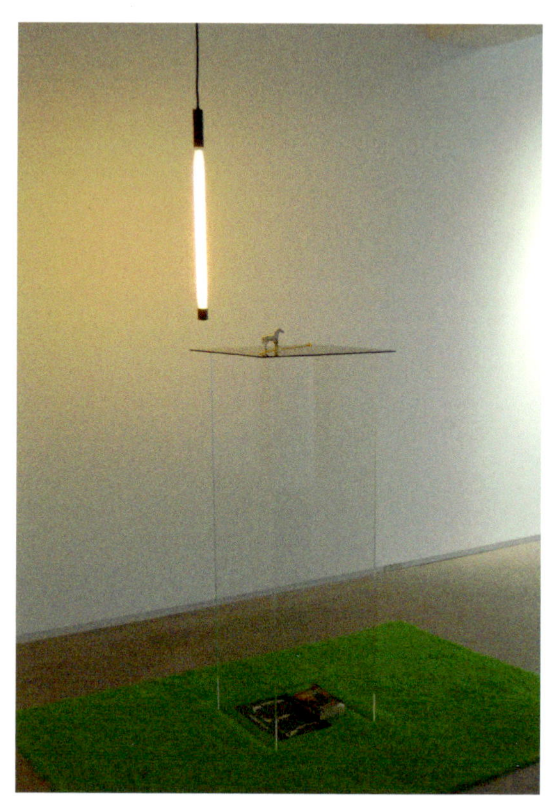

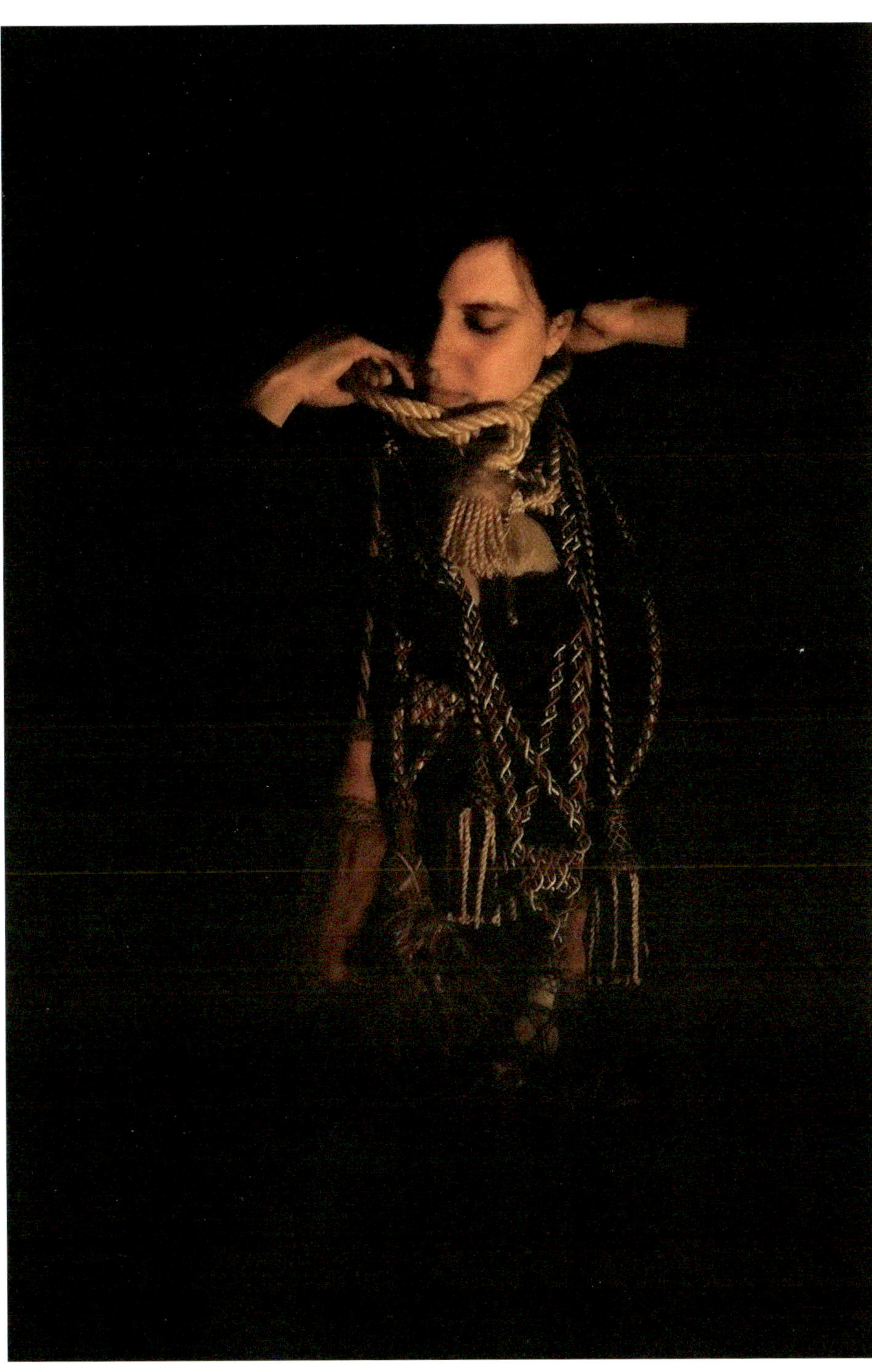

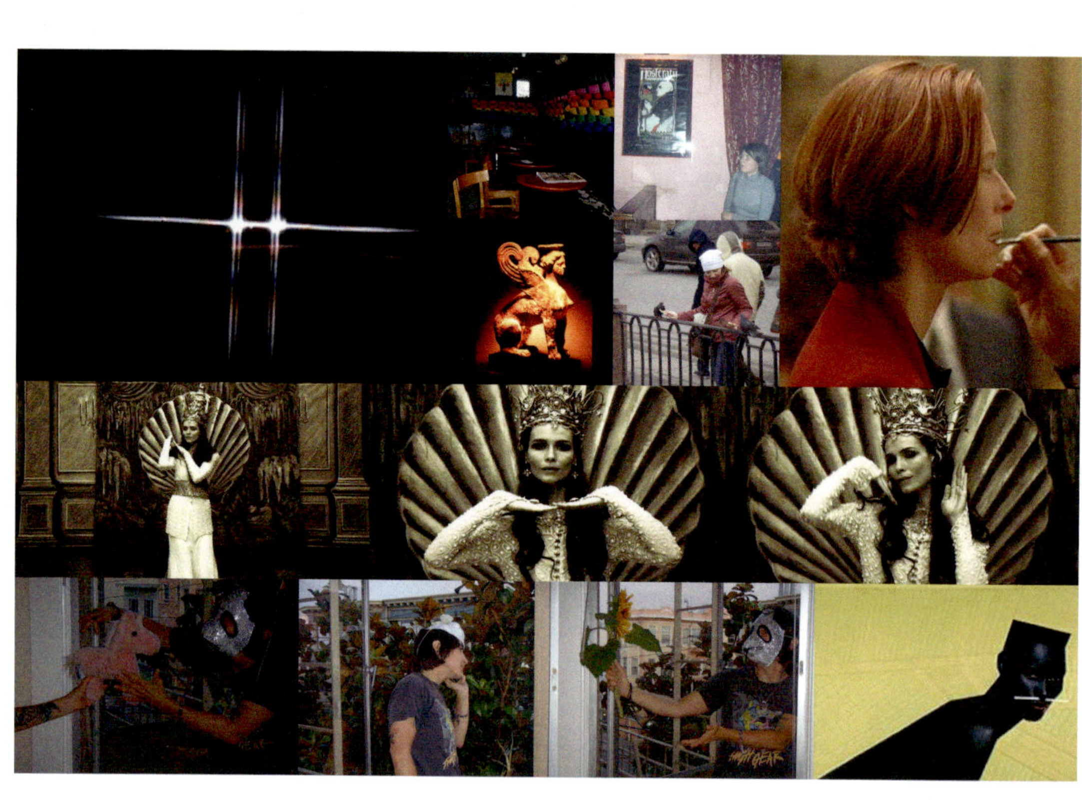

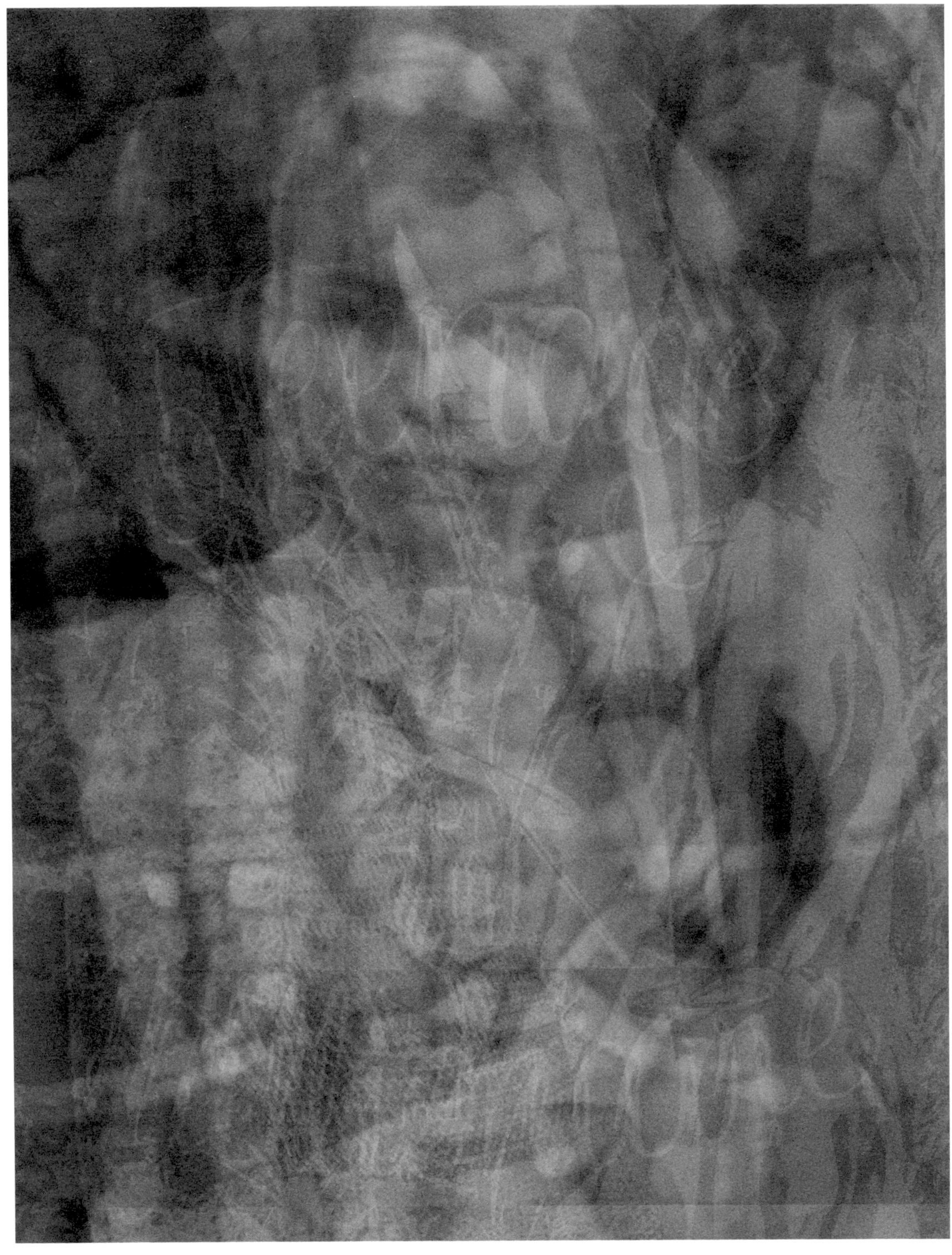

Kutluğ Ataman

*1961 in Istanbul
Lives and works in Istanbul

Solo Exhibitions (Selection)
2009 *Küba + Paradise*, Museum Ludwig,
Cologne
Mesopotamian Dramaturgies, Lentos
Kunstmuseum Linz
fff, Thomas Dane Gallery, London
2008 *Paradise*, Vancouver Art Gallery,
Vancouver; Harris Museum and Art
Gallery, Preston
2007 *Paradise*, Orange County Museum of Art,
Newport Beach; BAK, basis voor actuele
kunst, Utrecht
2006 *Küba: Journey Against the Current*,
organized by Thyssen-Bornemisza Art
Contemporary, Vienna. Exhibition travels
to thirteen destinations along the
Danube
*De-Regulation with the work of Kutluğ
Ataman*, Museum van Hedendaagse
Kunst, Antwerp; Herzliya Museum of
Contemporary Art
2005 *Küba*, Artangel, London; Theater der
Welt, Stuttgart
Perfect Strangers, Museum of
Contemporary Art, Sydney
2004 *Stefan's Room*, Lehmann Maupin, New York
Long Streams, Serpentine Gallery,
London; GEM, Museum voor Actuele
Kunst, The Hague
2002 *Never My Soul!*, Lehmann Maupin, New York
Long Streams, Nikolaj Center for
Contemporary Art, Copenhagen
Women Who Wear Wigs, Istanbul
Contemporary Art Museum
A Rose Blooms in the Garden of Sorrows,
BAWAG Foundation, Vienna
2001 Tensta Konsthall
Women Who Wear Wigs, Lehmann
Maupin, New York
semiha b. unplugged, Galerie Akinci,
Amsterdam
2000 The Lux Gallery, London

Group Exhibitions (Selection)
2010 Biennale of Sydney
Whitechapel Art Gallery, London
2008 Laughing in a Foreign Language, The
Hayward Gallery, London,
2007 2. Moscow Biennial
Turner Prize: A Retrospective, Tate Britain,
London; Moscow Museum of Modern
Art and Mori Art Museum, Tokyo
Istanbul Biennial
*Touch My Shadows: New Media Works
from the Goetz Collection*, Center for
Contemporary Art Ujazdowski Castle,
Warsaw
*Reality Bites—Making Avant-garde Art in
Post-Wall Germany*, Mildred Lane Kemper
Art Museum, St. Louis

2006 *The Grand Promenade*, National
Museum of Contemporary Art, Athens
Nature Attitudes, Thyssen-Bornemisza Art
Contemporary, Vienna
SNAFU: Medien, Mythen, Mind Control,
Hamburger Kunsthalle, Hamburg
*Without Boundary: Seventeen Ways of
Looking*, The Museum of Modern Art,
New York
2005 *Realität*, Seedamm Kulturzentrum,
Pfäffikon
2004 *Down Here*, Bergen Kunsthall
Turner Prize, Tate Britain, London
Carnegie International, Pittsburgh
The Future Has a Silver Lining, Migros
Museum für Gegenwartskunst, Zurich
Monument to Now, DESTE Foundation,
Athens
Flowers Observed, Flowers Transformed,
The Warhol Museum, Pittsburgh
Documentary Fictions, CaixaForum,
Barcelona
2003 Istanbul Biennial
Fast Forward, Sammlung Goetz
Collection, ZKM, Karlsruhe
Testimonies: Between Fiction and Reality,
National Museum of Contemporary Art,
Athens
Image Stream, Wexner Center for the
Arts, Columbus
Deste Foundation, Athens
Witness, The Curve, Barbican Art Gallery,
London
Tate Triennial, Tate Britain, London
2002 Documenta 11, Kassel
Bienal Internacional de São Paulo
FAIR, Royal College of Art, London
2001 Istanbul Biennial
Berlin Biennale
Narrative Affinities, GB Agency, Paris

Iñaki Bonillas

*1981 in Mexico City
Lives and works in Mexico City

Solo Exhibitions (Selection)
2008 *A sombra e o Brilho*, ProjecteSD,
Barcelona
Naufragio con espectador, Galería OMR,
Mexico City
2006 *PREMIOS COFF*, Sala Kubo Kutxa, San
Sebastian
2005 ProjecteSD, Barcelona
Intervenció en el Pabellón, Mies van der
Rohe Pavilion, Barcelona .
2004 *Five Minutes to Die*, Galería OMR, Mexico
City
2003 *Little History of Photography*, MUHKA,
Antwerp
2001 *Audiovisivi*, Galeria Boedone, Milan
2000 *Sala de Proyectos*, Museo de Arte
Carrillo Gil, Mexico City

1999 *Lighting*, Zacatecas 89, Mexico City
1998 Foto Apertura, La B.F.15, Monterrey, Nuevo
     León

Group Exhibitions (Selection)
2006 *Esquiador en el fondo de un pozo*, La
     Colección Jumex, Mexico City
     Accrochage VII, Galerie Meert Rihoux,
     Brussels
2005 *La reconstrucción del Lugar Común.
     Imágenes de Autor*, MACD, San José
     Detonantes, Oficina para Proyectos de
     Arte, Gaudalajara
     Prague Biennale 2
     Seeing Double, Bard College for
     Curatorial Studies, New York
     ECO, Arte contemporáneo mexicano,
     MNCARS, Madrid
2004 *Image Uses: Photography, film and video
     in the Jumex Collection*, La Colección
     Jumex, Mexico City; Malba-Colección
     Constantini, Buenos Aires
     Regarding Muybridge, ProjecteSD, Barcelona
     La Colmena, La Colección Jumex,
     Mexico City
2003 *Stretch*, The Power Plant Art Gallery, Toronto
     50. Biennale Arte, La Biennale di Venezia,
     Utopia Station
     Trabajo en Colaboración, Galería OMR,
     Mexico City
2002 *The Air is Blue*, Casa Estudio Luis
     Barragán, Mexico City
     Orden del Dia, VIII Salón de Arte
     Bancomer, Museo de Arte Moderno,
     Mexico City
     Zebra Crossing, Haus der Kulturen der
     Welt, Berlin
     *Axis Mexico: Common Objects and
     Cosmopolitan Actions*, San Diego
     Museum of Art
     Pictures of You, The Americas Society,
     New York
2001 *Tendencias*, VII Salón de Arte Bancomer,
     Museo de Arte Moderno, Mexico City
     1. Tirana Biennial
     Present, Museum voor Moderne Kunst,
     Arnhem
2000 *Contra el Muro*, Fortaleza 302, The Old
     San Juan
     Segundo Festival Internacional de Arte
     Sonoro, Mexico City
1999 *Ctrl + C/Ctrl + V*, Museo de Arte Carrillo
     Gil, Mexico City
     Frontera, Novena Bienal Internacional
     De Fotografía, Mexico City
1998 *Made in Mexico Made in Venezuela*, Art
     Metropole, Toronto

Gerard Byrne
*1969 in Dublin
Lives and works in Dublin

Solo Exhibitions (Selection)
2009 Lisson Gallery, London
     Green on Red Gallery, Dublin
2008 *Momentum 12: Gerard Byrne*, Institute of
     Contemporary Art, Boston
     Galerie Nordenhake, Stockholm
     x-rummet: Related Works, Statens
     Museum for Kunst, Copenhagen
2007 *1984 and Beyond: Gerard Byrne*,
     Contemporary Art Centre, Vilnius
     52. Biennale Arte, La Biennale di Venezia,
     Irish Pavilion
     Kunstverein Düsseldorf
     Lisson Gallery, London
2004 *In Repertory*, Project Arts Center, Dublin
     Artissima 11, Torino
2003 *Gerard Byrne*, Frankfurter Kunstverein,
     Frankfurt am Main
2002 The Douglas Hyde Gallery, Dublin

Group Exhibitions (Selection)
2009 *The New Monumentality*, Henry Moore
     Institute, Leeds
     *SLOW MOVEMENT ODER: Das Halbe und
     das Ganze*, Kunsthalle Bern
2008 16. Biennale of Sydney
     Not Quite How I Remember It, The Power
     Plant Contemporary Art Gallery, Toronto
     The 7. Gwangju Biennial
     T2 Torino Triennale *50 Moons of Saturn*
2007 *Perspektive 07*, Lenbachhaus, Munich
     Anachronisms, Bonniers Konsthall,
     Stockholm
     9e Biennale de Lyon
     Contour Biennial, Mechelen
     Alabama, Office Baroque Gallery,
     Antwerp
     The Art of Failure, Kunsthaus Baselland,
     Muttenz
2006 *Momentum—Nordic Festival of
     Contemporary Art*, Moss
     Bühne des Lebens – Rhetorik des Gefühls,
     Lenbachhaus, Munich
     A Short History of Performance Part IV,
     Whitechapel Art Gallery, London
     Tate Triennial, Tate Britain, London
     Don Quijote, Witte de With, Rotterdam
     *wieder und wider: performance appro-
     priated*, MUMOK, Vienna
2005 *Eindhoven Istanbul*, Van Abbemuseum,
     Eindhoven

Jay Chung & Q Takeki Maeda
*1976 in Madison, *1977 in Nagoya
Live and work in Berlin

Solo Exhibitions (Selection)
2008 *Hardy Boys and Gilmore Girls*, Cubitt,
     London
2007 *Hardy Boys and Gilmore Girls*,
     Künstlerhaus Stuttgart

2006 Galerie Isabella Bortolozzi, Berlin
Caducean City, MAMbo Museum of
Modern Art, Bologna
ARC Musée d'Art Moderne de la Ville de
Paris
2004 Marc Foxx, Los Angeles

Group Exhibitions (Selection)
2008 GASAG-Kunstpreis 2008, Berlinische
Galerie, Berlin
2007 *Pensa/Piensa/Think*, Centre d'Art Santa
Monica, Barcelona
Luna Park, Consonni, Bilbao
The California Files, CCA Wattis Institute
for Contemporary Art, San Francisco
Otra de Vaqueros, Laboratorio Arte
Alameda, Mexico City
Doomsday Celebration, castillo/corrales,
Paris
2006 *Pigment Piano Marble*, Maipu 327,
Buenos Aires
Data Mining, Wallspace Gallery, New
York
2005 *A Brief History of the Invisible*, CCA Wattis
Institute for Contemporary Art, San
Francisco
Parallel Life, Kunstverein Frankfurt,
Frankfurt am Main
Frieze Art Fair, London
Not a Drop but the Fall, Künstlerhaus
Bremen
*Julieta Aranda, Jay Chung & Q Takeki
Maeda, Melik Ohanian, Jozef Robakowski,
Miljohn Ruperto, Lawrence Wiener*,
Greengrassi, London
The Opening, Claus Andersen
Contemporary Art, Copenhagen
2004 1. Moscow Biennial
Utopia Station, Haus der Kunst, Munich
Always Already Passé, Gavin Brown's
enterprise, New York
*Shannon Bool, Jay Chung & Q Takeki
Maeda, Kersten Czmelka, Dirk Fleischmann*,
c/o Atle Gerhardsen, Berlin
Hyper Style, Loop Galerie, Berlin
Definitively Provisional, Appendiks,
Copenhagen
Buy American, Galerie Chez Valentin,
Paris
Make it New, Portikus, Frankfurt am Main
2003 50. Biennale Arte, La Biennale di Venezia,
Utopia Station
Definitively Provisional, Whitechapel Art
Gallery, London
2002 Manifesta 4, Frankfurt am Main
The Object Sculpture, Henry Moore
Institute, Leeds

Rodney Graham
*1949 in Vancouver, British Columbia
Lives and works in Vancouver, British Columbia

Solo Exhibitions (Selection)
2009 *Rodney Graham*, Jeu de Paume, Paris
2008 *IT'S ALL ABOUT BLACK AND WHITE*, Galerie
Rüdiger Schöttle, Munich
Donald Young Gallery, Chicago
303 Gallery, New York
2007 *Rodney Graham. Wet on Wet—My Late
Early Styles*, Lisson Gallery, London
Sprengel Museum, Hanover
(Kurt-Schwitters-Preis 2006)
BAWAG Foundation, Vienna
2006 Bergen Kunsthall
*A group of literary, musical, sculptural,
photographic and film pieces*, Musée
d'Art Contemporain de Montréal
2005 *Rodney Graham: A Little Thought*,
Vancouver Art Gallery; Institute of
Contemporary Art, Philadelphia
Donald Young Gallery, Chicago
2004 *Rodney Graham: A Little Thought*, Art
Gallery of Ontario, Toronto; MOCA—
Museum of Contemporary Art, Los Angeles
La Colección Jumex, Mexico City
2003 Kunstsammlung Nordrhein-Westfalen K21
Ständehaus, Düsseldorf
MAC, Galeries Contemporaines des
Musées de Marseille
2002 The Whitechapel Art Gallery, London
Music and Noise, Kunsthalle Zürich,
Zurich
2001 *Currents 29: Rodney Graham*, Milwaukee
Art Museum
Donald Young Gallery, Chicago
What is happy, Baby? Lisson Gallery,
London
2000 *… the nearest faraway place …* , Dia
Center for the Arts, New York
*Some works with sound waves, some
works with light waves and some other
experimental works*, Kunstverein
München e.V., Munich
Getting it together in the country,
Westfälischer Kunstverein, Münster
1999 *Cinema Music Video*, Kunsthalle Wien,
Vienna
Time Traced, Dia Center for the Arts, New
York
1998 Galerie Johnen & Schöttle, Cologne
Wexner Center for the Arts, Columbus
1997 47. La Biennale di Venezia, Canadian
Pavilion
1996 Lisson Gallery, London
Le FRAC Haute Normandie, Rouen
1995 Galerie Rüdiger Schöttle, Munich
303 Gallery, New York
1993 *Concordance of the Standard Edition*,
Galerie Micheline Szwajcer, Antwerp
School of Velocity, Lisson Gallery, London

Group Exhibitions (Selection)
2008 *The Practice of Everyday Life*, Fundación/
Colección Jumex; Museo Nacional de
Arte, Mexico City

*UN COUP DE DÉS. Bild gewordene Schrift.
Ein ABC der nachdenklichen Sprache*,
Generali Foundation, Vienna
*Real. Fotografien aus der Sammlung der
DZ Bank*, Städel Museum, Frankfurt am
Main
16. Biennale of Sydney 2008
*Blasted Allegories. Works from the Ringier
Collection*, Kunstmuseum Luzern, Lucerne
Reality Check, Statens Museum for Kunst,
Copenhagen
2007 *MACBA im Frankfurter Kunstverein*,
Frankfurt am Main
Brave Lonesome Cowboy, Villa Merkel,
Esslingen; Kunstmuseum St. Gallen
*Sympathy for the Devil: Art and Rock and
Roll Since 1967*, Museum of
Contemporary Art, Chicago
*All About Laughter: Humor in Contem-
porary Art*, Mori Art Museum, Tokyo
2006 *Beyond Cinema: The Art of Projection*,
Hamburger Bahnhof, Berlin
Le mouvement des images, Centre
Georges Pompidou, Paris
Whitney Biennial 2006, New York
Music is a Better Noise, P.S.1 MoMA, Long
Island City
2005 *The Imaginary Number*, Kunst-Werke, Berlin
*Superstars. Das Prinzip Prominenz in der
Kunst*, Kunsthalle Wien, Vienna
Ecstasy: In and About Altered States,
Museum of Contemporary Art, Los
Angeles
50 Jahre documenta, Kunsthalle
Fridericianum, Kassel; Domus Artium,
Salamanca
2004 *Sons et Lumières*, Centre Georges
Pompidou, Paris
All under Heaven, MuHKA Museum van
Hedendaagse Kunst, Antwerp
*Videodreams: between the cinema and
the theatrical*, Kunsthaus Graz
14th Biennale of Sydney
2003 50. La Biennale di Venezia
7e Biennale de Lyon
Golden Oldies of Music Video, MoMA,
New York
*Go Johnny Go!/The Electric Guitar—Art &
Myth*, Kunsthalle Wien, Vienna
2002 13. Biennale of Sydney
Rock My World, California College of the
Arts, San Francisco
Loop – Alles auf Anfang, Kunsthalle
München, Munich with P.S. 1
Contemporary Art Center, New York
2001 *Neue Welt*, Frankfurter Kunstverein,
Frankfurt am Main
Art/Music: Rock, Pop, Techno, Museum
of Contemporary Art, Sydney
010101: Art in Technological Times, San
Francisco Museum of Modern Art, San
Francisco
7. Istanbul Biennial

2000 *The Greenhouse Effect*, Serpentine
Gallery, London
Let's Entertain: Lifes's Guilty Pleasures,
Walker Art Center, Minneapolis
1999 *Millennium My Eye! Head Over Heals A
Work of Impertinence*, Musée d'art
contemporain de Montréal
*Regarding Beauty: A View of the Late
Twentieth Century*, Hirshhorn Museum
and Sculpture Garden, Washington D.C.
1998 *The Magic of Trees*, Foundation Beyeler,
Riehen/Basel
The Serial Attitude, Wexner Center for the
Arts, Columbus
Speed: Visions of an Accelerated Age,
Photographers Gallery; The Whitechapel
Art Gallery, London

Hilary Lloyd
*1964 in Halifax
Lives and works in London

Solo Exhibitions (Selection)
2008 Sadie Coles HQ, London
2007 Galerie Neu, Berlin
2006 Kunstverein München e.V., Munich
2005 Yorkshire ArtSpace, Sheffield
2003 50. Biennale Arte, La Biennale di Venezia,
The Henry Moore Foundation
2000 *Kino der Dekonstruktion*, Frankfurter
Kunstverein, Frankfurt am Main

Group Exhibitions (Selection)
2008 *Dispersion*, Institute of Contemporary
Arts, London
Une saison à Bruxelles, Dépendance,
Brussels
Films, Sadie Coles HQ, London
Art Sheffield 08
2007. *Die Blaue Blume/steirischer herbst*,
Kunstverein Graz
9e Biennale de Lyon
2006 *Canal Plus at Vilma Gold: Films, perform-
ance, music*, Vilma Gold, London
ATTITUDE, c/o Atle Gerhardsen, Berlin
Loveletter, Herald Street, London
Never for money, always for love,
Kunstverein Graz
2005 *Use This Kind of Sky*, Keith Talent Gallery,
London
*I Really Should … *, Lisson Gallery, London
2003 *To What End?* Center for Curatorial
Studies, Bard College, New York
Electric Earth, The State Russian Museum,
St. Petersburg
2002 *Gareth Jones, Hilary Lloyd, James Pyman*,
38 Langham Street, London
*Happy Outsiders from London and
Scotland*, Zacheta National Gallery
of Art, Warsaw
4. Gwangju Biennale

2001 *ABBILD*, steirischer herbst, Graz
Videonale 9, Kunstverein Bonn
The seat with the clearest view, Grey
Matter Contemporary Art, Sydney
City Racing 1988–1998: a partial account,
Institute of Contemporary Arts, London
2000 *Intelligence: New British Art 2000*, Tate
Britain, London
The British Art Show 5, City Art Centre,
Edinburgh; John Hansard Gallery,
Southampton

Kirsten Pieroth
*1970 in Offenbach am Main
Lives and works in Berlin

Solo Exhibitions (Selection)
2008 *Passengers*, CCA Wattis Institute for
Contemporary Arts, San Francisco
2007 Klosterfelde, Berlin
2006 display, Prague
2005 Secession, Vienna
Cubitt, London (with Henrik Olesen)
2004 Contemporary Art Gallery, Vancouver
2003 *From the Laboratory of Thomas A. Edison*,
Portikus, Frankfurt am Main
*I regret that a previous engagement
prevents me from accepting your kind
invitation to dinner at your home, on
Thursday evening, September seven-
teenth*, Klosterfelde, Berlin
2002 Mellemdaekket Projektrum,
Charlottenborg, Copenhagen
*There are two temperatures: one outside,
one inside*, Galleria Franco Noero, Torino
(with Henrik Olesen)
2001 Helga Maria Klosterfelde, Hamburg
Sparwasser HQ, Berlin (with Kirstine
Roepstorff)
2000 Klosterfelde, Berlin
rraum, Frankfurt am Main

Group Exhibitions (Selection)
2008 *This is not a Void*, Galeria Luisa Strina,
São Paulo
Art Focus 5, Can Art Do More?, Banit
Centre Jerusalem
Jahrgang Rausch, Atelierfrankfurt,
Frankfurt am Main
*When a clock is seen from the side it no
longer tells the time*, Johann König, Berlin
Home is the place you left, Trondheim
Kunstmuseum
Participation, Galerie Martin Janda, Vienna
Yes, No & Other Options, Art Sheffield 08
2007 *In Attesa Di Risposta*, Supportico Lopez
32, Naples
Curiosities Encountered, Grieder
Contemporary, Sils-Maria
Learn to Read, Tate Modern, London
Made in Germany, Sprengel Museum
Hannover, Hanover

Romantischer Konzeptualismus,
Kunsthalle Nürnberg, Nuremberg; BAWAG
Foundation, Vienna
Conditions of Display, The Moore Space,
Miami
Door Slamming Festival, Mehringdamm
72, Berlin
Absent Without Leave, Victoria Miro
Gallery, London
Elephant Cemetery, Artists Space, New
York
2006 *Subito Sera*, Galleria Zero, Milan
The Clinic a Pathology of Gestures,
Hebbel Am Ufer, Berlin
*When the moon shines on the moon-
shine*, The Breeder, Athens
Auflösung III – Entgrenzung, Neue
Gesellschaft für Bildende Kunst e.V., Berlin
*The Show Will Be Open When The Show
Will Be Closed*, STORE, London
on the move verkehrskultur II,
Westfälischer Kunstverein, Münster
Wrong, Klosterfelde, Berlin
2005 *Information/Transformation*, Extra City,
Antwerp
Not a Drop but the Fall, Künstlerhaus
Bremen
En Route: Via Another Route, Trans-
Siberian Train, Moscow to Beijing
The Need to Document, Kunsthaus
Baselland, Muttenz
2004 *Drafting Deceit*, apexart, New York
Gelegenheit und Reue, Kunstverein Graz
Never Never Landscape, c/o Atle
Gerhardsen, Berlin
Beuys don't cry, Galleria Zero, Milan
Manifesta 5, Donostia-San Sebastian
Socle du Monde Biennale, Kunst-
museum Herning
Tätig sein, Neue Gesellschaft für Bildende
Kunst e.V., Berlin
This much is certain, Royal College of Art,
London
2003 *Adorno: Die Möglichkeit des
Unmöglichen*, Frankfurter Kunstverein,
Frankfurt am Main
Spectacular: The Art of Action, Museum
Kunst Palast, Düsseldorf
50. Biennale Arte, La Biennale di Venezia,
Utopia Station (with Henrik Olesen)
GNS, Palais de Tokyo, Paris
2002 *Haunted By Detail*, De Appel, Amsterdam
2001 *retur*, Copenhagen
1. Tirana Biennial, Chinese Pavilion
2000 Iaspis Galleriet, Stockholm

Susanne M. Winterling
*1970 in Rehau/Oberfranken
Lives and works in Berlin

Solo Exhibitions (Selection)
2009 BAWAG Foundation, Vienna

Alliance, Sisterhood, and the Rope,
Hiromi Yoshii, Tokyo
2008 *Isadora's Scarf,* Parrotta Contemporary
Art, Stuttgart
Pattern Recognition of a Collar … ,
Silvermann Gallery, San Francisco
Precious Future II, National Center of
Photography, Saint Petersburg
2007 *i'll be your mirror, but i'll dissolve … ,*
Daniel Reich Gallery, New York
Eve's Arc and the feminist, Gavin Brown's
enterprise, New York
… they told you the future will be … ,
Moscow Center for the Arts/Moscow
House of Photography
2006 *White Light,* Julia Stoschek Foundation
e.V., Düsseldorf
2005 *A Skin too Thin,* Galerie Meerrettich, Berlin
Mise en Scene: In Swans World, Duolun
Museum of Modern Art, Shanghai

Group Exhibitions (Selection)
2009 Videonale 11, Kunstverein Bonn
Don't Expect Anything, Francesca Minini,
Milan
2008 *twice upon a time,* Galerie Andreas
Huber, Vienna
*Intermission of a new order, Intrude Art
and Life,* Zendai MoMA, Shanghai
Pollen, Neue Alte Brücke, Frankfurt am
Main
Conversations and Readings,
Silberkuppe, Berlin
Multiple, Ke Center for Contemporary Art,
Shanghai
5. Berlin Biennale
Opera, Late at Tate Britain, London
2007 *Migration Addicts,* Shenzhen & Hong
Kong Bi-City Biennale of Urbanism/
Architecture, Hong Kong
Kostbaarheden en Bijzondere Vruchten,
Aktualisierungsraum, Hamburg
Aspen 11, Neue Alte Brücke, Frankfurt am
Main
Josef Strau and Galerie Meerrettich,
Vilma Gold, London
Who, Kunstverein in Hamburg
Doorslamming Festival, Meeringdamm
72, Berlin
EHF Ein Überblick, Akademie der
Konrad-Adenauer-Stiftung, Berlin
Migration Addicts, Sculpture Projects,
Singapore
Kaufen, Staatstheater, Stuttgart
The Gallery Show, Extra City, Antwerp
2005 *Gifted Generation,* Hebbel Am Ufer,
Berlin
2004 Guardini Stiftung e.V., Berlin
Faxe Coni, Futura Project, Prague
2003 *Rituale,* Akademie der Bildenden Künste,
Berlin
As Soon as Possible, PAC, Milan
La Biennale di Venezia

2002 *Alien—Inside the Outside,* Austrian
Cultural Institute, Swiss Institute, New York
Prêt-à-Perform, Via Farini, Milan
Body Basics II, Württembergischer
Kunstverein, Stuttgart
2001 Videonale 9, Kunstverein Bonn
2000 Akademie Isotrop, Galerie Krinzinger,
Vienna
Scape, Foro Artistico, Hanover

Work and Image Credits

Isaac Mendes Belisario

Sketches of Character, In Illustration of the Habits, Occupation, and Costume of the Negro Population, in the Island of Jamaica (Kingston, Jamaica: Published by the artist, 1837[-8]), Yale Center for British Art, Paul Mellon Collection (selected images and texts of the original books)

p. 18   Part: 2, cover
p. 19   Part: 1, preface
p. 20   Part: 1, text plate 2
p. 21   *Red-Set Girls, and Jack-in-the-Green*, plate 2, lithograph 37.5 x 26 cm
p. 22   Part: 1, text plate 3
p. 23   *Jaw-Bone, or House John-Canoe*; plate 3, lithograph, 37.5 x 26 cm
p. 24   Part: 1, text plate 4
p. 25   *Koo, Koo, or Actor-Boy*, plate 5, lithograph, 37.5 x 26 cm
p. 26   Part: 2, text plate 1
p. 27   *Koo, Koo, or Actor-Boy*, plate 6, lithograph, 37.5 x 26 cm
p. 28   *Lovey*, plate 8, lithograph, 37.5 x 26 cm

Kutluğ Ataman

pp. 34–43   *Women Who Wear Wigs*, 1999, video installation, ca. 60 min.; courtesy the artist, Thomas Dane Gallery, London, and Lehmann Maupin Gallery, New York; photo credit: Uwe Walter, Berlin
pp. 34/35   Installation view: Tanas Berlin, 2008

Iñaki Bonillas

pp. 50–55   *A sombra e o brilho*, 2007, seventy-four typewritten texts on paper, twenty-four black-and-white kodaliths in lightboxes, documents: 19.5 x 13 cm each, lightbox: 30 x 42 cm each; courtesy gallery ProjecteSD, Barcelona; photo credit: Iñaki Bonillas Archive
p. 51   Installation view: ProjecteSD, Barcelona, 2007; photo credit: Silvia Dauder
pp. 56–59   *Una tarjeta para J. R. Plaza*, 2007, six digital prints on cotton paper, 25.5 x 20.5 cm each, private collection, Spain; courtesy gallery ProjecteSD, Barcelona; photo credit: Iñaki Bonillas Archive

Gerard Byrne

pp. 65–76   See captions on artist pages 66/67

Jay Chung & Q Takeki Maeda

pp. 82/83, 86/87   *Untitled*, 2009, corner vitrines, dimensions variable; courtesy the artists
pp. 84, 88, 89, 91   *She's Gone*, 2009, video, 3.30 min.; courtesy the artists

Rodney Graham

pp. 98/99   *Wet on Wet—My Late Early Styles*, installation view 2007; courtesy the artist and Lisson Gallery; photo credit: Henri Robideau
p. 100   *Untitled*, 2006, oil on canvas, 31 x 26 cm
p. 101   *Untitled*, 2006, oil on canvas, 45 x 36.5 cm
p. 102   *Untitled*, 2006, oil on canvas, 32 x 32 cm

p. 103   *Untitled*, 2006, oil on canvas, 41 x 33.5 cm
p. 104   *Untitled*, 2006, oil on canvas, 61.5 x 48.5 cm
pp. 100–104: Courtesy of all works Hauser & Wirth, Zurich and London, and Donald Young Gallery, Chicago; photo credit: Barbora Gerny
p. 105   *Untitled*, 2005–2008, thirteen paintings, various techniques, oil on linen, oil on polyester silk screen mesh, and oil on plywood, installation view: Sydney Biennale, 2008; photo credit: Ben Symons
pp. 106/107   *Lobbying Potatoes at a Gong 1969* (2006), film still and photograph (part of installation); courtesy of all works Hauser & Wirth, Zurich and London, and Donald Young Gallery, Chicago

Hilary Lloyd

pp. 114–123   *Untitled (Cut-Outs)*, 2006, slide projection, dimensions variable; courtesy the artist

Kirsten Pieroth

pp. 130/131   *Loan*, 2007, loan contract
pp. 132/133   Demounting the label at the Louvre Museum, Paris. Installing the label at Tate Modern, London, for the exhibition *Learn to Read*, Tate Modern, London, 2007; photo credit: Cedrick Eymenier
pp. 134/135   *Trophy*, 2008, bike courier on route from Manchester to Sheffield
pp. 136/137   Engraved bicycle pump awarded to the courier; photo credit: Lee Boswell
pp. 138/139   *Untitled*, 2008, installation view; photo credit: Nick Ash
pp. 130–139: Courtesy of all works the artist, and Klosterfelde, Berlin

Susanne M. Winterling

p. 146   *Untitled (The Pressure Behind Your Nailcolour My Dear)*, 2009, C-print, 45 x 30 cm
p. 147   *Daydream Nation*, 2009, C-print, 45 x 30 cm
p. 148   *Untitled (Part of the Circle I)*, 2009, C-print, 45 x 30 cm
p. 149   *Untitled (Part of the Circle II)*, 2009, C-print, 45 x 30 cm
p. 150   *Liberty and Sedation*, 2009, C-print, three parts, 20 x 30 cm each
p. 151   *Tooth in Roots*, 2009, C-print, 45 x 30 cm
p. 152 RT   *Illuzion*, 2009, C-print, 20 x 30 cm
pp. 146–152: Courtesy of all works the artist, and Daniel Reich Gallery, New York
p. 152 LT   *Untitled (the Big Illusion)*, 2009, mixed media installation, installation view: Hiromiyoshii, Tokyo, 2009
p. 153   *La Nouvelle Vague and the Thrill of It (from the Inside Out Series)*, 2009, C-print, 45 x 30 cm; courtesy the artist, and Daniel Reich Gallery, New York
p. 154   *The Glow of Nurture*, 2009, assemblage of footage material
p. 155   *Ivory Lilies*, 2009, photo collage, 39.5 x 30 cm; courtesy of Hiromiyoshii, Tokyo

This catalogue is published in conjunction with the exhibition

Little Theatre of Gestures
Kutluğ Ataman, Isaac Mendes Belisario, Iñaki Bonillas, Gerard Byrne, Jay Chung & Q Takeki Maeda, Rodney Graham, Hilary Lloyd, Kirsten Pieroth, Susanne M. Winterling

Kunstmuseum Basel, Museum für Gegenwartskunst, May 16 – August 15, 2009
Malmö Konsthall, October 10, 2009 – January 10, 2010

Exhibition in Basel
Director: Bernhard Mendes Bürgi
Curator: Nikola Dietrich
Curatorial assistant: Jacqueline Uhlmann
Press communication: Christian Selz, Giacomo Paravicini
Restorers: Peter Berkes, Sophie Eichner, Amelie Jensen, Chantal Schwendener, Caroline Wyss
Registrar: Charlotte Gutzwiller
Installation: Claude Bosch, Peter Lütje, Stefano Schaller, Andreas Schweizer, Käthe Walser, Martin Werner
Interns: Mareike Spendel, Deborah Johanna Kositzki

Kunstmuseum Basel, Museum für Gegenwartskunst
mit Emanuel Hoffmann-Stiftung
St. Alban-Rheinweg 60
4010 Basel
Switzerland
www.kunstmuseumbasel.ch

Exhibition in Malmö
Director: Jacob Fabricius
Press communication: Lena Leeb-Lundberg (Tel. +46 40 341294)
Staff: Ann-Marie Björklund, Angela Cesarec, Per Engström, Anna Holmbom, Nilas Hultman, Gerth Malmros, Cathrine Nilsson, Mårten Nilsson, Magnús Ólafsson, Magdalena Svensson, Stefan Tallberg, Peter Wallström

Malmö Konsthall
S:t Johannesgatan 7
Box 17127
200 10 Malmö
Sweden
www.konsthall.malmo.se

Catalogue
Editors: Nikola Dietrich, Jacob Fabricius
Editing assistant: Jacqueline Uhlmann
Texts: Dominic Eichler, Sarah Pierce
Copyediting: Alix and Bish Sharma, Ann-Marie Björklund
Graphic design: Müller & Wesse, Berlin
Production: Stefanie Langner, Hatje Cantz
Printing: sellier druck, Freising
Binding: Concella Verlagsbuchbinderei, Urban Meister GmbH, Aschheim-Dornach bei München

The email interviews between the artists and the curators were conducted from January to March 2009

© 2009 Kunstmuseum Basel, Museum für Gegenwartskunst; Malmö Konsthall (Catalogue N° 212); Hatje Cantz Verlag, Ostfildern; and authors
© 2009 for the reproduced works by Susanne M. Winterling: VG Bild-Kunst, Bonn as well as the artists, photographers, and their legal successors

Published by
Hatje Cantz Verlag
Zeppelinstrasse 32
73760 Ostfildern
Germany
www.hatjecantz.com

Hatje Cantz books are available internationally at selected bookstores. For more information about our distribution partners, please visit our homepage at www.hatjecantz.com

ISBN 978-3-7757-2436-4 (trade edition)
ISBN 978-3-7204-0187-6 (museum edition; only available at Kunstmuseum Basel, Museum für Gegenwartskunst)
ISBN 978-91-7704-118-4 (museum edition, only available at Malmö Konsthall)

Printed in Germany

Special thanks to:
Daros Services AG; Galerie Hauser & Wirth, Zurich; Galerie Johnen, Berlin; Galerie Klosterfelde, Berlin; Galerie Neu, Berlin; Geist (Oscar Mangione, Fredrik Ehlin); Vincent Lestienne; IASPIS (International Artists Studio Program In Sweden); Informationsteknik; Arzu Kraner; Kunstverein Düsseldorf; Lisson Gallery, London; Green on Red Gallery, Dublin; ProjecteSD, Barcelona; Studio Rodney Graham; Jan Verwoert; Käthe Walser; Yale Center for British Art, New Haven, Conn. (Elisabeth Fairman, Maria Singer, Melissa Fournier)

and to all the artists and the authors